As I Remember It

As I Remember It

RALF H. SIEGEMUND

Edited by Karen Siegemund, Ph.D.,
daughter of the author, 2021

Cover photograph of author and his father
by Frieda Siegemund, mother of the author, 1929

Cover Illustration by Endre Balogh, *www.endresart.com*

Book design by Maureen Mead, Olympia, WA

Published by Palisades Press, Pacific Palisades, CA 90272
PalisadesPressCA@gmail.com

Send all inquiries to the publisher

ISBN 9798-7-434-5024-4

DEDICATION

Unfortunately, dad never included a dedication in these memoirs.

*But I think it's pretty clear that he would have dedicated this book
to his wife Joan, our mom, who meant the world to him,
and
to those along the way who created and with whom he shared
the various "refugia" which protected him
throughout the catastrophe of the war and beyond.*

CONTENTS

EDITOR'S NOTE

When I was growing up, dad seldom spoke of what he'd gone through as a kid in Hitler's Berlin, of the war and the catastrophes that were part of his coming of age. Somehow, though, we knew the toll it had taken, we were aware of how those years had contributed to his worldview including a joyous appreciation for all that he had, and we had a sense, even though he didn't speak of it, of his constant wonder at the contrast between our childhood and his.

It was only when he'd finished writing his memoirs twenty years ago that he really started to share stories of his youth, and it's impossible to overstate how grateful I am to have finally heard those stories, and to have this remarkable manuscript. It has now been ten years since he passed away, and it has been an honor and privilege to realize his wish of bringing these memoirs to publication.

Editing such a work, especially posthumously, has been an emotional undertaking, but I am grateful for the opportunity to become familiar with dad's childhood and young adult experiences, as well as his intellectual efforts to tell his story as clearly and thoughtfully as possible. I've tried to use the lightest touch, not wanting to lose his voice; I have also avoided making any major editorial decisions as the idea of doing so without the opportunity to discuss, share or debate any big changes with him simply did not feel right.

In general, footnotes are his; those I added for clarity are indicated by square brackets and my initials.

So for the most part, this is as he had completed it. He wrote it in English, although of course German was his "Muttersprache," his mother tongue, and while his English was exceptional, the German speech patterns still come through. In addition, he was a scientist and an attorney, so the level of detail and emphasis on precision reflect those disciplines as well. In his later years, he'd also earned a Ph.D. in Art History with an emphasis on the origins of civili-zation, and this passion for history and for accurate and objective description are also apparent.

His primary concern in writing *As I Remember It,* I believe, was that, over time, the facts of what had happened in Germany generally, and Berlin specifically, during those exceptionally tumultuous years have been forgotten, or worse, distorted, and with fewer and fewer survivors of that time and place, it was increasingly important to him to document his first-hand experiences and have them "on the record" for anyone desiring to read a first-hand account.

These memoirs also serve as a timely reminder that evil doesn't come in with a bang. Rather, it creeps in, overshadowing every aspect of life, each step just a barely-perceptible adjustment of one's life, until one's world has changed, one's country is destroyed, and the joy and optimism of an earlier time have been whittled away and are somehow.... gone.

From a happy, carefree childhood, to the horrors of a catastrophic war, then to the rebuilding of a society, the book includes a wide range of experiences that set personal detail against a backdrop of a nation undergoing a cataclysmic destruction and renaissance.

But especially, it is a story of survival, of resilience in the face of incomprehensible and surreal catastrophe on every level, of gratitude, and, in the end, of turning to the light of opportunity and of freedom.

And it's an honor to share this story, my dad's story, with you.

– by the Editor
Karen Siegemund, Ph.D.
Ralf's daughter
Calabasas, California
June 2021

PREFACE
NO CELEBRITY SO WHY A BIOGRAPHY?

I began to write these recollections at a little after 7 p.m. on August 31, 1989, on the West Coast in California, which was the early morning hours of September 1st in Central Europe. Fifty years ago, a sizable portion of the then rather puny German army perched along the eastern border of what was known as the German Reich, ready to fall into Poland at the crack of dawn.

I remember very well the announcement over the radio – made by Hitler himself – at some time during the first day of September, 1939:

"Since five o'clock this morning our troops have been *returning* fire."

He thus dishonestly claimed that the German troops had responded to a Polish attack on Germany. This lie attempted to cover the true state of affairs, but it soon gave way to another lie: that Germany alone had started an armed conflict which soon burgeoned into what became known as World War II.

Even though certain historical facts are clear, it seems that it will take a long time before the participants to this scenario will recognize unequivocally that the second World War began when and because Stalin and Hitler agreed in a written contract, pact, or treaty (whatever one wishes to call this instrument of shame), to divide Poland. This cruel endeavor became known as the fourth division of Poland and the Soviet Union steadfastly held onto its share of the loot for many years.

Now, after the amazing turn of events of the fall of the USSR, the formerly eastern part of Poland has become a potential problem between Belarus, Ukraine and Poland – with of course Russia in the background[1]. Hopefully this unresolved problem will not contaminate the purge from the world of the evils of Communism. In retrospect, the position the Soviet Union took for so many years is quite a remarkable feat, considering the fact that it was the co-perpetrator to one of the most devastating periods in the history of mankind, and is still holding on to the spoils with impunity.

I make this point for one simple reason. The guilt and participation of the USSR in launching WWII was obvious then, but now appears all but forgotten. I fear it will take a long time before the truth in this matter will be generally recalled and accepted. And here I come to my point of departure for justifying this account of remembrances: If such blatant historical facts are so quickly brushed aside and seemingly forgotten, or at least classified as "historically insignificant," then my own experience and recollections are doomed to oblivion unless recorded[2].

I want to write my memoirs, autobiography, or whatever one

---

1 A great to-do was made about Chancellor Kohl's reluctance to accept the western border of Poland. My view is he shouldn't have, or should have brought up the issue of the eastern part of what was Poland prior to the 4th partition.

2 Of course it could be argued that WWII began when Germany obliterated whatever was left of Czechoslovakia after the Munich treaty. However the world swallowed that without protest.

may wish to call these memories of mine, for a very simple reason. I lived through and was witness to some very turbulent times. On the day Hitler committed suicide I was in downtown Berlin, just a few hundred yards from his bunker. In the preceding years I saw Berlin, my hometown, and metaphorically my own life, gradually reduced to rubble. Before that, I grew up observing happenings, registering them as best as I could for my age, but not always understanding their significance. In 1945, I saw a victorious and barbarous army sweep through my city in an unbelievable orgy of cruelty, hatred, and revenge. Admittedly I saw this with an indescribable feeling and intuitive sense of justice coupled with an unbelievable sense of gratefulness that the nightmare of the war was over. But so many things happened before, and so many things happened thereafter – not just in the great arena of politics and history (that too, of course), but also in some very personal relation to me. And these happenings are, I believe, part of History.

This is the reason, or justification, if you will, for my autobiography. I wasn't a personage of any importance whatever; I was just one of "the people," and in fact just a kid at that time. I don't have to justify myself in any political arena; I don't have to drum up excuses for what I did, how I reacted and why, what I condoned and supported, or opposed and despised. I don't have to justify my life (as biographies often do); and most certainly, I do not wish the world to know any asserted, outstanding or heroic deeds. I simply want to record what I personally witnessed, experienced, and remember of that time. I have noticed, or more correctly, I have learned how often many impressions of that period of time become more and more distorted. On the other hand, more and more I feel that there is a lack of understanding, of a sense of reality as to "how it really was". What I have said about the beginning of WWII is a good example of how distortions begin early and may never be corrected – at least on a local, private level.

History is often concerned with the acts and pronouncements of the rulers of the day on the one hand and with the amorphous general "stream of events" on the other, but only indirectly with the effect words, deeds and actions have on the "common people." The general flow of history is the composite of intertwined trickles of individual lives. And so, with the presentation of one of the trickles, I may at times offer something that on a personal level is representative of history, but at times that may be very different from what historians found when investigating the composite of all submerging streams. While I do not intend to be unduly critical of historians in general, some of them may have some intention to distort the situations they purport to analyze in the name of history[3].

Now let me make one point abundantly clear. I am not attempting to present a revisionist account of history, although I am sure I will be accused of that. I am not writing "history," in the sense of presenting a pattern of seemingly intertwining events interpreted as History. Rather, I will present a variety of very specific accounts, some of them "typical" in a very limited way, covering, for example, my neighborhood, school mates, my parents' friends, etc. I expect that the reader will glean from this account elements that may be at variance with the official, accepted view.

There is more to be disclaimed. I am not in the least attempting to relativize history; I am not presenting a post-modernist view, in the sense of presenting my personal experience as an exercise in the presentation of views that have social relevance today. Quite to the contrary, I will try as much as possible to present my experience without such an interpretive filter. My account does not serve as contemporary, socio-political service. It is directed only to people who want to know what happened in the private sphere of somebody who was there.

Among revisionists and post-modernists, there are people who try to make a point or prove a hypothesis and may take

---

3 Notably in our time, for example, Daniel Jonah Goldhagen

liberties – well, just a little bit – with the facts. They may wish to relativize facts to the point that the historical "facts" are assertions that serve a contemporary purpose. If these "historians" are assumed to be authorities by others, very easily the assumption arises that this or that point, fact, position, or whatever was advanced, has now been proven as having actually happened.

I think that it is for this kind of reason that I came across rather astonishing assertions regarding what supposedly happened in those years, but which do not seem to, well, jibe with the facts as I remember them. Let me be blunt: to me, post-modernists are people who, on the basis of a mind-set that, for example, was explored by the motion picture *Rashomon*, like to elect a story that suits their purpose. Within that frame I want to present one of the Rashomon accounts as I remember it, not as I wish it to be or have been. My memoirs are simply to serve as a kind of record of what I remember to have happened and particularly happened to me during a very critical period of time, namely the early 30's to the beginning of the 50's Germany. If the reader does not believe me, I cannot help it. But wherever possible, I will present an abundance of corroboration.

A scholarly evaluation of a historical period may find personal closeness to the events to be detrimental; a personal involvement may be, and in many instances, is indeed a drawback. However, I have said that I simply have no point to prove, no position to defend, and that, hopefully, lends credibility to my presentation.

But wait, I do have axes to grind as the metaphor goes, and I should tell you about them – even if that aspect may result only in a comparatively mild distortion. I know for a fact that I didn't kill anybody, but I certainly was not an innocent bystander either. I was indeed a participant, namely, in the daily life in Germany at that time. That vantage point gives me a position of objectivity – what exactly did I participate in?

Of course, I did not actively participate in the political affairs.

But I wouldn't say I was just a passive observer; I participated as a child, but with the actively-growing understanding of an adolescent. If I as a child misjudged matters, no honest person can condemn me. So, I feel free to admit any possible shortcomings on my part.

On the other hand, modern social scientists and historians (or should I say "so-called scientists"?) and others may have an agenda of their own—for example, to perpetuate an unprovable myth. For example, there is the "Christian" myth that the Jews are collectively guilty of deicide, or the myth of Germany's exclusive guilt in WWI. Another of these myths, put forth by Mr. Goldhagen and others—from their own, preconceived perspective—was the assertion that the Holocaust was a kind of inherent result of the German soul, that many or most Germans participated in these events.

My presentation is not an attempt to refute such generalized condemning judgment. I simply want to demonstrate, on the basis of my experience, the broad validity of the ancient Jewish saying, "Whoever saves one life saves the world." The people and scenarios I am presenting do not disprove, for instance, France's ridiculous claim as a victor of World War II, or that the Germans wanted revenge for World War I because they didn't succeed the first time, nor will I even come close to disproving Goldhagen's position. But I will demonstrate that, time and again, people endeavored to cope with life, for themselves, and in the process may have saved the lives of others and survived the ineptitude of those who purported to steer the course of history.

Finally, there is still another particularly important aspect. I do not report here on my recollections as "just" one of the people, or as one of the victims of national and global policies. I am reporting on the recollections of someone—myself—who was then in the process of growing up, of trying to understand the world around him, as a kid trying to make sense of a rather messy, grown-up world, and how it was to grow up in a political climate that deteriorated in every sense of the term. Just as anybody else did, I had to cope with the circumstances I found myself in. In the process, I actually became more acutely aware of the difference between right and wrong.

Considering the fact that on May 2, 1945, I found myself in the center of Berlin on which the Russians had trained about two thousand pieces of artillery, and considering further that a few hours later, I marched in a POW column towards the east, I wouldn't have gambled a penny on my own survival. But I managed to get away and I participated in the revival of Berlin right from the very beginning. So, again I have the benefit of an observational vantage-point in a very critical location. If I don't put down on paper what I remember, if others fail to do the same (how many of us are still alive?), what really happened in the field may soon be forgotten and become the subject of intended or unintended distortions.

A JUSTIFICATION OF PURPOSE

The Nazi era just happened to coincide with my growing up. I was five years old when Hitler came to power, 11 when World War II started, and 17 when it ended. I was in my early twenties when an era began that later became known as the German "economic miracle." This, of course was no miracle at all, but the German equivalent of what Churchill had promised to the British in 1940: a lot of blood, sweat, toil, and tears – which turned out to be not so much blood or tears at that time, but a lot more toil.

Obviously, my memory of the early part of the Third Reich is fraught with the uncertainties and distortions of childhood. On the other hand, for that exact reason, I am in a position to reminisce without the danger of encroachment of evaluative aspects that may tend to look at things in an apologetic, accusatory, or otherwise biased fashion. The self-centeredness of a pre-teen kid, and the absence of a developed, critical frame, ensure a considerable amount of objectivity in what is remembered. That said, the critical attitude of an adolescent teen ensures against any approving bias towards accepting the world of the grownups.

Now I come already to an important point. Maybe I do have something to say, something to report which will tell somebody who bothers to read it something that he or she may not get out of history books, if only for the reason that that particular author wasn't there. Remember, this is not intended to be a scholarly evaluation. In fact, I will shy away from reporting any matters I have not personally experienced. However, such experience often invite reflection.

And so, at some future date, this writing may be deemed a valuable source for a social historian to draw on. Coping with life during that time ultimately meant finding some way to stay alive physically but in a manner that was compatible with some form of dignity.

I was a child, and for me the Nazi era coincided with that period in one's life in which we develop a value system and begin to (or at least try to) understand the world that surrounds us. So, initially my account will reflect a conflict. To a child, the world is as it appears to him or her and is thus "all right"; but what happens if your own development of an understanding of what is right and your own intellectual evaluation are in conflict with what you're experiencing? That kind of conflict will indeed be a part of this account, but I hasten to add this conflict didn't turn me into a "neurotic," but rather enhanced my inquisitiveness.

This inner conflict was something which many of my contemporaries also faced, including my classmates and many others of my generation who attended different schools, but I do not know how many of them were even aware of the problem. I will, as best as I can, though, report on the information which was, for me, the source of that conflict.

What information, exactly? Here I arrive already to a point which people living today, that is, half a century later, will find difficult to understand, namely, how limited the information was that was available. We had no TV (yet); radio was very limited in its news content and it was, in general, of no interest to me, except on certain occasions which I remember vividly and will recount in due course. I don't recall when I started to read any newspaper, nor when I became aware of the fact that the press was controlled, but I do remember how, in late 1943, a teacher openly justified lying by the press. As a growing child you really didn't know what was going on in the world, particularly if you, as I did, lived in a very sheltered environment.

I am writing this story in the turning years of one century/millennium to the next one. Many things have happened since I began, and I have gained many new insights. But also, many distorted accounts about the era of my childhood have emerged. As I said in the beginning, the real beginning of WWII hasn't been generally acknowledged: the idea of Nazi Germany's sole guilt is too dear to politically motivated historians. After all, now that the second millennium A.D. comes to a close, we need to be on good terms with the Russian government. But that point isn't important; after all, my memoirs aren't in the least intended as a subtle excuse for some Germans' behavior, including the government's, during the Nazi era. Quite to the contrary, my own observations are limited to Germany, and that is bad enough. What I want to convey is an impression that people, myself included and to the extent I can remember, will try to cope with whatever situation they're confronted with. I'll try to paint a picture of that situation as I, a kid growing up, perceived it. And I will include people in the picture, again myself included, to tell the reality of how we coped.

I am a student of history and, thus, know only too well that it is difficult, nay impossible, to find out what the people in past ages really felt, strived for, wondered, rooted for – whether they were really ever enthusiastic about anything. Just let me posit two situations for comparison. In the middle of the third millennium B.C., tens of thousands of laborers dragged many stones across the Egyptian desert and hoisted them on top of each other. Were they the unlucky victims of a kind of slavery system, or happy participants in a soul-lifting exercise that ensured them a near-Pharaoh position in the after-life? Were they just on a higher wage scale, or did they simply have no choice at all?

As a second example, after WWII, some people suggested that classes at technical schools should be held to teach that the development of weapons was immoral. Leaving aside the completely unrealistic aspect of such a position generally, this "moral" position disregarded a very simple fact: During the war, people in Germany in important positions (for example welders, engineers, managers) could show their usefulness to hi-tech warfare by building weapons rather than becoming cannon fodder. Maybe Jesus or Gandhi or Buddha would have opted for the latter, but to teach that to people as viable approach to life is patently ridiculous. One of my early adolescent experiences was that evil is not in the choice when made, but rather in the system that makes such a choice a necessity for survival.

My story touches on several people who had to make such choices. In fact, many aspects of my account deal with choices that people I knew personally had to make. The choices were not necessarily earthshaking ones, just choices that life threw upon them. I observed these people and had a limited understanding of their struggle, but at the time, I didn't judge them and won't do so now. In this spirit, then, being one of the people, I will try as honestly as I can to report what I remember about growing up in the Third Reich and how I experienced its aftermath. Maybe the reader will glean here aspects of that era he or she may not get from history books.

The author with his father, Berlin 1929: joyous in a simpler time, blissfully naïve as to what was to come.

-1-

EARLY CHILDHOOD – A SHELTERED LIFE

I was born in 1928, a year which later appeared to be the last, really "good" year of the first German Republic; a year later, the world economy collapsed. On the other hand, I was born ten years after the German collapse that marked the end of World War I. In those ten years, Germany struggled through times which were made very difficult by vindictive victors of that "Great War," who still, even to this day, try to avoid admitting their responsibility for the continuation of WWI known as WWII. Thanks to the French statesman Aristide Briand and the German statesman Gustav Stresemann, the late 20s seemed to mark the beginning of a final, stable development in Europe – nobody worried about the Russians, as they were embroiled in the incompetence of their newly created system. However, stock market speculation (i.e. the age-old attempt to get rich fast) brought an end to post-WWI prosperity. Extracting reparations from Germany not only ruined that country, but that the American economy financed, through loans, the German WWI reparation payments – thus tying the German and the American economies together – created a connection that caused them to be mutually dragged down.

This development was so monumentally stupid that, even today, the extent of that stupidity is not fully acknowledged. The economic disaster of 1929 brought down the American economy, but American democracy was too well developed and thus was never really in any danger. However, the first German Republic collapsed, simply by failing to make the people believe that democracy was a viable system for solving their problems. Forgive me for backtracking a little here; obviously, I wasn't aware of these things while wetting diapers.

During my early childhood, the German First Republic went to pieces, but my own world – the circumstances of my living conditions – was very much intact. Of course, I had no idea what was going on and naturally lacked any understanding of it. But even more importantly, my life at that time was so sheltered that as far as I was concerned, it seemed nothing was going on to disrupt it. When I was born, my parents lived on the outskirts of Berlin in the Grunewald area in a housing development which grew out of the housing shortage at the end of WWI. The houses were modest, solidly built, mostly semi-detached but set in a forested region with a garden attached to each house, and basically limited for occupancy (at first) to civil servants. It was as typical a middle class setting as you can possibly get. Since practically everybody in this neighborhood was a government employee, the impending industry unemployment had hardly any effect on the people who lived there.

The turbulence of the political-economic arena in the late '20s and early '30s, therefore, just bypassed our area. Also, in the wider surroundings were many houses owned by wealthy people who likewise were not much affected by the increasingly difficult times. Thus, while in other parts of the city, Communist and Nazi gangs fought street battles, life in my sheltered environment went on very peacefully. Yes, there were beggars, but I didn't understand what they wanted. After all, we always had a maid who lived in the attic and, I might add, quite happily so. At that time, maids often came from rural areas, usually from around the town of Bunzlau, where my mother was born and raised. They often came from farms – not so much a rich farmer's daughter but the offspring of a farm hand. Living in the attic of a city house as a maid was an improvement over living in a barn as a farm servant! I do not remember ever not having had a maid.

I offer here a little more on the subject of maids, as a kind of an aside to social history. I remember several of them quite well; they were paid 20 marks a month, plus room and board. They had long hours and I think, once a week, a day or half a day off. From today's perspective, this would be an almost shameless exploitation of a poor, peasant girl. But keep in mind that, often, these girls had never had running water, flush toilets, or electricity, and to them, the telephone was some kind of Satanic instrument. Room and board were pivotal to the arrangement; the rest was pocket money the likes of which they never had before. Also, they weren't only maids but, in a way, household apprentices. They not only learned how to live a city life, but my mother also taught them how to run a "normal" household. My mother was an excellent cook and didn't keep her recipes a secret. Of course, these girls could already cook, but simple, peasant stuff and not my mother's refined cooking. And as things go, these girls soon had boyfriends and often got married. In several cases, they visited afterwards with their husbands and were very grateful for what they'd learned. Not that those skills are, on their own, important, but it does affect one's outlook on life. Remember, having a maid at that time was practically a requirement!

My father was a civil servant who originally worked for the postal department, and then transferred to the German equivalent of the I.R.S. He grew up in Löwenberg, a small town in lower Silesia. His father died when he was only three years old. He didn't get along very well with his mother, which I do not find surprising because I remember her as a pretty unfriendly person. She died when I was nine years old.

My father attended high school, which was rather unusual in those days, but he didn't graduate. Still, he was too well educated to become a laborer or craftsman and so he became a government employee with the postal department. Apparently, he enjoyed a considerable amount of freedom because his work was organizing local post offices in rural areas with no boss breathing down his neck. I was told that, in any village, he was always immediately made a part of the local elite, which in class-structured Germany was an important aspect of life.

At some point before WWI, my father met my mother, simply because his widowed mother married the brother of my mother's father. I hasten to reassure you that I am not the product of incest. My father's stepfather – that is, my mother's stepfather-in-law, is her uncle; there is no blood relation. My mother told me, however, that after her uncle married this woman, who had a son seven years older than my mother, she met this son for the first time but didn't like him at all, finding him rather obnoxious.

Then came World War I, and my father was drafted into the signal corps. I really regret that I never had a chance to talk to him about his WWI experience as he died when I was seven years old. He was around Verdun, which probably wasn't even surpassed in WWII, in terms of what one may call a protracted, localized massacre. Strategically of modest to low importance, Verdun became a kind of symbol of military prowess. The German side was commanded by the Emperor's son whose sole military qualification was that he was the Emperor's son. The battles in and around Verdun lasted for several years and were about as horrible as the battle of Stalingrad in WWII, except that the latter was over in a few weeks.

Anyway, my father (obviously) came out alive, came home, and courted my mother who found this survivor of the Great War no longer so obnoxious. They married and moved to Berlin. This move, of course, was very fortunate, from my point of view, never mind that I wasn't born yet, as the area of Lower Silesia, where my parents grew up, became Polish territory after WWII.

My mother's hometown is Bunzlau, which I will tell you about in depth a little later; it is a very intimate part of my childhood. My paternal great-grandfather and his forebears also came from Bunzlau. However, I remember very little about my father's hometown, Löwenberg. His father had died long before, and nobody liked my father's mother; we ignored and avoided her to every extent possible which she apparently didn't mind, the dislike being clearly mutual. These towns were small, but I do remember them having a very distinctive character; I remember walking the streets of Bunzlau and Löwenberg and sensing their having a more manageable scale than I was used to in Berlin. To me as a child, the much smaller dimensions had a distinctive appeal.

Now to turn back to my parents. The fact that my father was a civil servant sheltered him, and all of us, from the economic disasters that engulfed Germany in the early '30s. My maternal grandfather's plumbing business, which he'd inherited from his father and expanded greatly, was apparently little affected by the economic situation, so all of us were really unaware of the ensuing upheaval. Again, I have to add that this information was something I gathered – one way or the other – from my elders, as well as through personal experience. The latter is simply the result of my not remembering any upheavals: things were pleasant, peaceful, and quiet, indeed.

Like me, my mother grew up in a very sheltered environment. My maternal grandfather was a kind of local, fairly wealthy dignitary in the business world. They were part of the typical, bourgeois middle class; they had no real problems economically but apparently, the circumstances of her upbringing bored her out of her mind. I never asked her, but I'd wondered whether she married my father primarily (or at least, partly) to get the heck out of that environment and to Berlin! Berlin may have been, for her, a kind of heaven, when looked at from afar. Maybe all that is not fair, but the relations between my mother and her parents were, as far as I remember, always somewhat strained. My grandfather had a kind of tyrannical streak, and my grandmother kowtowed to him in an almost embarrassing fashion. My mother was, her entire life, a very resolute person except when she was with her father. I remember wondering where that determined person disappeared to when she was around him. My mother and her mother, when together, had a kind of conspiratorial attitude you might expect to find among slaves. It was only after my grandfather died that I learned that my grandmother wasn't a bad person after all.

So far, I have been offering these little sketches about my family as a kind of overall background; now I should turn to some specifics. The house in which I first grew up was a kind of row house, four-in-a-row and we lived in one in the middle. On the first floor were a single large family-plus-dining room and the kitchen, a master bedroom and my small room were on the second floor, and then the maid's quarters in the attic. I'll never cease to wonder why we needed a maid, but we always had one; as I said earlier, one *had* to have a maid. My mother was certainly not a lazy woman nor did she have a job, but she and the maid always kept busy in that little house. Of course, at that time, labor-saving devices and most household appliances were unknown.

I remember "wash day," a day of major upheaval for which we hired, in addition to our usual help, a "washer woman." The laundry was done on a grand scale, I believe once a month, with these three women doing the family laundry which had accumulated during the preceding month. Sheets were boiled, and there was a big copper vat with a furnace permanently installed underneath in the basement, and other large, flat vats for rinsing. The entire garden was used up to hang up that stuff (we didn't have a dryer; I don't know whether such a thing actually existed at that time). Later, all this laundry was run through a manually-operated rolling mill kind of contraption.

What an undertaking! I remember all of this as one of my earliest memories because of the enormous to-do it brought about. My father, of course, stayed away; I never found out whether he used this as good opportunity to have a night out with the boys – I hope he did. However, I don't want to give the wrong impression; as far as I remember, my parents had a very good marriage.

Maybe I should add here a bit about modern things. We did have gas for cooking in Berlin, as well as in Bunzlau, and I guess, throughout Germany but in Bunzlau, my grandmother's kitchen was equipped to be heated with wood and coal. I do remember that, with the skill which my grandmother possessed, you could have a much higher and well-controlled oven temperature, as well as a very evenly heated surface griddle when you used wood and coal. We didn't have a refrigerator but in the summer, the ice man regularly brought huge chunks of ice to go into a well-insulated box, and food was placed into a space surrounded by that ice. It worked very well.

No doubt I was always in the way, but we had a lovely garden. In the back of the house, we had a nice patio with a lawn behind it; behind the lawn were some bushes which surrounded a seating area, a kind of patio without the concrete. Behind that seating area was more lawn, and then my little heaven. Since Berlin is part of Prussia, and all of main Prussia has very poor and sandy soil, all of this was, from my point of view, a big sandbox. There was a little bit of topsoil, but not far down, wherever you dug, you soon reached nice, clean, yellow sand. There were other boys of my age in my neighborhood and for some reason, they all came to play – dig, really – in my backyard.

Down the street we were on, across from our house, was the beginning of a rather large forest with little hills, and some open space for sledding on in the winter and for roaming around in the summer. That forest was of continuing interest to me even after we moved to a different street. Also across the street was the school which, in later years, would come to dominate my life and about which I will talk later at length. I remember, one summer, a band of gypsies camped right there, and I was not allowed to go out there because they were supposedly stealing children – all very exciting in an otherwise, very uneventful setting.

In the house next door lived twins, Acki and Heini, who were born just one day after I was. I don't really know why, but I remember that I played very little with them, except in our sand. On the other side lived a family including a daughter, Renate, who was about 5 years older than I, and who regarded me as her little brother. I am still, to this day, in contact with her even though her family moved away when I was just a few years old. I did have a friend my age, who lived around the corner, Peter Bäcker. He too came digging in "my" sandbox. After some years he moved away, and we never went to school together. Behind our garden lived a family with several girls whom I ignored. Generally, I don't remember much neighborliness; it seemed everybody kept to himself. I don't believe that this had anything to do with politics. I'll come to this aspect later, but the entire atmosphere was clearly one of "live and let live."

My early childhood fell into a time which was roughly one-and-a half decades after World War I. Well, it didn't have a number then; it was just The World War. All of the men of my parents' generation that I knew, and who had been in that war, obviously were glad that they made it back and were only too happy to embark on a normal life. By the time I was running around, all of them were clearly happy that they had accomplished something; it was a kind of German, post-WWI boom equivalent. Most acquaintances of my parents, and not just in my neighborhood, were civil servants and quite content to embark on a peaceful life. I bring up this point, because after WWII, the impression has sometimes been given that during the thirties, the Germans were drooling for revenge of WWI, that they were out to conquer, and what-not. Well, not in my neighborhood and not among my parents' friends.

On what basis can I say this? Children hear and learn about the world – and from the adults – more than the adults want them to know and realize. I don't believe that my mother and her friends talked about the war; they certainly didn't gloat over tales of heroism. As I learned, rather, quite the opposite – war is nothing but suffering; they, of course, knew that and simply didn't want to talk about it.

I need to interject an important point here, and it's something almost incomprehensible to the people of today. Besides occasional photographs in the newspapers and newsreels (provided you went to the movies often which my parents did not), people really didn't have the opportunity to get a real-life impression of any politician. I don't believe that people had an inkling of the demonic power that may have emanated from that man; anyone living today has had the opportunity to see him on history TV shows many, many more times than contemporaries could have.

I personally do not have the slightest recollection about Hitler taking power; it didn't affect my life one way or the other. Particularly, the Nazis taking power didn't affect my neighborhood. Admittedly, I was only five years old, and that limits your scope of observation. But I have observed my own children and presently, my grandchildren: five-year-olds are very observant; of course, they don't understand many aspects of what is going on, but they do remember scenarios. And on that basis, I feel free to assert that Hitler's taking power wasn't noticed in my neighborhood. Whatever the adults may have talked about, there was neither jubilation nor any public despair. But maybe there is more to this: If there had been commotion or excitement, I possibly would remember. After all, Hitler didn't gain power by a revolution, but as the leader of a party that formed a coalition government. A careful look at history books shows that on Jan 30, 1933, just another government was formed – a déjà-vu affair, we'd seen this before. Since television didn't yet exist, it couldn't bring the Nazi's victory parade into people's home. Life just continued as usual, as if nothing had happened.

Since my father, being a civil servant, was expected to join the Nazi party, he did. Whether he ever believed that stuff of which the great politics of that time was made, I have no idea. It sure did not affect the friendship I had with another little boy my age, Thomas Berliner. His father was an attorney and as the name indicates, he was Jewish. That, of course, didn't mean anything to me, until one day, shortly after I had started school, a new friend from school, Eberhard P., the son of a local Super-Nazi, an unemployed lawyer, told me that I shouldn't play with Thomas because he was Jewish. I find it remarkable that I remember this event, including the point that I had not the slightest idea what a Jew was. And so I tried to ask Eberhard what that meant. Well, he didn't know either – we were six years old, so this lack of knowledge of ethnic details may be excusable–until he enlightened me that Jews are people with crooked noses. I was quite flabbergasted and actually (and this is very important) found this perfectly ridiculous; first of all, why shouldn't I play with someone who has a crooked nose, and besides, Thomas had the cutest up-turned nose you can imagine. So much for my introduction to anti-Semitism. I wonder whether this little episode was a kind of antidote, a spiritual vaccination, making anti-Semitism ever so ridiculous[4].

I don't remember exactly when Thomas left, but the Berliners left Germany for London quite early in the Nazi era. Actually, there were quite a number of Jewish children in our neighborhood, and they all sort of disappeared, even well before the Holocaust so I am sure they all made it to safety, at least at first, unless they moved to one of the neighbor countries; I do not know about that.

So, politics hardly entered my life in these years, largely due to the geographic setting, i.e. the highly sheltered environment in which I grew up. We lived not too far from the site on which the

---

4 [In my opinion this is a crucial lesson: the inoculant power that a single encounter like this can have. It in part explains today's "cancel culture," the ensuring that such inoculations not occur. – KS]

Olympic stadium was being built for the 1936 Olympics. Within walking distance from our house, about five to 10 minutes, was a main boulevard called Heerstraße (meaning Street of the Army). It was and still is about as wide as the Champs Elysées in Paris, and at least twice as wide as Wilshire Boulevard in Los Angeles or Broadway in Manhattan, and leads literally straight to the Brandenburg Gate and into the center of the city. The stretch from Brandenburg Gate toward downtown is called *Unter den Linden* (meaning Under the Lime Trees).

A five minutes' walk from my house to the Heerstraße actually took me to a train station for the railroad line passing under that Boulevard. The railroad was a part of Berlin's superb public transportation system. The elevated train system was immaculately clean, something I didn't think notable until I came to New York. There also were streetcars running on Heerstraße as a part of a very extensive network of streetcars. We thus had very easy access to other parts of the city, to downtown and, primarily, to various shopping and business areas on the West Side of town including the famous Kurfürstendamm (or Ku-dam).

My immediate surroundings were these tract-houses built after WWI in the Grunewald, the forest facing our house. Along the Heerstraße from the train station towards the outskirts were very stately and frightfully expensive villas. In the opposite direction from the train station, that is, towards town, Heerstraße was lined with, as well as flanked by, side streets of expensive apartment buildings. Since we were at the edge of the Grunewald forest, there were other developments nearby as well as along that edge. All this created a very sheltered environment, far from any poverty.

The closest movie house was about 20 minutes away; shops one could walk to were few and far apart. I don't know whether zoning had anything to do with that. However, among fancy apartment buildings, just a bit away from the Heerstraße, we had an open street market twice a week. Believe it or not, that market is still there, same days and hours. That was and still is the place to get the freshest produce and continues to be frequented by ladies in fancy fur coats as well as maids. Before I went to school, my mother often took me along to the market. The highlight of my days occurred when my mother asked a potato salesman, for a very modest fee, to bring all the stuff she had bought to our house and I was allowed to sit next to him on a horse-drawn wagon. That was an era of simple pleasures; after more than 65 years, I still remember these rides. On a daily basis the milkman came each morning, and so did the "roll boy,"[5] some young fellow who hung a bag with fresh crisp rolls on our outside doorknob. Once in a while, a scissors and knife sharpener came by with a gadget that was operated by foot-pedals, and he sharpened whatever was given to him for that purpose. Indeed, nothing exciting really ever happened, not in my early childhood anyway.

The train station itself holds a number of memories. Very early on, and actually throughout the years, it was for me a kind of gateway to the world. Seeing the trains roaring into the station, and the stationmaster seemingly controlling them, was always exciting. When I was late and the train had already begun to roll and the doors had shut automatically, it was difficult to get on, but in later years it was a kind of thrill to jump on and pry the doors open to the adults' frowning glances. I also remember there was an attendant in the station to whom you had to present your ticket for punching before walking onto the platform; he knew everybody and everybody knew him, and he always had a smile and a friendly greeting.

Outside the station a policeman stood, guarding who knows what. Several of our maids were quite friendly with them. In later years, but still before the war, our guarding police "force" consisted of an elderly cop, usually riding a bicycle while being accompanied by a very large, very friendly German Shepherd. In the winter, this

---

5 Brötchenjunge

cop's duty was to make sure that the sidewalks were duly swept and kept free of snow. Beyond that, the only crimes he had to pursue (in my memory anyway) were when we boys were again riding around on our bikes in the evening without a headlight. (He never caught us shooting at streetlights.) At the beginning of WWII, the policeman was drafted to police the Warsaw Ghetto; he ended up in an insane asylum.

As I mentioned, my father died when I was 7 years old; we had just moved to a bigger house, but whatever I remember of him – which is very little – occurred while we lived in Lözenalle in the smaller house. Nearby, there had been a great deal of excavation left over from when the railroad tracks were built, and a lot of sand was piled up to create a simple but fairly high mountain where my father took me quite a number of times for kite flying, particularly in the fall. Later, during WWII, four heavy anti-aircraft guns were placed on that hill. When we heard the shooting (well, when our house started to shake from the shooting), we knew "they" were above us. In the beginning, the four guns shot salvos, but then the hill started to slide so from then on, they shot one gun after the other in cyclic repetition, more or less continuously. That noisy racket, too, is part of my childhood memory, but I'm getting ahead of my story.

My relationship with my father is difficult to recall, but a few aspects stand out quite vividly. One was his infatuation with automobiles, a luxury item at that time and, of course, he couldn't afford one. Not too far from our housing development was one end-portion of a speedway for auto races called Avus. He took me there, not to sit in a high-priced stand but to some place where there was a hole in the fence. When we climbed through, we stood just next to the track – officialdom wasn't much concerned about general safety then. And from there we admired the motorized monsters roaring by in a blur, just a few yards away from where we stood. Unlike the Indianapolis racetrack, or the Nurburgring or the Monte Carlo track, the Avus was more than six miles of straight track in each direction, with very tight curves at the ends. We stood about one mile down from one of the curves, so the cars had already attained full speed when they sped past us.

In retrospect I marvel at my father, a law-abiding civil servant, crawling with his son through the bushes to seek out a forbidden but unparalleled vantage point for viewing the auto races. Was it a kind of catharsis for him to relive the trenches in a manner that tied the thrill, not to destruction, but to pleasure, and to make sure that I could safely experience it? Well, my psychoanalyzing my father may not be fruitful. I hardly knew him, and I write this after more than half a century. I would just like to say that this is one of the fondest memories I have of him. Maybe I'm glorifying him excessively, but not until I began writing these memories did I realize how much I've missed him all these years.

I also remember a few visits with him to the downtown area of Berlin. Later, I would see more of it, but in my early childhood, downtown Berlin was a kind of far-away land – a talked-about, but not much seen, place. One particular visit stands out. My father and I were bumming around, and he had a silhouette cutter make a portrait cut of me. I remember when it was made; it still hangs as a picture in my living room, more than 65 years later.

-2-

ELEMENTARY SCHOOL – A NEW SHELTER

At that time, Germany did not have anything like a Kindergarten so school started for me when I was six years old, and what a school it was! It was quite a distance to walk, at least for little kids, about three-fourths of a mile. I think that it was close to what one might call a "little red schoolhouse," except that it consisted of three wooden, one-story structures painted red, each with two classrooms which could hold about 30 to 40 children, for just four grade levels. In all, there were four teachers, one of whom was the principal. As such, the school was an interesting reflection of the local class structure. Grammar or elementary school normally had eight grades and generally, after four years of elementary school, about twenty percent of all students nationwide switched to high school. However, in our area, almost all students did so it would not have been worthwhile in our area to maintain a full, eight-grade school.

As I have indicated, it was an era of simpler, and may I say, more human relationships in many facets of life. In our school, the fourth graders had as a project to jot down a list of items the next entering first graders were supposed to have and bring to school. Mind you, not a computer print-out or a type-written, Xeroxed sheet of instructions, but a hand-written list, written by a nine-year-old to be given to a kid a few years younger. I got mine in 1934 and still have it. I have no idea who wrote it, but I rather regret that my children and grandchildren never experienced anything similar. But maybe I am unfair; it may well be that today, there are other projects which tie kids of different grades and ages together in a common bond.

My elementary school years covered the mid-thirties, a time of considerable political change in Germany, but we students were not aware of any of it. Did our elders try to shield us from the affairs of state and avulsions of society? Quite possibly so. The political-social antagonism of what was, in fact, a decaying society was kept from us. We were taught what was right and what was wrong without political, demagogic coloring. I do not remember ever being taught that somebody, anybody, for whatever reason, was bad or evil. I deem this to be one of the most important aspects concerning my early schooling and actually of my later years, too. We simply weren't taught to discriminate against people for whatever reason, involving beliefs, origin, background, etc. Maybe this was an anomaly in our area, a rare exception although I doubt that. I simply want to report on my experience.

The list of things we needed to begin school I mentioned above included a slate board with a little sponge. So, aside from learning in the usual way, we learned to write on a slate board. Later on we wrote with real ink pens, each desk having a little well and we didn't make big messes (at least not all the time). One of our four teachers taught singing. I still remember his superb bass voice, and he also played the guitar. It was a school for sheltered children in a sheltered environment; we were never made aware, for any reason, of any trouble.

What I remember most from my early school years was an

annual summer festival. Because of its smallness, the school obviously had only a small budget. In fact, the city paid the teachers and some janitors, and owned the rather simple buildings so I don't know whether there was any budget at all for the principal's discretionary use.

In order to raise money, they held the summer festival which was made up of a play staged by the fourth graders. For us kids, this was, of course, quite an important event. But far more important was what we'd consider an afternoon brunch – main courses with salads, elaborate open-face sandwiches, and of course "Kaffee und Kuchen[6]." All of the mothers contributed to what had become, over the years, an open competition among them in gourmet food preparation. It was all homemade and put the finest delicatessen and cafés to shame. People came from far away to attend – of course all the parents, but many more. It was always a rousing success. The cost base for the school was zero and the prices were what the traffic could bear. Considering the quality of what was offered, that could be quite a lot. And the festival ended each year with a procession with lanterns.

As a consequence of its success, our little school acquired a sizable budget and saw significant improvements every year. One year, a wading pool was built. In another, a bobsled hill; another year, we got our own little indoor/outdoor gym. One of the most spectacular sights was a terraced garden with unbelievably beautiful and well-kept flowers. In short, it was a growing little paradise. Did I mention already that it was a sheltered environment? Maybe that was an understatement.

Anything as significant as street gangs fighting, unemployment – well, just don't read the papers. I certainly didn't – well I couldn't in the years when there was still something worth reading. As I have said, to us children, it was a peaceful world and may I conjecture that our parents kept it up, not quite yet as a make-believe sham.

---

6 coffee and cake.

-3-

A MODERATELY INTERESTING NEIGHBORHOOD

I was in second grade when my father died from a heart attack, which was apparently brought on by overexertion during gardening. There was big funeral, but it is somewhat blurred in my memory; it is very unfortunate but I just was too young to keep a lasting impression of my father except for the few memories mentioned earlier.

A few weeks before my father's death, we had just moved into a new house in Marienburger Allee. It was larger, a three-bedroom house, which had three stories and a garden which was a little smaller than at the other house in Lözenallee.

This new house is what I really consider my home because I lived in it – with a few interruptions – from 1935 onwards, during the entire war and thereafter, until I went to America in 1956. As before, I had my play heaven with the local sand, and my friends still lived around the corner including Eberhard who had tried anti-Semitism on me. But since little Thomas had left, there was no opportunity for further enlightenment on the subject. But let me tell a little more about various people who lived nearby.

Next door, and also in the next two houses beyond, lived three families of which the man of the house was blind from war injuries. Particularly our next-door neighbor, Mr. Schwaia, was a fascinating person to me. He walked in the garden next to ours with such a sure step that often, when people visiting us saw him, they could not believe that he was blind. He hosed the garden and never sprayed the street or even the sidewalk. How did he know? I never found out. He had a good job with the city; his wife took him every morning to the railway station and picked him up in the evening. In later years, on several occasions, particularly during the war, I took him to the station in the morning and picked him up in the evening when his wife was sick. It was amazing how sure-footed he was.

In the house next to his lived another of these "war-blinds." He always went to work by himself. Every house in our development had front fences and posts. The man had a cane and used it as a kind of scanner sliding along the fences and counting the posts as obstacles. It worked really well in all those years; once in a while, he miscounted and then went into the wrong house, but very rarely. People knew him, of course, and helped him home – he did not like that at all.

Obliquely opposite lived some kind of bigwig in the Opel company, the German General Motors affiliate. He often test-drove stylish looking, newly developed cars. (I understand that Opel had hoped to compete successfully with the VW, and later, after the war, they actually did.)

My mother had comparatively little contact with that family. To give an indication of this, as it happened, the wife died sometime in the late '30s, but my mother didn't know about it for almost a year. I guess, by and large, my mother had a complex mixture of traits. On the one hand she was extremely sociable, the kind one calls the "life of the party." But often, she could be very stand-offish. We really had hardly any contact on a personal basis with any of the neighbors, but that (as with so many things) changed after the war began. Then, of course, people were often drawn together – or became mortal enemies.

The houses in which we lived were part of the same development, as I said, of which one aspect was, of course, a certain commonality in style. However, in the Marienburger Allee to which we moved, a certain portion of the street – about seven or eight houses – were built in this particular style on one side only. Bigger, customized houses were built on the other side. Not that it made any difference as far as I was concerned, except later, that became important when the occupation forces moved in. The Opel executive lived in one of these houses, and next to them lived what was, in a way, a long-time friend, Eberhard von Werne. But our relation was, let's say, somewhat variable. He was very proud that he could trace his lineage back to a Roman centurion and that in the Middle Ages, his ancestors were knights but became robber barons[7], so the Emperor demoted his family to a mere "von." We played a lot together, went to the same elementary school which I described already, and when it was our turn to put on a play (1937) for the summer festival, we staged "Snow White," and he was the Prince. I was supposed to play, believe it or not, the witch; but there was a girl in our class who was even "witchy-er" than I, so I had to put up with just being one of the dwarfs. I was vindicated in a way, years later in high school, when we staged *Faust* and I was Mephistopheles.

Returning to a description of our neighborhood, I now turn to an aspect which is peculiar or, one might even say, inexplicable. In one of these larger houses lived a Jewish family whose name I have forgotten. On our side of the street, a few house away, lived a Jewish gentleman, Mr. Reinhold, with his daughter, and several houses still further, there lived an elderly Jewish lady (elderly, mind you, from the point of view of a child; so, everybody over 25 qualifies). I do

---

7 He was particularly proud of that aspect!

not remember her name either, but she was known as the "duck," on account of her somewhat waddling walk.

The entire street had, on both sides, about sixty houses, so, it wasn't very large. Well, these Jewish neighbors lived there when we moved in 1935, and in 1945, when the war was over, they still lived there unharmed. I don't believe that I ever saw any of them wearing the infamous yellow star; and I don't think that this could be due to inattentiveness on my part, because I noticed the star on other people. What am I really saying here? It is one of those situations that can easily be turned into a despicable polemics – into "proof" that things were not as bad as portrayed later: if all the Jews in our area were left untouched during the war, then maybe not many of them were. This is, of course, horribly fallacious. The fact of the matter is that maybe the Nazi machinery was just imperfect, and maybe it (the machinery) depended, to some extent at least, on citizens' co-operation which was not forthcoming in our area.

In 1945, when the Russians stormed Berlin, the Jewish gentleman, Mr. Reinhold, became temporarily a kind of local administrator, a kind of go-between for the local people and the Russians which was a very tricky position. I believe that he really did what he could to prevent excesses. All in all, on a very local scale, civilized behavior at least mitigated against the primitive brutality that often prevails, or seem to dominate, on a grander "historical" scale. But that was the world I lived in and is, in that regard, just an example.

A few houses away, on a kind of cul-de-sac, lived a couple named Schleicher. I'm not exactly sure of the family relation, but they were parents-in-law of a Mr. Dohnányi, as well as of the Reverend Dietrich Bonnhöffer, who also lived on the street; both were very prominent in the resistance against the Nazis. Both were executed after the uprising in 1944. The Dohnányis had two boys, Klaus and Christoph, who for some time went to my elementary school. I think I played with them for some time; one went to the same class as I did, the other one was a bit older. One, Klaus, was, not too long ago, Mayor of Hamburg; the other, Christoph, is a well-known conductor, and presently, I think, with the Cleveland Symphony Orchestra.

There were still other important or noteworthy people living in our street. Directly across the street lived Bruno Aulich, a conductor of the Berlin Radio orchestra. He had a pretty daughter I gawked at while I was in my early teens. In the house next to Aulich's lived a member of the Board of Directors of Siemens, Mr. Scharnofski. They had rather flamboyant habits and entertained the neighborhood by nightly hitting a gong to call the family to the dinner table. Then there was an Undersecretary of "I do not know what." We had little contact, though, with all these important people, and they all[8] left Berlin well before the end of the war.

Somewhat in anticipation of things to come, a few houses down the street lived the family Öchsner; their son Klaus went to elementary school with me, but later to a different high school. He was Luftwaffenhelfer[9] towards the end of the war, just as I was, but he vanished in some area near Berlin. Literally for years, Klaus' mother went to that area and volunteered in exhuming and identifying soldiers killed in action (there were many in and around Berlin), hoping to find her son. Somehow, it's hard to say whether it was good that she didn't find her son because, at least in later years, all she could have found was an extensively decayed body.

Why am I dwelling on this? I liked Klaus very much; in elementary school, we were fairly close friends, but then he went to a different high school. I went to a more liberal school, about which I will narrate quite extensively. He went to a neighboring, "elite" school called the Mommsen Gymnasium. Neither of us knew, of course,

---

8 Except the older Schleichers

9 Literally translated, it means "Airforce helper"; a rather cumbersome word, it applied to boys who were drafted into the air-force. I will talk about it later at great length as it applied to me, too.

that the latter school had a very pronounced Nazi orientation; it was the age-old conflict for the parents, seeking status or substance. The high school I went to was clearly a source of substance rather than a show place as the Mommsen Gymnasium was. I strongly believe that if Klaus had gone to my school, he may well be alive today. The same holds true for another friend of my early years, Detlev Seifert. I will talk about him in another context later.

Also, a few houses away lived a family named Trader, whose son Jürgen, was a grade below mine. He was exceedingly smart, but as soon as the war was over he became a devout Communist, one of the very few I know of and certainly an oddity in my generation, at least among my acquaintances.

At the end of the street lived what, potentially, could have been a super-Nazi. He was second in command of the infamous "Arbeitsdienst," some kind of labor conscription all young people were subjected to, for men to serve for half a year preceding their military service. Luckily, I was spared that kind of utterly disgusting, thinly disguised slave labor. By making this evaluative statement, am I not going beyond my own experience? I want to emphasize that I try very hard not to "supplement" experience gained in the past with knowledge gained later; that would be nothing but hindsight reasoning, exactly what I want to avoid. However, I will time and again come back to the fact that I grew up in a kind of golden ghetto, but the reference to the slave labor conscription is an important point for the following reasons.

This particular man, I think his name was Tolens, was part of that "movement" by means of which Germany was, by and large, converted into essentially a network of camps. The underlying concept was that of organized labor, "organized" encompassing, for example, labor service by enforced conscription of 18-year-old boys/men. I suspect that, in part, it was a way at that time to get at least young people off the labor market, so as not to compete with middle-aged people who had been looking for work. In retrospect, I find the attitude of many of our parents' generation, including my mother – that it's good to get the young people off the street – quite despicable, and excusable only by the ignorance about the slave camp facilities.

Much has been written about the German concentration (KZ.) camps, with an emphasis on limited and specific groups that were interned in that fashion. But, in fact, in the early '30s, an internment system began to be developed, such that, sooner or later, many people went through one kind of camp or another. Men conscripted to the armed forces went to barracks; later in the war years, labor camps sprang up everywhere. The degree of guarding and watching were different in different kinds of camps, but the concept of confining people and restricting their freedom of movement was similar and became prevalent throughout Germany. The labor force camps were, of course, not as bad as the "regular" KZ's. Am I relativizing matters? Not at all; there were degrees of confinement and relatively different aspects of stricture, but confinement is confinement.

I am not writing abstract history here. Rather, I am trying to explain how the conscription and slave labor became gradually noticeable, visible, and unfortunately, even acceptable. What do I mean by "noticeable?" My story covers at this point the middle part of the thirties, a few years into the Nazi era. And indeed, more and more people appeared in uniform: brown, black, mustard and even the gray of the Army and the bluish of the Air Force began to appear more often. I began to appreciate, gradually, the meaning of this, that is, the militarization of civilian life[10]. The uniform became a noticeable fact of life and, in time, was accepted, while as to me, it evoked gradually a rebellious attitude. Like the slave labor conscription, the preparations for what was to come took place everywhere, in secret at first, under all kinds of cover (like getting young people off the

---

10 [Because of this association of uniforms with militarization of civic life, neither my brother nor I was permitted to join any of the scouts organizations. Uniforms and the quasi-military nature of scouts was nothing our parents wanted to be part of our lives –KS]

streets). At that time, I didn't understand what was going on. So, I will gradually come to my growing aversion to the regime in power, as this story progresses.

As my home and school were far away from the rough parts of official politics and public life, it happened that the glamorous parts were not far from our bourgeois neighborhood. For example, the Olympic stadium was indeed not very far from home and school. The spectacle of the Berlin Olympics in 1936 is still something I remember well. Since our family lived so close to the area of festivities and sport events, we and many others had offered rooms in our house to visitors. I have a somewhat hazy memory of a multimillionaire from South Africa spending a few days in our house, and he left my mother a whole booklet of event tickets. I don't know what she did with it. Of course, I vividly remember the excitement of it all. The marathon runners, as well as the long-distance walkers, passed the next corner, and we could see this without much ado, i.e. paying for tickets. I also remember, in retrospect, that there was no security of any kind. And why should there be?

As an interesting aside to the Olympics, they occurred just a few months after the German army re-occupied the so-called demilitarized West Bank of the Rhineland. Just another bluff Hitler called. Interesting, how today's historians make much of the event as Hitler's first wrong-doing. Obviously, he viciously tore the Treaty of Versailles apart, I think beginning with the stopping of paying reparations. Clearly, he had the support of the German people for this, and even more importantly, at that time there was international silence and acquiescence. There just wasn't much fanfare, and who would do anything just a few months before the Olympic games? That the games served well as a propaganda tool was, of course, something of which I was not aware.

I mentioned already the main Berlin boulevard which was called Heerstraße, near where I lived at the outskirts of Berlin and rather close to it; in Downtown Berlin, that street became the well-known "Unter Den Linden." The Brandenburg Gate, a rather ominous landmark, straddled the boulevard and separated the "outskirts" from the downtown area. This boulevard was, of course, primarily planned for parades and other pageantry during the monarchy, well before WWI. Later it became the pompous access road for the Führer, as he was going to infatuate the world leaders, an endeavor in which he largely succeeded. Within walking distance from where we lived was an underpass where the boulevard crossed over the Railway particularly for the regular elevated / surface trains of the municipal train system of Berlin. Because of its location, the train station located here was used for Mussolini's first reception in Berlin. He arrived in Berlin, I think, in 1937 by train, and from the train track/ Heerstraße intersection, he was then driven for the entire length of the boulevard into downtown, traversing indeed the entire city. I wonder whether this kind of spectacular hosting is going to be resumed in the capital of the reunited Germany.

I remember the arrival of Mussolini quite well because we kids crawled all over the place to get near the station and around the barriers that were set up. Things were not that cozy with Italy at that time, but security wasn't tight at all. In any event, I did get close enough with other kids to get a glimpse of the two dictators together. Though I didn't see it directly, I still should add here an amazing feat accomplished by the railroad engineers.

Mussolini and Hitler arrived in separate trains, and the trains ran alongside each other at the same speed, so that the two dictators could talk to each other through open windows, as was duly recorded in the news-reels. Then, just a few minutes before arriving at the station, Hitler's train pulled ahead just slightly to stop half a minute or so prior to Mussolini's arrival, with Hitler's door at an exact spot where there was red carpet. He crossed over to be exactly where Mussolini's door landed when his train stopped; the doors, of course, had to be in exactly the corresponding spots. With today's electronics, that would be no problem. But controlling steam engines at such a positioning accuracy is a near impossibility. But when dictators give orders!

Well then, on they went, with the boulevard lined with flags, all the way to downtown. In less than 10 years, most of the houses on that road of pomposity were in ruins. But in later years, it became one of the first streets with traffic lights controlled in both directions such that if you drive a particular speed, you will hit green lights all the way to the Brandenburg Gate.

Back to the Heerstraße and my neighborhood in the '30s. Up to the early war years, Hitler rode down that boulevard for adulatory purposes relatively often, I would say several times a year. Of course, we kids were always gawking at the spectacle, which repeated itself with stupefying monotony. Still, it was always a "good show." But now I must recount an interesting aspect, of the kind which the world at large would rather forget.

We all know how, after World War II, "everybody" all over the world always "knew" how bad Adolf Hitler was; "they" all were always opposed to him etc., etc. What utter rubbish. The world kowtowed to Hitler. How do I know that? Not from personal experience, but just look at any newspaper from the '30s. But much more telling is the following observation.

I will never forget the sight of a *very* slowly moving open convertible car, with Hitler standing in the front, very erect, completely motionless. No matter how perfectly cushioned a vehicle might be, a person can stand in it without holding on and without being in danger of being thrown to and fro only when the vehicle is moving quite slowly, and that was indeed the case. In other words, he offered absolutely *the* perfect target. Consider: President Kennedy was sitting in his car, and it was not creeping along Dealy Plaza when he was shot. Crack-shots literally had hundreds more times the opportunity to get rid of Hitler but at that time, nobody ever made any attempt to assassinate him. There was no protection whatsoever. How come? Obviously, it was apparent that there was no need for protection. These demonstrations were a symbol of seeming invulnerability, power and strength, far different from the scum that brought him into power. Where were these alleged opponents? This is a typical example of post-modernist revisionist history. It suits the purpose of its proponents because the opposite, the truth, is just too embarrassing. You have to dwell on the well-recognized, unsurpassed evil of Adolf Hitler, and so you just ignore how much he was adulated and that it would have been very easy to eliminate him; but it was never attempted at that time. I mention this specifically because I witnessed, time and again, the slowly-moving, erect figure in the front of his car, a perfect target – how easy would it have been to assassinate him.

-4-

SOME INTERESTING PEOPLE (TO ME)

I'm sorry to say that my father's death in 1935 when I was seven years old was not as traumatic an experience as one might suspect; I guess I was too young and possibly, in one's early age, the father is just not around much. Here, I might add that, because of his expertise in complex accounting, the Nazi party used him and his spare time to keep the finances of the local party group in order [11]. In any event I cover now the period which, on one hand, was my pre-teenage years, coinciding on the other hand with the immediate pre-WWII years.

Following the death of my father, my mother decided to rent out one room to respectable gentlemen, never to any women, and the poor chaps who applied were subjected to tight scrutiny and screening as to their respectability. I will talk on and off about some of them

---

11 [Dad often mentioned how, in a twisted way, it was a good thing his father had died before the real horrors of Nazism and the war came about. Extricating himself from the party might not have been possible, certainly would not have been easy. Dealing with that during the war, and certainly after, would have changed this story in ways we can't even imagine. As his father had died, connections to the party no longer were a factor in the family. – KS]

because, for no known or anticipatory reason, some of them were very interesting people. The first one to stay was a Mr. Conradin, a Swiss student of means who always poked fun at my mother but without ever insulting her or otherwise misbehaving. That was, of course, exactly the right "medicine" for her, after the sudden death of her husband, my father. I remember Mr. Conradin only vaguely, but I do remember his cynical attitude towards the Nazis. You may ask, why he was in Berlin? The answer, of course, is very simple. Germany was still an intellectual powerhouse, as far as its universities were concerned, in spite of the exodus of many learned people. I, being a boy of eight or nine years old, did not fully understand his attitude towards the Nazis, except that probably for the first time, I encountered someone critical of the political ambience in which I grew up.

He married a girl from around the corner and left Germany with her, well before the war started. We visited them and their kids later, after the war. And here, I might add a sad, local statistic. Her father was one of many whom the Russians put into concentration camps at the end of WWII; I don't know of any individual who lived in our development whom the Nazis put into a concentration camp who then didn't return. A strange coincidence? Perhaps; it certainly doesn't disprove the Nazi atrocities, just that one has to be somewhat careful with generalizations. But by contrast, many people of our area were put into camps by the Russians and *none* – not one of them – came back.

Back to our roomers. In 1938 or thereabouts the room was let to a Mr. Junker. Believe it or not, in a subtle way, he made our house into some kind of meeting place for, well, exactly what? A conspiracy, a revolution, a palace coup? Well, not really any of the above, but preparatory for any of them. It shows how difficult it is to pin down and categorize labels on aspects of history. One should remember that the mid '30s was, on one hand, the early Nazi-period; but World War I had ended less than 20 years before, and in the minds of many, the Kaiser had abdicated rather recently under the dictates of WWI's victors. There was (and this I know from historical studies) still a very strong monarchist sentiment throughout the country[12]. So, what I have to report next is not as ludicrous as it may sound at first glance. And that is this: there were groups of monarchists who strongly believed that they could turn Hitler into just a tool, a kind of stirrup-holding knave, and our boarder Mr. Junker was one of them.

In 1938, there were several meetings in our house attended by a few, well, nuts? Among them was His Imperial Highness, one of the grandsons of the last Emperor. They planned the new government of Germany, with our roomer to be the next Minister of Justice. Apparently, these people believed that His Highness just had to snap his fingers at the right time, and this painter bum from Vienna would, of course, step aside. I mention this because, at that time, the arrogance of the nobility was still very strong. The belief that a noble person is almost biologically a somewhat superior species was genuine and any student of history should never forget that it is only very recently that such a belief is no longer held on a widespread basis[13].

In my childhood, I most certainly got still the tail-end of that belief. This is also the reason that my relationship with Eberhard v. Werne was always somewhat clouded. He genuinely believed himself to be a somewhat better person than the rest of us (and I have reason to believe that he still does).

Regarding his Imperial Highness, I am glad to report that my mother served him (and his cause?) delicious, coffee ice-cream, which he appreciated and enjoyed in our garden. Notice my memory of details: the monarchist bug had undoubtedly infested me, too. Luckily, the whole political concept was so utterly foolish that it either was never discovered or was swept under the rug by the Nazis as a

12 Not too long ago there was demonstration in Moscow's Red square with people shouting "long live the Czar"

13 But I am convinced that this belief is far from being dead.

completely unimportant matter; in any event, neither my mother nor I were shot or hung as conspirators. His Imperial Highness was killed in action as a German officer and what happened to the rest of "his government" I do not know. So the brush with the great politics passed us by.

-5-

VACATION (BACK-TRACKING A BIT)

I now turn to other aspects of my "private" life's description in the prewar years involving primarily vacation times, travelling, and a kind of "home away from home." Before I come to the latter, let me report that following the death of my father in 1935, there was a change in our summer travel for two years. Previously, we had always gone for the summer to my grandparents, about whom I will tell below; but in 1936, my mother took me to a Spa at the North Sea near the Isthmus of the Elbe River, in a little village called Duhnen. There, I saw the ocean for the first time and, of course, was overwhelmed. But what was even more astonishing was this.

We arrived in the evening and there it was, the North Sea in all its splendor. In the morning, after we got up, I looked out of the window, but no ocean; it was all gone! This was my first encounter with the tides, which are extraordinarily strong in that part of the world. If you walk out with the receding waters and just keep walking, you will not make it back safely; the water of the tide moves in much faster than you can walk. Well, I stayed nicely near the shoreline, played in the sand and, sadly, I have to admit, I had all but forgotten about my father.

In Duhnen, we stayed in a pleasant inn, which was a novelty to me. There was a cheerful dining room with a very busy waiter whom I remember quite well. The rooms were simple but very nicely furnished. The inn stood a little bit off the center plaza of this village with a very picturesque, cased well in the middle of the village plaza. All that was still there when I visited it 50 years later and rekindled very happy memories. The times, and the war in particular, had passed the place by; well, not quite – the inn had been expanded but not changed in its rustic style. There were some new fancy Strand-hotels, just as boring as the ones they replaced.

This trip was, to some extent, unusual. In those days, people generally, particularly families, didn't travel much except to relatives' homes. But the middle class, I guess, was beginning to discover that, at least occasionally, one doesn't have to travel to relatives and lodge with them; there are other options. One thing that was helpful in this case was the closeness to the beaches of the Baltic Sea, making traveling easy and fairly economical. So this experience from my childhood reflects the beginning of this novelty in middle class life-style. It probably came into being some years after WW1: a summer vacation to a resort or spa was no longer something just for the rich but for the middle class as well, yet there was no mass tourism. Staying in a hotel or inn was something affordable and acceptable, and you didn't squander hard-earned money.

Did this have anything to do with the improvement in the German economy in the '30s? No doubt, to some extent, but as I have mentioned, we and many others of assured income weren't affected by the economy's ups and downs. Travelling at that time was not so much a matter of being able to afford it but an attitude change. Am I unduly generalizing? Perhaps, but I do know that this trip broke a pattern I knew others were following as well: the annual visit to the grandparents. Of course, we had to visit my grandparents too; otherwise they would have been mortally insulted. I do remember that my schoolmates and friends all followed that same pattern, except maybe a few. Going to a resort just was an exception.

I will come to my regular visit to the grandparents (the home away from home) shortly, but I'd like to dwell a bit on these first ventures into a different world. It included a boat ride to an island called Helgoland, not too far from our beachside resort. Once it had belonged to Great Britain, but the last German Emperor traded for it by giving Britain the island of Zanzibar, offshore of Tanganyika, in return for Helgoland. I will never forget our visit: it was a beautiful day and as our ship approached the bright red rocky island sticking out with rugged, vertical edges from a very blue ocean, a shining, silver Zeppelin passed over it. It was spectacular, even by our, present day over-saturated standards.

Another event, memorable to me at least, was a visit to sightsee one of the prides of the German merchant marine, the "Europa." For a while it held the blue ribbon, meaning that it was the fastest ship on the North Atlantic runs. Maybe my current fascination with the Titanic had its origin in this visit. It wasn't as spectacular as the Titanic, but still exhibited significant class differential. Present-day cruise ships don't come even close to the luxury of the first class; though the "Europa" was already toned down from the ridiculous splendor of the Titanic, it still had clearly the solidity of the teak-mahogany age, not yet the plastic-glass pretension. So, I have a vivid memory of a bygone era – not just of its splendor, which was still present but somewhat muted. I also remember very well the third-class accommodations: simple, but decidedly better than on the Titanic, and also considerably better as compared with the congestion prevailing in today's "steerage" on jumbo-jets.

The year following this wonderful oceanside vacation, my mother and I went to a mountainous area along the border between Czechoslovakia and Germany called the "Riesengebirge," or mountains of the giants. Well, it wasn't quite that spectacular. The mountains were modest hills, but still they presented a very lovely area, well developed and with many restaurants. We hiked a lot, and I still remember many parts, many of the inns, and even individual hiking paths. It wasn't as overwhelming to me as the Alps were on a subsequent trip. This particular trip in 1937 to the Silesian Mountains led us also to many little towns which I knew already. I will come shortly to that quite distinctive part of my childhood, the visits to Silesia. Most importantly, we didn't know it yet, but 1937 was the last year of peace. To my way of thinking, WWII had a precursor in 1938, when German troops occupied the Sudetenland, the mountainous region along the border with Germany. Before that, the Riesengebirge had been a part of the Czech/German border region.

My mother and I enjoyed the freedom of togetherness. Two years previously, she had lost her husband; I was now nine years old and obviously didn't take his place. But I remember an incident one evening, when my mother fainted and collapsed because of what turned out to be food poisoning. I didn't panic but summoned help, and she recovered quickly. That incident may have created an important bond.

Closer to home we took occasional trips on a small excursion ship up and/or down the Havel River. Berlin has a very pretty, natural surroundings, with many lakes which are interconnected by rivers and canals. Boat rides there were certainly peaceful and for me, even if they were too long or somewhat boring, still memorable to this day.

Two particular vistas and fun places stand out. There was Potsdam, with its castles and palaces built by Frederik the Great; in particular, I remember Sans-Souci with its splendid gardens, beautifully kept and revered by the people. I'm not sure last time I saw Sans-Souci during this period, probably just shortly before the war. It was like a homecoming when I saw the grounds again in 1994; nothing seemed to have changed, except that the tea pavilion was newly gilded in honor of the then-forthcoming visit of Queen Elizabeth II.

The other fun place was Wannsee, a bay along the Havel, with a very fine beach, almost like an ocean-side beach, with a nice, shallow area for kids to splash in without danger of drowning. This place wasn't far from home, and we went there quite a number of times. I don't remember when it closed in the war. In a rather sinister way, I suspect that the Nazis really were against anything that was fun and not useful in a historic-glorifying manner.

On weekends, my mother always sent me off to the movies. German movies in the thirties were just as phony as in the U.S.: Don't show reality to the people! But amazingly enough, the Nazis tolerated Mickey Mouse who had just made his debut and was shown in Berlin quite extensively. It still amazes me what one saw in this funny little mouse; a kind of escapism? But why would little kids need escapism? Maybe from the adult world? Or just to enjoy the fantasy. In any event I still remember the Mickey Mouse movies. In retrospect, I believe that, even without the war, sooner or later, the Nazis would have found reasons to keep Mickey Mouse from us; after all, it spelled f-u-n, and that they couldn't stand unless it was decreed from above.

-6-

BUNZLAU AND VISITS IN THE SILESIAN MOUNTAINS

The preceding chapter was a kind of interlude emphasizing what I experienced in terms of extracurricular activities in the two summers after my father's death. I now will go back to the mainstream of my life, which is probably quite typical for the middle class. I remember, from my earliest childhood, that during the summer, we always traveled to my grandparents on my mother's side. I think, and have said so already, that was the usual thing to do in the middle class, at least among the people I knew. After my father's death, we broke the exclusivity of that pattern of the "normal" summer vacation. For me, that was, of course, interesting; for my mother it was essential. And with this, I turn to that "normal" vacation pattern which for me was in itself quite interesting because of the basic differences of the setting compared with my Berlin home.

My grandfather was, by and large, a very stingy person, aside from being mostly a stern sourpuss. Possibly, I am a little unjust here and judge the matter by today's standards. At that time, he was probably regarded as just being thrifty. However, he did have a car. Today, this may not seem to be much to say about a person, but at that time it certainly was. In the U.S., Henry Ford had already introduced the car as a people's appliance, but that wasn't the case in Germany (the Volkswagen was already on its way; but in the thirties, it was still in the planning stage, not on the road). Anyhow, an automobile was quite a rarity at that time. I traveled by car only during our visits with the grandparents. However, this wasn't all of his "capitalistic" lifestyle display. My grandfather didn't drive; he could not drive and never even bothered to learn. So, one of the workers in his plumbing business had to double up as "chauffeur" on weekends.

I've never been able to figure out whether my grandfather had that car only for rare weekend excursions, because he sure did not need it for business in the little town of Bunzlau. (The van for crafts-men was not invented yet.) Also, when he visited us in Berlin he always took the train; why, I don't know. I don't believe it was any cheaper, and it would have been nice if, once in a while, we would have a car in Berlin. During our annual visits to Bunzlau, we did occasionally travel by car into the mountains, though not very far. But, for me, this was, of course, quite an adventure. In addition, my grandparents didn't like to walk, so we would be driven from home in Bunzlau to a restaurant for lunch, then to another restaurant for "Kaffee und Kuchen" and then back home. I don't recall whether there was ever any occasion to do a little hiking. Still, the mountain and forest views were very nice. Amazingly, however, when I visited a part of that area again, in 1992, I couldn't remember anything except a church, "Kirche Wang." The church had been built in the Scandinavian style; a very enjoyable memory for me, until I came close and heard a Polish Catholic service taking place in this strictly Lutheran setting. It was certainly a moment when I regretted that 1992 trip down "memory lane."

My mother didn't enjoy these very short trips to the mountains one bit. Whether she just didn't like the trip, or whether this was part of her general dislike of her parents, I will never know. In any event, and as I have already reminisced, in 1937 my mother and I went to the Riesengebirge by ourselves, by train and bus. We did a lot of hiking in all these areas, which we had previously just visited by car for finding a place to eat. We had a really good time. Another trip without my grandparents took place in 1940 and covered the same general area, but from the other side of the mountain range. The crest line of the Riesengebirge had been the border between Germany and Czechoslovakia. Obviously I was very little affected by the then-brewing political storm. However in 1940, half a year after the war had started, we still didn't feel much of any fallout, so we traveled again to the "mountains of the giants," but now on what had been the Czech side, which I must say was at that time exclusively German-populated, even without ethnic cleansing.

Of course I didn't understand all that at the time, but with these simple visits and the impressions I gathered even as a child, much later I came very close to realizing the enormous difficulties that aggravated the problems of political-ethnic minorities in a country, particularly when, in a limited area, the "minority" is really the major-ity. (For example, the Chicanos are the majority in south east L.A., the African-Americans are the majority in Harlem, NY.) And so it is all over the world, notably in Africa, particularly in those parts across which mindless politicians drew borders, creating problems. Of course, the attack, or whatever you may call it, on Czechoslovakia in 1938, was very wrong, but so was the dictate by WWI's victors, decreeing that part of these mountainous regions, though almost exclusively inhabited by ethnic Germans, was to be made part of Czechoslovakia.

Anyhow, when I visited this area in 1940, the focus of the visit was a lovely town called Spindelmühle. All seemed peaceful in every respect, and nobody would have believed that, in a few years, that area would almost literally drown in an orgy of blood. I have to add here, in a somewhat cynical fashion, the following, historical footnote: Since the victims of these orgies were Germans, the world didn't care at all. At the end of WWII, it was acceptable to speak only of German atrocities, not of atrocities with Germans as victims. Some day, that part of history will also be written and maybe the term Holocaust will be applied also to those many millions of Germans who were murdered during the final weeks of the war and beyond, just because they were Germans. No, I didn't witness any of this, but recently Mr. Havel, the Czech president, has apologized to the German nation for the atrocities the Czechs committed against Germans after WWII; this surely is a good sign for the future. At the end of WWII, all of Eastern Europe suffered primarily from the Red Army and also from each other, and they descended upon anybody of German origin. I understand that these Sudeten Germans I have been talking about were particular victims of Czech pogroms. But during my visits in 1940, and later again in 1944, there was nothing but peace and tranquility and the beauty of the mountains.

-7-

GRANDPARENTS AND BUNZLAU

I may have given a somewhat distorted impression of my summer visits to my grandparents in Bunzlau, Silesia. I was much too independent a person to be significantly influenced by my grandfather's sourpuss attitude and my grandmother, but it did affect my mother. My grandfather had a kind of attitude that made everybody jump, except me: I just looked away when he cast a furious look around. As I got older, he seemed to respect my not being intimidated by him. In my younger years, my grandmother was a kind of non-person, totally overshadowed by her husband and echoing him. In my mind, she actually became quite human after he died in 1943. I had no trouble with her though, as she believed me to be very well behaved all the time. I recall though just ignoring her.

My grandfather had a plumbing business which he had taken over from his father and greatly expanded. Let me add here a small aspect of social differentiation and the craft's history. Strictly speaking, my grandfather was a plumber, however he detested that relatively modern term. In the past, a person working with tubing, faucets valves etc. was called a coppersmith, which ranked somewhere in between the regular (vulgar) smith putting shoes on horses, and a goldsmith. So, my grandfather was a coppersmith. His business was quite substantial: he installed and improved the water supply system and sewer system in the town of Bunzlau. And so he called his business an "installation operation"[14]; completely leaving open what was being installed. In any event, he was very diligent and a very smart businessman, as well as a skillful craftsman and planner. Not only that, but my grandmother helped him in the planning stages. She had no formal education beyond elementary school, but people tended to think that she had some kind of engineering degree. By the end of the first world war, my grandfather was already quite wealthy, but the inflation of 1923 wiped it all out; otherwise, he certainly would have died a millionaire. But whatever he had retained and regained was wiped out entirely by W W II.

The place where my grandparents lived was very interesting, at least from my point of view, as it was so vastly different from my hometown of Berlin. I was used to more or less modern houses and correspondingly modern surroundings – shops, many, quite glitzy, department stores, houses of friends, grand government buildings etc. Now, the house in Bunzlau was very old. I don't know exactly how old it was, but I do believe that it had stood, at that time, for at least several hundred years. It had fascinating, thick walls, about two to three feet thick, built for eternity. It had spooky stairways that were hardly lit and had no windows; there were creaking floors, perfect to let one's imagination run wild. There was a vaulted basement which was always very cold and in my early years, reminded me of storybook dungeons.

In the front part of the house, on the first floor, there was a so-called "good" room; the parlor room with no purpose, that was never used, I don't know why, but it did have an uncomfortable cold, overall appearance. On the other hand, I do remember some beautiful pieces of furniture, gems in today's world, had they survived.

---

14 Installations-Betrieb

Then, there was a totally useless middle room, just for storing stuff and behind that, open towards a rear court, was a general-purpose room where life took place. It was my grandfather's office, a kind of office for a secretary; and in the afternoon and evening, it was the family room, very homey and comfortable. A few days a week, it served another purpose. My grandfather never shaved himself, so a barber came and shaved my grandfather while he sat in the middle of that room. This is one of the funnier memories I have from these visits in Bunzlau, but much more interesting was the area behind the house.

In the back, there was a work area with a garage, storerooms, and a real workshop with a real fireplace, anvils, vises, lots of junk, and stuff such as iron rods, tubes, and who knows what. There, I learned how to forge, and that I did; I forged swords, not too sharp though, but with good points. Though I am generally a rather clumsy person, I don't believe that I ever burnt myself seriously; I must have been fairly skillful in my metal-working ventures. I actually got pieces of metal red hot and through a lot of banging on an anvil with sparks flying all over the place, I got them to stick together, that is, I must have successfully welded them together. We had nothing like that in Berlin.

On one side of my grandparent's house was a bakery run by a friendly man named Krause, who had two hopelessly ugly spinster daughters. Quite a number of times, I was allowed to watch him baking. When does a big-city boy ever have a chance to be happily scared by the blazing fire of an oven looking like a "mini" hell?

On the other side of my grandparent's place was a frame and windowpane shop , that is, the workshop of a glazier. The front shop room was alright, but in the back rooms, there were always pieces of broken glass. I didn't go there often, even though they had a son a few years younger than I; he mostly came over to our place to play. Safety didn't seem to take a central role, with the kitchen and dining area located right next to where glass was cut.

Around the corner was a park with a statue of Prince Kutusov, the Russian general whose troops liberated the area, and in fact, most of Europe in the waning years of the Napoleonic wars. This is actually an interesting reminder that the role of Prussia in that part of history has been (understandably) grossly exaggerated in Germany. The real military winner in that war was the Russians. Most Germans like to forget that, by and large, Germany kowtowed to Napoleon (just read Henry Kissinger's dissertation, *A World Restored*")[15]. Not surprisingly, the statue was still there when I revisited Bunzlau in 1992.

In the opposite direction from my grandparent's house was a kind of public garden area which led to the railroad station. The station was an Express Train stop station for trains from Breslau, the capital of Silesia, to Dresden and on to Munich. To get to Berlin, however, we had to change trains twice. But it was also a time when porters were always where you needed them.

The entire town of Bunzlau was small but had several movie houses and even a stage theater and a theater season. I do have a very fond memory of that little town, possibly because its dimensions were easier to comprehend by a child than the vastness of rows and rows of houses in Berlin. I believe that, without being told (my folks were not that literate or poetic), in Bunzlau I really began at an early age to experience what is commonly called "a sense of history". We lived not far (only about 500 feet) from the center of the town, which had a rather stately town-hall and a marketplace or plaza around it and was surrounded by stately and quite interesting, though not spectacular, old houses with nice facades, fairly elaborate roof structures and doorways. The town-hall had an octagonal tower with a not-quite onion shaped top, rather typical for Eastern

---

15 Just as the French "forgot" that Austerliz was the last battle/war they ever won against the Germans.

Europe. There was an archway in the middle of one block leading to a street with a — well, *the*—Café, and there were many shops around the plaza. Nothing was really comparable to the picturesque houses along the Romantische Strasse in West Germany but still, it was enough of a unique layout as far as I was concerned, to get an idea of what a town in the past had been like for a long time.

In later years, I found that set-up to be increasingly interesting. But while I was a pre-teen, I preferred to go into the forests surrounding the town. The town was small and typical for Europe with everything crowded and bunched together, so the forest and a river were not too far. The woods were very dense, with lots of blueberry bushes. Before leaving this subject (I will return to it when covering the late war years), I should mention that Bunzlau was known for a widely-distributed, rather high-quality ceramics. The pottery was manufactured by families who had their own typical, traditional patterns. Because of this practice and industry, the town was rather wealthy. Some of the pottery traditions continued after the war in West Germany, but such a tradition cannot really be transplanted. Related to that was something I don't know personally, but I have read: Bunzlau was also a center for forging ancient, Near Eastern pottery!

My grandparents were kind of upper class in the town, so as in Berlin I was in a quite sheltered environment and, of course, I naturally took that for granted. In other words, not being in a somewhat sheltered / privileged position was a way of life simply unknown to me, in Berlin as well as in Bunzlau. I emphasize this aspect of my life, and again for a variety of reasons. I grew up in a class society which shaped me and whose very existence and justification I never questioned. Please remember the limited amount of information that was actually available; "one" simply didn't know what the other classes were doing. Also, when I was confronted, later in the war, with the real world beyond my *refugium*, I think I had sense enough to seek as a goal a return to some sheltered society. Indeed, while I am writing this, I am again living (and hope for quite some time) in a sheltered environment on the West Coast of the U.S.A. My son wanted, at one point in time, to escape from it, and so he did. But he returned after he had married – you just can't beat a golden ghetto.

The ambiance of Bunzlau did, however, present an amazing contrast to my hometown, Berlin. Above, I painted a somewhat glorified picture of my home away from home, but it wasn't always that glamorous. In Bunzlau, we always ate in the kitchen and at exact, preordained times. Eating in the kitchen was not appropriate for the big city boy I was, nor for any other people of comparable "lifestyle"[16]. I may have romanticized the old, even ancient house in Bunzlau, but its toilet facilities were abominable, actually outside, in the back of the house, reached only by walking along the workshop area all the way to the back. That was really a pain in the neck, particularly when it rained. And so, am I contradicting myself? Not at all; remember Versailles had no toilets at all! And so, the lack of amenities had nothing to do with the fact that I lived in an upper class, though seemingly ancient, shelter whenever I was in Bunzlau. Well, I liked it a lot, I had a few friends and the proximity of everything resulted in a great variety of things to see, to visit, to gawk at, to play with and be otherwise entertained; and so it was, indeed, a home away from home, different but still homey.

My grandparents were quite conservative, still believing in the monarchy (a belief which I found intriguing) and believing the Nazis to be a silly bunch of bums; that, too, was intriguing. The deadlier aspects of the Nazis had not yet materialized, and the little town of Bunzlau, as many small towns, had been spared the political strife and confusion that had led to the Nazi takeover in the first place. How do I know that? Of course I didn't in my pre-teen years, but

---

16   This is an interesting cultural "aside:" the dinette in the kitchen is commonplace in American society, but unheard of in Europe, and why should it have been; in middle class society, it wasn't Mother who put the food on the table but the maid with an apron, and to shorten the number of steps for her would not have been a matter of concern to architects.

later, I became quite aware of the differences between small towns
and big cities. A particular funny incident stands out. I heard – but
don't know whether it's actually true – that there was just one Jewish
family in Bunzlau (that part is probably true) and the man of the
house applied for membership in the Nazi party; well that's a kind of
believe-it-or-not situation. In any event, in later years, my emerging
political views served as a kind of bridge to a better understanding
between my grandparents and me, particularly my grandmother
after her husband's death. On the other hand, as the years went by
and my political awareness grew, I also became increasingly aware of
the political and cultural isolation of a small town; people just had
no real idea what was going on.

There's not much else to report about these annual visits except,
of course, that in the beginning of each stay, there was a train trip
from Berlin to Bunzlau and in the end of the summer, we returned
again by train. As I'd noted before, I don't understand why we were
not driven in Grandpa's chauffeur-driven car both ways; the distance
was just a little farther than L. A. is from San Diego, or from New
York to Philadelphia. Well, if we had gone by car I wouldn't have
had the pleasure and experience of train rides. I will never forget
these monstrous steam-engines and the commotion they caused
when the train entered any train station, particularly a covered one.
I think Monet has captured incomparably well that kind of a scene,
in at least one of his *"gare"* pictures. The huge wheels, the puffing
cylinders, and the infernal but somehow so exciting noise, I will never
forget it! It's difficult to separate earlier from later visits, because in
Bunzlau itself, nothing ever changed, but surely the steam engines
form a part of my earliest memories; the wheels were much larger
than I was. All that alone made the trip worthwhile.

My maternal grandparents had a kind of peaceful moroseness,
but my paternal grandmother, in the neighboring town of Löwenberg, was obnoxious. My father's father had died long ago, and my
father's stepfather was completely disinterested in the family he had

acquired even though he was the brother of my maternal grandfather. Once every stay in summer in Bunzlau, there was the obligatory, but very short, visit with the paternal folks, and that was it. Actually, that was a very good arrangement: why put up with people, even if relatives, if you have absolutely nothing in common? My paternal grandmother died in 1937; my paternal step-grandfather vanished at the end of the war. I simply had no connection to this line of my family.

My grandparents usually came to Berlin for Christmas. Why they took the train and didn't have themselves driven with all the baggage, I will never understand. The chauffeur could have brought them and driven their car back the same day, to return a week or so later. In any event, their arrival was preceded by the arrival of numerous packages with food. Why my grandmother thought she or we couldn't get that stuff in Berlin escaped us. In addition, in my grandparents' opinion, excessive eating was definitely called for. In Germany, Christmas Eve is the main event of decorating, with lighting the Christmas tree as a kind of culmination; and then, there is the piling-up of presents. For most people, there is also a modest meal. The main meal came Christmas Day, with the familiar overeating. In our house, my grandfather insisted on a 3-main course dinner: polish sausages with kale; duckling with red cabbage and dumplings; the third I have forgotten. Later, I learned that my mother dreaded Christmas because of this excessive to-do. Like most parents, she wanted it primarily to be a leisurely exciting, fun day for me, with all the expectations and presents and decoration, etc. I remember that she did her best, and she made sure that I wouldn't lose out and indeed, I never did. As a result, she worked herself to near exhaustion. I think the maids were usually sent home to their families. My grandmother, of course helped, but then came this old grand-aunt with her husband as an additional guest. The "operation" was truly phenomenal and my mother, without showing it, was too exhausted to enjoy any of it. One year, she dared to hint that, maybe, one dinner course would do but that suggestion invited great reprimands from her mother for being an ungrateful daughter, combined with threats that "they" would not come at all, etc., etc. It really sounds ridiculous, but when the war came, my grandparents stayed home, and we had a leisurely Christmas – or a while, at least.

In years past, I have often thought about visiting Bunzlau again, just one more time. Or would it be better just to stay with my memories, remembering the town as it was, because what there is now may have no relation to me or my family. But doubts on this point lingered on; after all, something must be left, it cannot be all gone, right? Well, as I have hinted already, I did visit the town in 1992, 48 years after I had seen it for the last time. I was shocked and amazed, bewildered and confused. On one hand, the town's center was exactly as I remembered it, except the writing on the walls was Polish and the people spoke that language. It was an indescribable, emotionally confusing situation. Everything looked the same, but nothing reminds you that it was once a German town. A very peculiar mixture of what seemed a grand scale forgery of culture history, but then it seems as if everything was as it should be for the people *now* living there. The architecture is not that much different from Polish architecture, as I found out during a later visit of Poland proper in 1995. The railway station in Bunzlau was exactly as I remembered it; the green tiles, the swinging doors, the busy-looking, track patterns, but then the writing of the announcements, the time-tables had no relation whatever to anything I could recall.

I don't want to dwell on the fact that it was devastating to see that my grandparents' house was no longer there, and even the street patterns had been changed; but then I was glad, because there is nobody living in any place that I could claim my own, there wasn't anybody I could have accused of living where he didn't belong.

Should I have stayed away? No, quite to the contrary; I plan to go there again, at some point in time. My immediate childhood environment may be gone, but the town is still there, and in that sense, I claim its memory as vividly as possible and that includes, for me, all that is left. I also visited Löwenberg, my father's hometown, but there was nothing at all left for me to remember.

-8-

MY ENCOUNTER WITH NAZISM AND THE "JUNGVOLK"

My personal exposure to the "Great Era" came in three rather different aspects in 1938: one was quite specific and elaborate; the second is of interest in a more general sense; the third one concerned me personally and had to do with the time when I reached the age to join the Jungvolk, the early Nazi children's organization.

The first item, an elaborate involvement, concerns our exposure, in the Nazi era, to the radio. To today's readers, this may not sound like much and so I have to include in my narrative a certain strain of culture history. In the thirties, the radio had become a common utility, and politicians everywhere availed themselves of this unique opportunity to reach people in their homes! It was not as vivid and potent, of course, as television would prove to be, but to hear somebody speak is quite different from reading a transcript in the newspaper. Of course, the movie houses' newsreels were the forerunners of TV news coverage, as far as pictures and visual scenes were concerned. But the newsreels and related documentaries were just excerpts seen in isolation; they never gave any sustained coverage of any of his speeches[17]. Generally, in the mid-to-late '30s, the primary media was radio and like everybody else, I was exposed to Adolf Hitler's oratory.

It's too bad that the ability to make voice recordings was not in existence in Lenin's time[18], so it is difficult to compare him with Hitler. So, I must leave open to whom the top slot of oratory belongs, but there is no doubt in my mind that Adolf Hitler was at least one of the greatest orators of our times. No doubt, Franklin D. Roosevelt and Winston Churchill were magnificent speakers, and the world has heard, ad nauseam, a few oratory tidbits of John F. Kennedy. We all know the drivel of Clinton and Nixon, the awkward concoctions of Johnson, the theatrical eloquence of Reagan, but also the eloquence of Major and Blair; but none of that is genuine oratory.

We are now able to see, in short sound bites on TV documentaries, a few minutes of Hitler's physical gyrations and wide gesticulations coupled with yelling and offering, dispassionately viewed, a sequence of rather ridiculous postures.

These somewhat farcical displays serve admirably to inspire the question: how could an entire people succumb to such a person, who in these short clips looks like a clown? Even though I never saw him speak, I did hear him quite a number of times over the radio, and I also remember different scenes from newsreels pertaining to different parts or phases of his speeches, and so I can, with some justification, recreate in my mind the mesmerization that emanated from his speeches. It surely came through on the radio; in a live situation, it must have been truly astounding. As a child I was intrigued by his

---

17 This was not quite true in all cases. Leni Riefenstahls, glorifying in full movie length the Nazi-party rallies in Nuremberg and her subsequent, undoubtedly brilliant motion picture report on the Olympic games in Berlin 1936 may have helped movies and TV, as well as the Nazi propaganda machine, in an indiscriminate fashion.

18 Strictly speaking, this is not quite correct. Edison had invented the phonograph earlier, I just do not know whether anybody had set up the elaborate equipment needed to record Lenin.

voice, but in my younger years, I had little connection to anything he said about the past. I should add here that my mother, and sometimes friends of the family, would listen together to his speeches (for whatever reason, I don't remember). They were indeed mesmerized, but my mother admitted, at some point, that the speeches did become boring because of repetition; they followed the same pattern (today we would say they were derivatives of the same script).

The speeches began always in a halting, low, very quiet voice, presented in an almost stooped posture (I saw that in a documentary). This was the way he always began to narrate his humble beginnings, but he skipped his bumming around in Vienna and avoided anything that could be interpreted as an admission that he was basically a lazy person – as can be drawn from Speer's memoirs[19]. Then came his subsequent call to arms with his voice now growing a little stronger, and his supposedly magnificent war record (which he coyly minimized). Then he spoke about some injury from gas exposure, duly dramatized but still low-key. But then came the humiliation of defeat, his calling to become a politician (which he appeared to see as an endless sequence of speeches; no work, but he never said that). The voice grew louder when talking about his struggle for power, denigrating in any possible way German politicians' attempts to guide Germany from an empire to a democratic republic. As time went on, his speeches included additional and increasing mentions of "his" successes. Little did we know that, in many cases, he had no idea what he was talking about. But seemingly, he was leading Germany to greatness, and since the former enemies from the World War let him be and let him tear apart one treaty after another, his always forceful conclusions, presented in a wildly gyrating and screaming manner, were seemingly justified.

Now, if you hadn't listened to the ever-so-gradually controlled

---

19 [*Inside the Third Reich* by Albert Speer, an architect and member of Hitler's "inner circle" who was convicted of war crimes at the Nuremberg trials – KS]

increase in volume and agitation, you wouldn't know that he had worked up to his wild finale for an hour or so, carrying the audience, as well as many listeners, along. I am convinced that many listeners and/or viewers were not listening but wallowed in mesmerization, breathing in the aura of the oratory. So, by the time his speeches came to an end, he did have his listeners stirred to a frenzy. Whenever you see, in a short TV clip, the wildly gesticulating man, you see exactly the mental state and mood of the audience as the result of the hour-plus long speech. How do I know this? Simply because I remember my own reaction, after having listened to the man on radio without seeing him. I wasn't in a frenzy, but readily understood then how it could be, just from the screams of the audience. Did I *believe* what he said? Not that I remember, but I want to answer that question very carefully and very deliberately.

Remember, I heard these speeches while I was between about eight to 12 years old. Their factual simplicity seemed convincing, in the sense of a well-presented lecture, particularly about the short-comings of the republic he had, in fact, overthrown. But on the other hand, I became quite interested in those individuals who were maligned by him, because several of my parents' acquaintances didn't share Hitler's view on several of these people. I remember, for instance, that G. Streseman, who was repeatedly German foreign minister prior to the Hitler era and at some time chancellor, was held in great esteem; I also heard of Friedrich Ebert, the first president of the Republic and of Heinrich Brüning, the last Chancellor prior to the Nazi take-over, and how he had tried to hold the decaying republic together. I also remember very well that Hitler's derogation of these and other people was not echoed in school.

On the other hand, I don't remember any of the people I knew, who liked certain personages from the republic era, ever voicing the opinion that, in their mind, they had caught Hitler in a lie concerning facts. Any negative reaction was due to Hitler's evaluation of the situation, not because he presented false facts. I'm not saying that he didn't. I'm saying that I wasn't in a position to judge the veracity of Hitler's presentation and that the grown-ups around me, who were neither dummies nor immoral scum, never disputed these facts. But bear in mind that, to Germans, the injustice of the Treaty of Versailles and its aftermath was a fact, not an opinion.

The second aspect is my observation of people's reactions to the political scenario, as I could understand them, as I approached age 10. I do remember seeing anti-Semitic propaganda in the form of cartoons. How they affected other people I don't know, but to me, they were very funny, in a totally ridiculous way, because as far as I was concerned, there weren't any people like that; there just was no relation to reality. I don't know how that stuff affected the grown-ups, but its very grotesqueness couldn't possibly have been taken seriously – except by the most gullible and people of modest intelligence.

Somehow related to this, is people's reaction to Hitler's book, *Mein Kampf* (my struggle). I wonder whether, in the long run, this isn't a very tragic matter. People more or less openly voiced the opinion that the book was awful regarding the way it was written. But I think it was a common detail that people had not read the entire thing, only portions of it, and had stopped precisely because it was so awful. I haven't read it either, except portions of it, which indeed I found bland. But I understand that, unabashedly, Hitler outlined in a somewhat guarded a manner a blueprint for the future, his willingness to destroy the "Jewry" (das Judentum) and to start a war. But, because of the poor quality of the presentation, it was disregarded.

Also of some importance is the acknowledgement one could hear – I did hear – that Hitler had put people to work, serving apparently as a kind of justification for his rule to continue. After the war, one was given the impression that the drop in unemployment was the result of re-armament. At the time, I didn't know about that nor did anyone else in the country. But history has shown since then that that was just post-war propaganda meant to hide the fact that Germany's initial, military success was, in fact, accomplished by a very inferior army.

A third recollection is that I distinctly remember how scared people were in 1938, when the so-called "Sudeten Crisis" arose. Of course, I had no idea what that meant, nor what the preceding "Anschluss" or annexation of Austria meant. But I do remember this: My mother and I were walking home one evening, and in one area, they were installing anti-aircraft guns. I asked her what that stuff was for. She said she didn't know (how could she?), but she was very scared. I also remember the high esteem the adults in my life had for the British Prime Minister, Neville Chamberlain. Never mind how history has treated – condemned – his appeasement. The people believed, they hoped that he had restored peace for our time. How ironic that, in our time, most people despise him for having compromised liberty. But I think that, in the mind of many honest, befuddled, confused Germans, Chamberlain did appear as a savior. Well, I know I shouldn't generalize beyond my own experience, so I'll simply offer my own experience and what I heard people – friends and family – say: they put Chamberlain into a position of a savior. I also remember that there were, in places, public outbursts in gratitude for him, and later, I read that the Nazis were very disturbed by the public outpouring for a man who seemed to have saved us from our own government.

The fall of 1938 – the "appeasement" year – ended with the infamous "Reichskristallnacht," the night of the broken glass. Absolutely nobody I can remember ever talked about it. Since, in the immediate vicinity of my home there were no stores at all, nothing was mutilated. However, synagogues were burned down, and one of the ruins loomed ominously along a well-traveled, commuter train line. I'm glad to report that the houses of Jewish people in our area weren't damaged, stoned, or even burned. Again, nothing bad happened in our privileged area. To what extent our elders were aware of ominous goings-on, I don't know. I don't believe that Jews were rounded up in our area. The subject was certainly not discussed in school.

This is probably the right point to go back to other aspects of my sheltered life in the late '30s. At some point in time, the secret police must have started to round up people. They'd already done it in 1933. Were my elders aware of it? I don't know; there was some talk about concentration camps. I didn't know what that meant, but can one say that German's culpability began when they ignored this phenomenon? People apparently knew about them but ignored them. I've tried as hard as I can to remember when fear began to creep into people's lives, when it was deemed advisable to keep your mouth shut. That fear of being reported, with unknown consequences, did exist after the war began; actually, for quite some time after, too. But when did it begin? There was no mention of any rounding up of people – it was unimaginable in our sheltered neighborhood.

The fourth aspect of my exposure to Nazism involved the youth organization called Jungvolk (meaning… not very imaginative, rather simplistic and thus effective… "young-people"). To go back a little, the Nazi youth organization was originally the equivalent of a youth gang. I doubt that there was much difference between them and the Harlem street gangs or the gangs in South Central Los Angeles, except for the political, rather than territorial, set up. Prior to 1933, these gangs of Nazi kids arose in tough neighborhoods, battling other toughs, which were known, I think, under the name "Red Banner." Well, remember the description of my childhood neighborhood; of course, nothing of that kind was anywhere to be seen before the Nazis came to power, and not for a while afterward. So, the Nazi youth organization was something basically unknown to me prior to, say the American equivalent of the 5th grade – or 1938. There may have been some of this gang activity, but certainly very unobtrusive.

But what did happen was this. With a stroke of genius, in the mid-'30s, the Nazis simply merged all other youth organizations into the Hitler Youth and its subsidiary for younger kids, the Jungvolk. So, and I remember this very distinctly, in our neighborhood there suddenly was this Nazi youth organization – except that it had nothing to do with the Nazis! Why do I remember that? Very simply, starting at age 10, boys joined up through what today is called peer pressure (i.e. any boy who did not want to be known to be a "sissy.")

But still, we did have a lot of fun. Well, maybe that is not quite correct as a sweeping statement; one has to be careful with generalizations. I am talking about myself. First of all, no politics were involved; we weren't expected to battle other thugs, nor were we set up to annoy others, particularly adults (e.g. Jews!) as has been often reported. It simply was no part of organized juvenile delinquency. What did we do? We roamed around in the forest nearby, played all kinds of games, played soccer a lot, did a lot of hiking, sang traditional folk songs, attended sports festivals; well, that's all I remember. At that time, I didn't experience any Nazi ideology "teachings," not the slightest suggestion of harassing Jews or other "disbelievers." But mind you, I'm talking about 1938 and '39, just before the war. And I'm talking about my own experience; elsewhere, it was probably different.

Also, these were the years when I had just entered high school, and there were a few kids in school who weren't members of the youth organization. I remember one in particular, Horst Scheunemann, who was clearly not a sissy by any standard. Later we became fairly close friends and I learned that, to him, that outfit was nothing but a bunch of thugs he didn't care to associate with. He had grown up in one of those tough neighborhoods where Nazi and Communist gangs were battling each other in the streets, and he despised them all; to him, there was no difference. And in retrospect, of course, I agree. But that was a different world for me; the class distinction held, and the overt thugs just lived and stayed outside of the territory of the "respectable people" (just as no gangs can be found where I live now!).

Let me dwell on this a bit more because of the highly ambivalent aspect of the subject. In my first year or so after I had just joined the Jungvolk, we had a leader, Jan. Because of the Nazi's assimilation of other youth organizations, Jan had become a Jungvolk leader. Since the turn of the century, lots of different youth groups and organizations had come into being. Hiking groups, religious groups, and also political groups of different persuasions; all of them had been "unified" by the Nazis. Jan had been in the so-called Wandervogel (migrating birds) movement. So, he just continued what he had been doing before and kept politics away from us. We adored him, because he let us do all the things boys of our age needed and wanted to do: roaming in the forest, playing soccer, roughing it a bit here or there—it just was great. He took us on weekend trips where we hiked through the countryside, we slept in barns, washed in very cold water with courtyard plumbing. It was very different from our sheltered existence at home, but quite appropriate for boys of our age to experience. Well, that was just a year or so before WWII; soon, Jan was drafted, and he was one of the early war fatalities. I feel strongly in saying, "Jan, wherever you are, you did a lot of good."

Maybe I was lucky, but in 1939 and '40 or thereabouts, a group was set up to sing. I had a good voice and was asked to join. The Vienna Boys' Choir we were not, but once a week, we practiced in one of the opera houses. These were not Nazi songs, but complicated, folk song canons. Our practicing is one of my fondest memories. About a hundred boys singing in the beautiful, acoustic ambience of an opera house is something I still have not forgotten.

Suffice it to say, I enjoyed my early Jungvolk experience; it seemed to have nothing to do with the Nazis except that, in retrospect, the Nazis used the inherent goodness, honesty, and decency in people, for example our leaders and many aspects of German cultural life as bait. At that time, that is, the late '30s, you can say that I was among those who were caught without knowing it. My early encounter with the Jungvolk was fun and, to put it differently, involved nothing I would have to be ashamed of then or later; but it ain't over yet, and a good part of my account will involve or relate to my gradual awakening to the stark realities around me.

-9-

HIGH SCHOOL – ANOTHER SHELTER

Now, I must return to the "mainstream" of my story. Previously, I talked about the elementary school I attended and about which I have so many fond memories. In the fourth grade (I don't remember whether this was early spring 1938 or late summer 1937), while the preliminaries to World War II were already in the offing, our class went on a weekend outing which I remember for two reasons.

One was during a boat ride on a shipping canal. Suddenly, the skipper picked me up and made me "take the wheel." I didn't do much steering, but I almost exploded with pride (never mind that others got their turn, too). That canal was one of many waterways in Germany; it connected the River Oder with the River Havel, which in turn is a tributary to the Elbe River. Shipping bulk goods by waterways was and still is an important aspect of Germany's transportation system. Because of elevational differences between the rivers, there had been a large number of locks. A few years before our excursion, all these locks had been replaced by a single ship hoist. Two canals ends met at the hoist at an elevational difference of about 120 feet. That difference was bridged by a trough-shaped elevator, into which one or several barges or other boats floated and, by lowering and raising the elevator hoist, the trough was aligned with one or the other canal ends. A true technical marvel, even to us sophisticated city kids. I visited it again in 1995, and it was just as magnificent as it had been then. I wondered, however, how it survived the war. If it had been destroyed by bombs, it would have interrupted a very important transport path, but also there would have been an ecological catastrophe of major proportions.

In 1938, I entered high school, or the Gymnasium, whatever label one wishes to apply to higher educational institutions in many parts of Europe. The school I entered would be called the 5th grade in the U.S.A. It was, as far as facilities were concerned. more of the same as the elementary school, but on a grander scale. But not only that, the Waldschule, as it was called, was an institution of its own. The school was not (as is often the case in Europe) concentrated in one, rather dismal-looking, brick structure, a kind of better-looking army barracks or prison[20]. Rather, the school area covered a large mostly forested area. Scattered under the trees were little huts, just simple wooden, one-story structures which each held two or three classrooms of normal size. Each would hold about 30 children in a comfortable setting. It was actually quite similar to my elementary school buildings, including their red exterior. There was a gym, which I believe was the largest structure. We had a stone building for Physics and Chemistry classes, and a dining hall, which was also used as an auditorium. Next to the auditorium was an open seating area, but with a roof-like covering, so that one could eat outdoors during the summer. On the grounds, there were so many trees and bushes and shrubbery, we couldn't see these other buildings from

---

20 In all fairness I should add that there were some nice and even picturesque school houses in Germany, but not that many.

our regular classrooms[21]. The entire school grounds and area for about 400-plus kids covered about 25 acres. Weather permitting, we took our chairs and had class outside.

The entire make-up of the school was very unusual, I think generally, for Germany and here, for a variety of reasons. First of all, it was at that time one of the few if not the only co-ed school, not only in Berlin, but possibly in all of Germany. It was unheard of otherwise, and I am certain, many people frowned upon that feature. In addition, it was a school which the kids attended all day. We had regular classes in the morning, a mid-morning snack, and after the instruction classes were over, we all did our homework in our home classroom. Next came lunch. The preparation of the meals was under the control of the wife of the principal, Mr. Krause; it was almost a kind of family enterprise. We knew her very well, and she knew us. Mrs. Krause often went to the produce market at 5 am, to get fresh vegetables for us.

Following lunch, we had a one-hour resting period; we lay in rather simple, easy chairs – always outside – and when necessary, we wrapped ourselves in blankets; when it rained, there was some sheltered area to put the chairs under. We didn't always like this rest period too much, or even at all, because after all, only babies take naps in the afternoon, but it was a good opportunity to catch up on reading assignments. Most importantly, though, this was a wonderful opportunity to catch up on rest, relaxation, and sometimes sleep. As the war progressed, and nightly sleep was increasingly interrupted by air raids, these afternoon rest periods may have made all the difference to us, not to be caught up in a terrible pattern of incessant anxiety.

Following the rest period, we had an afternoon snack: coffee

---

21 The school system is a little different; classes basically stayed in their home room and only for special courses, like physics, chemistry, art, music and biology, we went to different rooms with lab facilities etc.

and simple open-face jam or marmalade sandwiches. After that, we played on the school grounds or in the huge forest area behind the school. Outdoor playing in the afternoon was, to some extent, organized but in a very relaxed fashion; nobody *had* to play anything nor in any specific way. Most importantly, the morning class teachers turned into play buddies in the afternoon, without ever losing their authority. I am convinced that this kind of school attracted only certain personalities as teachers who would put up with this additional afternoon work for which they didn't get any extra pay (but once in a while, a day off)! It didn't seem to hurt them – most of them lived to their nineties and now, in 1999, one of them is still alive. Of course, many of the teachers were what you might call "characters," with demeanors that we liked to mimic but never in a derogatory fashion. Of course, there were also "losers" among them, some were outright obnoxious, even sadistic. But by far, most of them were held in adoring reverence and esteem.

Maybe by today's standards the available activities were not that numerous, but they seemed to be at the time. First of all there was a kind of swimming pool; not very large, but it was a lot of fun in the summer. On a different note, some kids had little garden plots where they planted flowers, and some vegetables like radishes. Others did experiments in the physics lab, and still others built model planes or did other arts and crafts. There was always something going on on the sports field. In the winter, that sports field was hosed down and was turned into an ice-skating rink. One of the sports teachers, a Mr. Reimann, did the watering at 10 p.m. or even later on the previous day, so that it would be frozen solid in the morning. Of course, there wasn't much grooming in any manner, but that rink was lots of fun. It was quite funny: in the summer, we were, for some obscure reason, not allowed to walk across the sports field with regular shoes. But in winter, the same field was completely messed up in any imaginable way just to get a fairly level water surface. Ah well, we did enjoy it, and who should expect consistency?

The forest in the back of the school was the Grunewald I mentioned earlier when describing the setting of my house. Actually, the
first house I lived in was a few feet away from the entrance to the
school. The rather large Grunewald forest extended to the Havel
River, many miles away, all within the confines of Berlin. Strictly
speaking, the school grounds were part of that forest and even today,
there is just a low fence separating the school from the publicly acces-
sible forest, one of the great recreational facilities of Berlin. As I have
said already, quite often I went with others and teachers to play all
kinds of games in the forest. Among the many, different games was
the so-called "Schnitzel-jagd." It's almost untranslatable: the best I
can offer is "hunting for clues." A first group of us vanished into the
bushes and placed clues as we went along; they weren't obviously
placed. A second group followed looking for these clues. It was a
favorite game, which tested ingenuity in finding hiding places and
separately in finding the clues. Now, if you are so inclined, you may
discover in this game aspects of military strategy – decoy and deci-
pherment. Not so at all. The first group was supposed to place the
clues "fairly," making it difficult but not impossible for the pursuer
to find them, which is quite anathema to military thinking and
undertaking. This school taught us fairness, not how to be connivers.

As a corollary and in a literal sense, I had very few, other after-
school activities; the school was really our world. Another sheltered
environment within a sheltered environment. I think back on this
school with great fondness; I have retained a continued attachment
to it which persists to this day. I still have more to dwell on here,
in order to make sure that this *refugium's* emotional significance is
understood.

In 1985, there was a kind of anniversary of the school, and a
very large number of "old timers," including many from our class,
was there. It is exceedingly difficult to describe the character of this
school; its specific character didn't survive the post-war era on account
of the social planners' zealotries, at least as rampant in Germany as

they are in the U.S. That is really unfortunate, because I regard my school as one of the kinds of medium through which democratic tradition survived in Germany. First of all, the setting was of course ideal at least for, as we would say today, ecological reasons. In later years, when I saw for one reason or another other schools in Berlin or elsewhere, I shuddered at the sight of many big, stone structures with their tiny schoolyards. Even in the US, with lots of space available, some of the schools my kids went to were ant hills and cluttered by comparison; only my daughter Karen's boarding school[22] in a Boston suburb, which she attended for two years, had a comparable spaciousness, and I believe a commensurable scope in spirit.

So, my idyllic surroundings of home and elementary school continued, at least at the beginning and through the first years of WWII. Just prior to my first year in high school, there was the "Anschluss[23]." While I was in the fifth grade, the Sudeten crisis arose which was "resolved" by the infamous Munich conference; several months later, Czechoslovakia was dismantled completely. I have no recollection that it affected us in school; particularly, there were no tirades against the dismembered nations. During the sixth grade, WWII began in Poland, with staunch resistance by the Poles, and later, there was the French campaign. I remember distinctly wondering what made it so short. All this meant nothing to us. I don't remember any victory celebration nor any class discussions along those lines. For the most part the war, including all of its dangers, was just ignored. Not entirely though; as younger teachers vanished,

22 [Dana Hall School in Wellesley, Mass. And I must add that the high school my own children attended, Rocky Hill School in East Greenwich, RI, was also spacious and also had a campus notable for its natural beauty. We are all fortunate to have attended schools with grounds that are uplifting. – KS]

23 Much has been made of this and obviously Hitler's method of achieving it was despicable. But it should not be forgotten that in the early twenties the Austrian parliament had overwhelmingly voted to seek fusion with Germany. In the 50's when I visited Tyrol, there was open discussion that it would have been better if Austria had stayed combined with Germany.

they were replaced by older ones called out of retirement who had little sympathy for the regime.

Geography was taught by a lady, Ida Richter; we called her, affectionately, Ida. She had a rather accentuated way of speaking, which lent itself very much to mimicry. She really was one of the cornerstones of the school, particularly as far as afternoon activities were concerned. We learned where countries, rivers, mountains, and specific areas were in the world. Today, I often wonder about the ignorance many people exhibit in this regard. In the '60s and '70s, when Vietnam was much in everybody's mind, I wondered whether the entire perspective of a domino theory, etc. had to do with the fact that many people had no idea where Vietnam was.

In the lower grades, we had learned details about Germany, and in the next grade, we covered Europe, as it was or had been, irrespective of any front lines. In our school lessons, Europe was not divided into conquered and not – (yet) – conquered territories. As I have hinted already, the unity with Austria was accepted as natural; the way it had come about (i.e. the bullying tactics of the Nazis) was not known. Soon, we had a classmate from Vienna, Herbert Knauthe, whose funny accent we enjoyed. I visited him in 1995 in Vienna and still have close ties with him. With the Anschluss, abominable as it may have come about, came the overlapping awareness of history and the Holy Roman Empire of German nations. I didn't know then that it was neither holy, nor Roman, nor an empire, and only some of its constituents were German nations.

Biology was taught by a very small lady with an inherently funny bearing, Ms. Meuß. She did look a little like a mouse, and again, she was a kind of solid fixture for the school. I have to say, though, that I did not learn much about biology. But she supervised two activities in the school. I said previously that whoever wanted could have a little gardening plot; I think I had one several times and learned more than in class. In addition, occasionally we had to do gardening on the school grounds as a kind of low-level punishment for some things we'd done, and actually, I learned a lot on these occasions about botany—more than I remember from class.

For quite a number of years, we had a history teacher, Mrs. Henrici, covering the period of that Empire. She taught us real history, not any supremacy of the German people, but of a people living in a rather loosely organized state torn apart by petty feuds and religious strifes, with apparently better-developed neighbors to the west. We learned about the Magna Carta and the great Queen [Elizabeth I] during Shakespeare's time; we learned about the French economy, and that Fredrick of Prussia may have been "Great" because he copied it and brought craftsmen from France to the country his wars had impoverished. Officialdom was somewhat in a quandary how to teach / polemicize the Prussian / Austrian disputes. The textbook we had was outdated, with its "position" oriented from the Prussian perspective, but Austria was now part of Germany. Our teacher, by her nature, took a position of pure neutrality (that's what history is supposed to be) between Maria Theresa and Frederick, emphasizing that Frederick was ultimately saved by the German-born Russian Empress. We covered thoroughly the American and French revolutions, not so much about all their battles but what they really meant and stood for. Without ever explicitly saying it, she taught us democracy.

Prior to Mrs. Henrici, we had a Mr. Pleisner as history teacher, who later taught us religion. In Germany, that was a legitimate subject for public schools. Mr. Pleisner didn't teach us much religion (in retrospect, that was wrong), but he told us Bible stories in a very interesting, historically-founded but also metaphorical manner. Religion was a proper field to be taught in school and quite possibly the major source for teaching us morality. His classes were quite interesting, and he never taught us Nazism as a cult / religion or worldview (Weltanschauung). Incomprehensibly, he left our school for a position with a so-called Napola[24], a Nazi-run boarding school to train future slave-masters. Possibly, he took the job to avoid the draft.

Did these teachers allude to what was going on in Germany? That German history was at variance with the contemporary scenario? No, they didn't, because how could they have known? The school taught us to be decent human beings, but without contrasting it with the world outside the schoolyard. It is difficult for people later to understand, but how could they have known what was going on? You don't teach rumors, innuendoes, gossip in institutions of learning and at the time, that was all we had of what had been happening.

Our art teacher was a scurrilous fellow, an artist who taught because he couldn't make a living with the kind of art he practiced; we didn't know that, and he didn't dare to teach us outright modern art. Still, we learned a lot of art history and in the afternoon, he had his easel up somewhere on the school grounds, painting the way he saw the trees, the shrubbery, houses, the sky. I do remember wondering about it; it wasn't abstract, Dada-ism, cubism or any of these kinds of radical, 20th century departures from the conventional. Rather, it appears to me in retrospect to be a kind of post-impressionism.

The various English teachers we had left their distinctive marks. To this day, among the classmates I am in contact with, our favorite was Mr. Klein. He was also our "homeroom" teacher, starting in the fifth, and I think, also for some time in the sixth grade. He was very young; I believe this was his first job and we, his first class of students. We adored him; he started us on the English language and I think he did a wonderful job. Unfortunately, no sooner had the war started than he was drafted. I remember some in our class crying when he said good bye. We lost track of him; we had hoped that he would re-appear after the war, but not a word.

---

24 The movie *Europa Europa* showed that kind of school in all its despicable splendor.

Next, or soon thereafter, there was the Baroness von Örzen. She, too, was a very good teacher and offered a great variety ranging from American folk songs, catchy stories, and even, in the early years, some poetry. She was a woman of some bearing. However, she wore very short skirts (for the time) and usually sat on the head table, with her very good-looking legs crossed and in clear view – a fact not lost on us adolescent boys. Was that distracting or intended to get our attention? As I said, I do remember her sitting there and did learn a lot – a well-rounded education.

There were some other teachers, and among them, outright losers. But, in an overall balance, that didn't matter, except that I feel we were short-changed by an incompetent, unpleasant, and even outright sadistic music teacher. Even paradise has its flaws. But is there another side to the coin? One always expects it, but in this case, the situation is very peculiar; it concerns the principal of the school, Herr Director Krause. He was commonly called Chef (well, "chief" is not the best translation, and "boss" has too many, other American connotations; some may apply, others may not, but to leave it un-translated doesn't work, either, because in English, a chef is a cook. And so I will use the term "Chef," with the understanding that this does not mean a capitalized cook. I, thus, may actually contribute to the, well, myth of the man and a uniqueness of his own creation[25].)

Some time ago, I made a short presentation on an aspect of divinity and observed that the Western way of looking at a monotheistic God is pretty much fixed by Michelangelo's representation of Him in the Sistine Chapel: an elderly, benevolent but stern and determined-looking Caucasian male. This image I compared with the Sumerian views of, for them, an important deity, Inanna; a young mischievous and playful, happy go-lucky, black woman. The first

---

25 [I believe the best translation in this context would be Headmaster, or Head of School. – KS]

description of a man in authority fits Chef Krause quite well. He "ruled" the school in a rather autocratic fashion, so that all of the wonderful features of the school, as I have described them, were not diluted by contemporary events. He was the kind of man who could make people cringe just by his looking at them but the need did not occur very often. He cultivated his image very cleverly, particularly to minimize the actual need for sternness.

Whenever he inspected the school grounds (and that was quite often), he was accompanied – preceded, actually – by his German shepherd Biene; of course, he knew that and so did we. So, whenever we saw Biene, we stopped whatever no-good things we had been up to, and when Chef Krause majestically appeared, everything was in order – no fighting or yelling or other "disorderly conduct" and we diligently returned to doing whatever we were supposed to be doing. In all those years, I never saw him discipline anybody; undoubtedly, he may have on occasion, but basically the system worked. You may object that this was a system of maintaining order through fear; some kind of Teutonic terrorism. Not so, because what was there to fear? We never found out what punishment he may have meted out when coming across some misconduct, because it seemed he never did. Nothing but simple, solid, good psychology.

Chef Krause cleverly cultivated a cult of personality. In the morning, we all walked past his office and we were to salute him, which he graciously acknowledged, dimly visible through a window in his office. A little Hitler in his own right? Not quite, just an authoritarian figure who, as it happened, shielded us in his own way from the outside world. His birthday was a kind of Fourth of July celebration. The noon meal on his birthday was special and elaborate, which was quite important as soon as war time shortages began to creep into our daily life. A play was put on, I think there was even something like a parade, speeches were made, songs were sung, and then Principal Krause, sitting on a very elevated chair, read some stories to the school. We still talk about this "event" today.

I have to be careful here not to interpret his role in the light of present-day knowledge. Still, I venture to say that through his stern and autocratic attitude and behaviorism, and, yes, his rather pompous demeanor, he kept the school running, and he kept a bunch of adolescents in line without invoking the then-prevalent militaristic stupor which he was able to keep out of the school exactly because of his attitude, demeanor and behavior. Am I glorifying him? Yes, to some extent at least, because it was exactly his autocratic way of running the school, as we observed, that kept discipline in a benevolent way; I believe that this same attitude simply worked to keep the authorities at bay. He was in charge and nobody would take that away from him.

He got away with it throughout the Nazi era precisely because, just as Mr. Schindler (he with the "list"), he very prominently displayed the emblem of the Nazi party on his lapel. Just as Mr. Schindler saved "his" Jews, Chef Krause saved a lot of us, not so much from physical destruction, but from becoming less than human.

Am I a bit drastic here? Perhaps, of course! I am not comparing Krause with Schindler but I do believe that there are certain similarities. One way to rectify something in a bad system from within is, you have to seemingly fit into it. Mr. Schindler saved "his" Jews by ostensibly being one of the Nazis. Without that, he would have had "no standing." Krause's prominently displaying the Nazi party badge must have convinced "them" that he was one of them. I believe that this, together with his autocratic demeanor, lulled them into believing that everything "was in order;" it was, but not the way they meant it.

Under his overall guidance, but leaving all the details and initiative as well as creativity to teachers and students, the Christmas Season (Advent) became something very special and memorable with candles, a play, and lots of singing. Again, as the war progressed, this emotionally soothing event was very important to us, as I know now.

Yes, lip-service had to be paid to some official events; a few times during the year, we all had to assemble, and of course we had to sing the national anthem on Hitler's birthday. However, in our school, Hitler's birthday celebration remained a colorless event compared with the to-do over Principal Krause's birthday and compared with the pomp and circumstances that was practiced elsewhere.

Hardly anybody ever came to school wearing the Hitler Youth uniform. Again, who really knows how Chef Krause kept the party bosses at bay, the often despised "gold pheasants," as they were called in their decorated mustard color uniform? But thanks to him, as most of Europe gradually fell under the control of the Nazis and their local collaborators, we enjoyed a life of peace as if nothing happened; the Nazis were kept outside. We no longer had Jews in our school because by the time I entered, Jewish children by law had to go to a separate school. But we had quite a number of so-called "half-Jews," with only one parent being Jewish. I understand that, in other schools, they were made unwelcome, but not in ours. As the war progressed, they were supposed to leave, too. I don't know how Chef Krause managed it, but somehow, by placing them into lower grades, he was able to keep them; we had one in our class, and nobody even considered this as being something special.

-10-

WAR: A MILDLY INTERESTING BACKGROUND STORY

I have talked a lot about aspects of my life as if they were little affected by the outside world and actually were continued into the early war years, thus giving the impression that nothing else really happened; from my point of view, that was more or less true. My school, my summer trips to Bunzlau, some additional vacation, visits with family friends and their visits with us, just continued into the first war years as if nothing had happened. But in a way, and below the surface, it was really the beginning of a kind schizophrenic-like existence. Of course we were affected by the war, even if we denied any effect; in a way, we ignored the war as much as possible. And so I must return to September 1, the day which I referred to in the beginning; it was the day we heard over the radio that, as of five o'clock in the morning, our troops returned enemy fire[26]. I don't remember how the grown-ups were affected by whatever specifically had led up to that day. I positively do remember, and have said so already, that the mood everywhere after it began was very somber and subdued. There was the propaganda (I do remember that) of

---

26 "Seit heute früh um 5 wird zurückgeschossen"

Polish atrocities against Germans in Poland, and that these Germans had to be liberated. Did the German people believe it? I simply do not know.

Often it has been said, after the end of the war, that the German people had been enthusiastic about the opportunity for revenge for the Treaty of Versailles' punishing terms following the loss of the World War (it didn't have a number then). Quite possibly, there were some celebrations, but I don't know any; I don't remember any outpouring onto the streets, nor any parades or rallies or any other mass hysteria, not even after Poland was defeated. After all, the World War had just ended 21 years earlier. I don't believe that, in the beginning, there was any expectation other than a skirmish with Poland. I didn't know at that time but I know now, since reaching middle age, that twenty-one years are quite a short period of time.

When England and France declared war on Germany, the benevolent attitude towards Chamberlain about a year ago was forgotten. But to my mother, her friends, our and their families, and I guess all of our parents' generation, memories returned of things they'd hoped to forget for good. Memories of shortages generally, particularly of dairy products and meat; then, there was the infamous turnip winter of 1917, the lack of coal, but also of sickness everywhere; they remembered all of these things. The men mostly just clamped up with memories of the trenches. I have a very vivid memory of the quiet desperation that clutched my parents' generation; there was no jubilant recounting of whatever victory there may have been in the past, but instead there was just a solemn, "not again."

Rationing began right away, though it was quite liberal at first; I don't remember any actual food shortages, but people generally lived more frugally than today. My mother's income was quite limited (we still had a maid, even well into the war years) but she was an excellent cook; a good meal doesn't have to depend on fancy and expensive ingredients. Any shortages were selective and not much noticed. In our school, of course, we continued to have a morning snack, lunch, and an afternoon coffee break. That had never been fancy anyhow, and it simply continued without change. Clothes were also rationed, but in our age, boys in their sub-teen or early teen years had very little interest in clothes[27]. I couldn't care less what I wore, as long as it was warm in winter and cool in summer, and it was. For some reason, women's hats weren't rationed, and my mother amassed about 30 of them; why, I do not know.

For reasons I don't recall, but at some time before the beginning of the war, my mother was strongly urged to take up at least a part-time job. Having a maid was an added "incentive." Who did the "urging" and how it was done, I don't remember, but in retrospect, this was obviously done in anticipation of a significant labor shortage, once the "war" would begin (as was expected by Officialdom). My mother's taking up a job didn't affect me because I was in school all day. Her job did, however, have interesting side effects. My mother was assigned to a job in what may have been one of the first displaced persons, or refugee, camps of the era. It wasn't really a camp but a building somewhere in town, which was converted to take up and to temporarily house and feed refugees. My mother was soon elevated to a kitchen manager, under the top guy who ran the place.

Who were these refugees in 1939 and '40?

They came from different places, but I remember only the more interesting ones. There was, early on, a group of Germans from Brazil who had been expelled. I met one of them and remember him well: a tall, very pleasant, easygoing fellow, no rabble-rouser, but obviously quite naïve. He'd tried to organize a Nazi party in Blumenau, an ethnically German town in southern Brazil, so the Brazilians kicked him out. Then there were Germans from the part of Poland now occupied by Soviet troops. There were Germans and others from the Baltics, after the Soviets took them over and assimilated them into

---

27 We didn't concern ourselves with "cool" clothes.

the USSR. Then there were still others; for example, Ukrainians who had been exiled from the Soviet Union after the early 1920s because they'd established an independent Ukrainian state. I met a Ukrainian professor who became a friend of the family. He was very nice and told us a lot about the history of the Ukraine and of Eastern Europe in general. He befriended us for several years and then left suddenly, but he'd brought to us the notion of peoples and countries to the east, which I had no idea existed.

So, there was some fall-out from the war: to me, this was an interesting supplement to what we learned in school. It certainly "widened my horizons," as the saying goes and added to the pleasant memories of my childhood. But clearly, I was only seeing the brighter side of a terrible circumstance.

I don't remember how long my mother held that job in the refugee facility. But at some point, the facility was relocated outside of Berlin, and she was assigned (at that time you had no choice) to another job, in the city's Social Services department. She was a case worker but didn't talk much about it at home; probably I wasn't too interested. Was it arrogance on my part, or a tacit attempt on her part to continue to shield me from the lower classes or from the Nazis? I don't know. But a particular event stands out, because it shook her deeply and was my first real encounter with the abysmal side of Nazism.

One day a case was assigned to her that originated with the Gestapo. A man was to be taken out of a concentration camp. At that time, I'd heard of that kind of institution but didn't really comprehend that it wasn't just another kind of camp. I believe it was Sachsenhausen. The man was to be turned over to some foreign organization or the Swiss Red Cross. The man was apparently in bad shape, so my mother hinted, and was to be restored to health. However, his condition was such that he couldn't be just booked into a spa or sanatorium; on the other hand, it was already well into the war and health spa facilities were either crowded by the public or taken over by the military. So, it took considerable organizational skill, finesse, and power of persuasion to get the man placed to get good health care without having to explain why he needed it. Apparently, my mother did the job very well but was quite shaken by it.

After everything was done and the transfer was completed to everybody's satisfaction, the Gestapo offered my mother a job as a social service worker, presumably to handle similar cases on a regular basis. She didn't tell me at the time, but later she explained how much she'd agonized over the decision. Off hand, you might say almost automatically "no way." But matters aren't that easy. First of all, you didn't say no to the Gestapo. At that time, details of what they were doing weren't known, but there was an ominous aura around them. On the other hand, there is the old Jewish saying, "Whoever saves one life, saves the world" so shouldn't she have taken the job with the Gestapo and do whatever she could? Obviously, I'm glad for her and for me that she somehow managed to decline particularly because, after the war, having allied herself with the Gestapo would have made things very difficult. But was it the *right* decision? Isn't the very fact that I am/was glad about her decision a kind of moral capitulation? Isn't it shocking that this kind of issue could even arise?

In conjunction with her job, my mother met a Mrs. Ide, whose husband was a high school art teacher. The two ladies became close friends; the Ides played a large part in my life toward the end of the war and beyond. They present one of the paradoxes outsiders have a difficult time grasping. Both Ides were members of the Nazi party but in their apartment they were able to hide a Jewish girl. She was introduced as the maid and made it through the war; afterwards, she left for New York and was never heard of again.

A major happening in the spring of 1940, or a bit earlier, of course, was the rapid defeat of France. It was very bewildering to our parents' generation: an armistice was announced a month-and-a-half after comparatively little fighting, and just 20 years after WWI's four-year, stalemate carnage. There was, of course, the boasting about the invincible German army under the divine guidance of the "greatest army leader of all times," Adolf Hitler. I remember, however, wondering about the fact, admitted in radio and reported *ad nauseam* in the newspapers, that the German soldiers were marching and marching and marching into France – 40, 50, 60 kilometers and more per day, day after day after day, so there was not much fighting. How come? Post war "history" tried to elevate the German army to an unbelievably strong force, when in fact, it was, at that time, still quite puny. The French, admittedly, had, at the same time, the strongest army in the world, but were running away. The German army's marching was the dominant theme and there was not much of any fighting except in Belgium and in a region under the command of a Colonel De Gaulle who promptly beat the Germans wherever he encountered them. But that was a limited encounter and did not stem the tide of the needlessly retreating French.

Little did we know that the French were given orders to retreat, retreat, retreat. Ever since De Gaulle, and still today, the French refuse to admit that they were the victims of betrayal; the French generals wanted to cooperate with the Nazis, which they did. We didn't know these details at the time, but the Vichy French turned into some kind of Nazi ally. As I said, the fact that the German army just seemed to walk into France made me wonder at the time and is of course consistent with what came out later, any French denial notwithstanding. As a funny corollary, I had an aunt who was not much enthused with the Nazis, but she, like the rest of the people, were puzzled by the stunning victory which should have resulted in an early end to the war. And so she bought victory decorations, as presumably there would soon be a shortage. Well, there never was, even though there was some kind of victory parade in the summer of 1940, but that was quickly forgotten.

There are some other aspects of the war I must touch on. While the Battle of Britain was fought (as we heard in the radio and read in the press, before I learned how to listen to "enemy" radio), and while the qualitatively superior British Spitfires decimated the German Air Force (which we learned much later), we had our first air-raids. This was nothing exciting since there was initially no actual bombing.

However, Hermann Göring, the leader of the German airforce, had announced that his name would be "Mayer" if Berlin or Germany would ever be bombed[28]. Well, he was called Herman Mayer after that. It was still political joke-telling time; later, there were none. However we heard the thundering of the anti-aircraft guns, and that is when the artificial hill my dad and I used to visit to fly kites started to slide. Closer to town, there was bomb damage which became a regular local tourist attraction but whatever was destroyed was very quickly rebuilt. For us kids, there was something new: pieces of exploded shells. But soon we became selective and centered on "attractive collector's items:" pieces of copper from the exploded anti-aircraft grenades. The copper had something to do with gun guidance but why we deemed this valuable, I don't recall.

For some reason, some bureaucrats probably took their cue from London and they started to evacuate schoolchildren from Berlin; other cities, particularly in the highly industrialized Ruhr district, were also involved. It was voluntary at that time, and the regular schools continued as before. It would have been too drastic to close down all schools, so about half of our class left late in 1940. I stayed and others who did so, too, liked to think of ourselves as the more sophisticated ones. In any event, we did form a closer tie, which persists to a considerable degree today. I speak of, notably, Wolfgang Baecker. There were then a few air-raids but anybody who stayed and continued a "normal" life (or so it seemed who stayed) didn't regret it. About half of the kids of our grade went to something called Kinderlandverschickung, or the KLV camp, an abbreviation

---

28 That's like saying "I will eat my hat."

for "sending children into the countryside" – but that wasn't considered an evacuation. The boys went to a village in Thüringen called Schmiedefeld and stayed there a few months. The girls went to a town far away in Upper Silesia, Dramathal. The places were quite simple and basically makeshift, but some private quarters existed. Apparently, many of the girls were retrieved by their anxious parents and brought back to Berlin before Christmas.

These facilities didn't compare with those assigned to a neighboring school, the so-called Mommsen-gymnasium. For some reason they deemed themselves superior, perhaps because it was a Nazi-dominated school. The principal boasted at one point that his school was free of half-Jews: he'd had them removed as early as possible. The entire school was evacuated to Zakopane, a well-known Polish resort in the Carpathian Mountains, after the town, or at least the resort facilities, had been "ethnically cleansed." After the war, there wasn't even an attempt to continue the school.

In the beginning of 1941, all of our classmates were back, with the result that they were significantly behind those of us who remained in Berlin. But that was soon ironed out. At that time, things were not yet falling apart, but the war showed its effects here and there. For example, there was a government-organized effort to reinforce the basements of private homes. In our street, one basement room in each house was reinforced with thick posts. We had a basement room of about 150 square feet and it was shored up by six posts each about a foot thick. I imagine they're still there, as it would have been too much trouble to take them out.

Most importantly for me, however, was that very gradually, and for a number of reasons, I began to question what was going on. I don't recall specifically when it happened, but people began to be afraid. Afraid of what? It probably began to dawn on some people that questions of "right" and "justice" were becoming (actually, had been for quite some time) less and less important in favor

of abstractions such as the "holy fatherland" and "germanhood[29]."
Right at that time (i.e. in the '40s) came the edict that Jews had to
wear a yellow star on their clothing. I didn't see many, but those
who did wear it tried to hide it, for example by reading a paper while
walking or having an arm raised, seemingly to blow their nose. In
my naïveté, I wondered what all this was about. Again, it was something the adults ignored and didn't talk about, but still it occurred
to me that this must have been humiliating to those who were the
victims of that order.

---

29 Deutschtum

-11-

WAR: BUT THE SHELTER STILL HOLDS

I will now turn to the ominous year 1941. School life was still good, the normal routine continued with the annual glorification festival for Chef Krause's birthday; there was some obligatory ritual on Hitler's birthday, which eventually petered out but I don't remember when. There was, however, unabated, the pre-Christmas season with all its candlelit splendor. Because of food rationing, there may have been fewer cookies, but as the war droned on, it was during this period that we particularly appreciated all the to-do. As I mentioned previously, the earlier, temporary evacuation strengthened the bond between those of us who remained. And with it came, gradually, talk that was critical about aspects of public life as we understood it.

At this time, we were 13 and 14, our early teens, adolescents with confused emotions and the beginning of critical understanding. Was there trouble with our parents' generation? Not that I remember, certainly not by today's standards. Life for the adults was generally stressful, while we kids were in school all day. Foremost, on the outside, was the apparent increasing overall militarization and regimentation. Our parents had nothing to do with it—not directly anyway (I don't wish to whitewash them for their contribution to the rise of Nazism). And there was none of that militarization in school. There was discipline, of course, but without the military regulation as there was in other schools. We were aware that, indeed, things were different in our school compared with the outside, and the same was true at home, and so there was nothing really to rebel against as far as our immediate life scenario was concerned. School and home remained the focal point without being questioned, because, undoubtedly, we felt instinctively how desirable that was for us.

Let me be a bit more specific on the "teenage" issue. I certainly don't mean to create the impression that we were perfect angels. Of course not: we played our pranks in school but never terrorized the teachers. We drove some of them to exasperation, but nothing was excessive. I think, intuitively, we didn't directly or indirectly consider "them" as enemies to be outfoxed at all cost.

Today, it's customary that teens coalesce and vociferously complain to each other about how bad their parents are ("they don't understand anything"), except that, increasingly, parents aren't even talked about, because "everybody knows" they're beneath contempt. We had none of that; not, as I have said, because we were "so good" but I think we realized that the world around us was beginning to come apart and that teachers, school, and home were what were holding our world together. Our attitude shouldn't be generalized though; quite to the contrary. Later, we learned (and to some extent, already sensed) that the Nazi youth organizations often quite purposefully drove a wedge between the kids and their school and parents. We were spared that because, through the school, we were, to a great extent, screened from this malice.

Of course, we tried alcohol; I remember I almost choked on my first sip of hard booze, whatever it was, and I found beer singularly awful. Wine was hard to come by; my mother hardly had any. Cigarettes, I tried: awful! Again, they were rationed, and kids didn't get any. My mother must have gotten some, but I think she used them as barter or even bribe, which, of course, was helpful. Some kids in school may have sneaked a smoke here and there but that was very rare. By and large, I don't remember ever having experienced any frustration with what school and home had to offer. The blackouts and some shortages were bothersome, and in earlier years, I had trouble getting more equipment for my train set, which was very annoying indeed, but it clearly was not my mother's fault! I didn't have a bicycle except for an old broken-down contraption – it was difficult to get spare parts – but I considered that as very minor and certainly no reason to get angry with my mother or the teachers. To some, the Jungvolk may have been a kind of defusing activity, provided you didn't mind the military aspect, which most of us did. I'll talk about that shortly and how it affected me.

There's very little to add to the "teenage problem:" school and home remained a focal and anchoring point of a peaceful existence amidst growing changes elsewhere.

During the 1940 Christmas season, there were great hopes generally that the war would be over "next year." In terms of any war effort that school children had to contribute to, I think today we'd call it recycling. We collected old newspapers, bottles, and cans from people, except that there weren't many cans – German housewives didn't like canned stuff – nor were there bottles, because there was not much to drink anymore; the Coke culture came only after the war. Recently, I visited with a former classmate of mine, W. Dieter Luz; he still has his old report cards, and in one of them, there was the remark that he had failed to reach the paper collection quota. I don't remember whether or not I did; it didn't matter to us one bit, and I am convinced that the report card writer was just required to put something. It certainly didn't affect Dieter's standing in school.

The spring offensive in the Balkans wasn't taken seriously. We knew from our history studies that there was always trouble in the Balkans. But the June invasion of the Soviet Union shattered all expectations of an early peace. It was as if a great shudder had crept over everyone. In spite of what appeared to be an endless stream of victories, even the most unsophisticated observer of the map was immediately stunned by what was clearly a rapid dissipation of the German army over an ever-expanding territory. Increasingly people moaned, "*Wir siegen uns zu Tode*," which is difficult to translate but which can perhaps be closely rendered as, "We will conquer ourselves to death."

It very soon became apparent that the German army was ill-equipped to cope with the Russian winter. No sooner was fall upon us than an urgent call was made for people to donate warm clothes, coats, socks, scarfs, gloves, whatever, as they needed it right away. This certainly didn't help morale or peace of mind. The winter of '41 to '42 was particularly cold, with lots of snow everywhere. We kids, of course, liked the snow, but it certainly didn't help the German war effort. Officially, of course, the disaster wasn't acknowledged, but enough filtered through with the mail soldiers sent home. Officially, the catastrophic loss of life on the Eastern front, particularly near Moscow, was, of course, kept from us. On the other hand, it was clear from the lack of "progress" that the offensive had come to a grinding halt. The pitiless manner in which German troops were sacrificed was equaled by the ruthlessness of the Soviet high command (and vice versa). Again, we didn't learn this officially at the time, but here and there, information trickled back from the front.

The official story, at the onset of the campaign against Russia, was that the Russian army had been preparing to attack Germany, and so the attack on the Soviet Union was a "justified" preemptive strike. As I have said at the outset, my main concern is my own remembrance. However, for reasons of perspective, I have to refer occasionally to some later reflection, particularly when the situation is of an unbelievably flagrant nature. In 1941, two of the most evil kinds of empires faced each other. That they would be at each other's throat was and is a matter of virtual certainty. It doesn't matter at all who struck first. That was a matter of tactics[30].

Well, of course, we wondered how had Germany won these unbelievably swift victories, in which one Russian army after another was encircled and taken prisoner? Yes, of course, Adolf Hitler was the greatest strategist, army leader, etc. etc. of all times, but it was quite obvious that the German army had encountered Soviet chaos, a country really unprepared for anything, and certainly not ready for an impending attack on Germany. The German strategy of encirclement of Soviet units was the result of precise and superior military strategy on the part of the German High Command. How did I know that? At that time, I began to read the newspapers, and they were very precise on this point; after all, as long as you're winning, you can afford not to lie. Of course,we didn't know then that Hitler tried to meddle in the generals' affairs, and that he was unsuccessful. Even that dilettante couldn't argue with the obvious success of the generals he so greatly despised – this we, of course, learned later.

We also didn't know that, a few years earlier, Stalin had eliminated most of the highest ranking officers of the Red Army, and just like Hitler, he too was meddling in the army's affairs. But Stalin had the freer hand and had nothing to fear from his army. At that time, Hitler had to soft-pedal; he still was afraid of the army, and he hated the high command. Hopefully, at some future time, a historian with sufficient information will write about how these competing incompetents were shored up on both sides by well trained and talented military people. There were only a few of them on the Russian side, but many on the German side so the Russians had to wait until Hitler's incompetence began to dominate the German command. This, I believe, began in 1942, when the Russian climate, the vastness of the country and the Russians' patriotic reaction to the cruelty of

---

30 After all, on a smaller scale, who cares in a moral sense, whether Al Capone murdered Moran in the St. Valentine's Day Massacre or whether it was the other way around.

the SS all combined to finish off the German army a few years later. The dissipation of the German army in the Russian – Ukrainian vastness was frighteningly obvious to us, as I vividly recall. Somehow, the winter stabilized matters temporarily, but with the German army stalled before Moscow, early victory was again far, far removed from reality.

The disaster in Russia overshadowed the declaration of war against the US. The latter didn't play any significant part in our thinking; after all, there was the Atlantic in between, and as time went by, there was nothing noticeable of what was to become the redoubtable, American war-machine. We didn't know that it would take some time to develop.

-12-

WAR: NOW IT DOES AFFECT US (SOMEWHAT)

Before continuing with aspects of war and remembrance, and how the people reacted to it, I want to look at a different development in my life, running more or less in parallel. First of all, it was during that time (i.e. upon the disastrous extension of the war into Russia), that in school we covered the real history of the 18th and 19th centuries. It was taught by Ms. Henrici, whom I already mentioned. She taught us about the 1848 fledgling and abortive German uprising in an appreciative manner; the preceding Napoleonic wars were shown from a perspective the Prussians had no reason to be proud of, and even Bismarck was not excessively glorified. Our English lessons became more interesting, as they centered on all kinds of short stories. I already mentioned Baroness von Örzen. She even read with us some Western stories and also some English history, but we were short-changed on Shakespeare, probably because the German translation was competing with German authors, and Shakespearean English is a bit hard for beginners.

We began, however, to appreciate Schiller and tacitly understood one of his famous plays *"Die Räuber"* (The Bandits) to cover what later became known as freedom fighters.

During this time also, my interest arose in physics and technology, and this overshadowed, in terms of personal interest, the unfolding of "great events of history." Here I have to refer to a teacher, Mr. Franke, who for some reason, kindled in me an interest in mathematics, and soon I became his star pupil. It's possible that he was a bad teacher, and I was just at the age and maturity when my interest in math would have emerged no matter the quality of the teaching but in any event, he was a man one had or should have looked at with great compassion, an attitude adolescence doesn't have towards adults in great abundance. He had been in the trenches in WWI and following some artillery barrage and explosions, he'd been buried under sand and rubble for quite some time before being rescued. Not surprisingly, that incident had shattered his nerves. Occasionally, he had a nervous tick; we called him the Cod[31].

Much to our shame, I have to confess that we occasionally made fun of him and, in a rather sadistic fashion, enjoyed his outbursts. I talked recently with my friend and classmate Wolfgang Baecker about an incident in which he, Wolfgang, was the victim of one of the Cod's / Kabeljau's outbursts. Wolfgang noted that Chef Krause's aloofness, though very effective in most cases, was quite improper here as he should have addressed our class and others and told us about Mr. Franke's war injury, appealing to our decency. Kids are often mean but rarely really vicious, and I'm sure things would have been much different after a stern lecture. However, Chef Krause's aloofness might have been a streak of arrogance which did help to keep the Nazis out, but, on a personal level, it was clearly inappropriate.

Other than that, we worried about Latin words and English vocabulary, that is, basic aspects of an education. Geography became

---

31 In German, Kabeljau

increasingly interesting and each year we covered a different continent. I wasn't an excessively diligent student, but math and physics came easily to me. I continued to enjoy frequent afternoon outings, an occasional lab class and sometimes, we had to work on the school grounds, not just for punishment, but to help keep them neat, trimming bushes, taking care of weeds, etc. And so, our *refugium* remained intact.

Of course, in the summer of 1941, there was our annual trip to Bunzlau which, however, I began to find a bit boring. Berlin was still a glamorous city and to me as a growing boy, it became increasingly so, even with all the war problems inevitably affecting big city life. Also, my grandfather's car had been confiscated for the war effort so there were no outings anymore into the mountains. This year, however, my mother had planned a trip to the Alps, to a little resort village near the Swiss border. This was quite a change from the regular trips. It began with a very long train ride from Bunzlau to Munich – there were no Inter City Express (ICE) trains yet, just good old steam engines. In Munich, I stayed for the first time in a luxury hotel, towering right next to the railway station. All other stays before had been in some nice but modest inns in the country; this now was something new. I mention it because hotel service was still available in spite of the war and was by no means makeshift but up to a high standard, as I came to learn later. When I compare this with hotel stays in later years, well into the '50s and '60s, it was quite on par even then.

The next day, we continued our journey on an unforgettable train ride into the Alps proper. Trains in Germany were generally driven / pulled by good old steam "horses," but south of Munich and into the Alps they were electric which was not as spectacular as the steam engines but cleaner and alluring in other ways. I distinctly recall that they accelerated faster. Going into the Alps, we didn't cover the really majestic part (Großglockner, Ötztal), but the mountains are magnificent compared with the modest Silesian mountains. The train ride, even just along the Inn Valley, was so very different from what I was used to. This part of Austria was, and still is, a province (now it's called a state) called Tyrol. The inn where we stayed was elegantly rustic. Everything was interesting, the food quite different, and there was plenty of it – no shortages of any kind – and the people spoke a fascinating dialect.

We did a lot of hiking from one vista point to the next, but to me, one of the most interesting sites was a walk on a high road, well above the bottom of a gorge. One side was Austrian, the other, Swiss. The road was, in fact, hewn into the rock on the Austrian side. When looking across the gorge, we could see on the Swiss side what looked like caves, level with the street on which we were driving. In the caves, we could see heavy guns pointing straight at our road. If Germany had declared war on Switzerland or just marched into that country (that was the customary way then), that road could have been demolished in a few minutes. And there weren't and still aren't that many roads in North / South direction across the Alps. Any repair would have taken very long, and the Swiss would undoubtedly interfered with any repairs. Fortunately, none of that happened while we were there nor at any time later.

We also visited Innsbruck and I enjoyed a beautiful town without the paraphernalia of war, nor was there ever any hostility toward Germans. The annexation had been a questionable affair, but western Austria was very German-oriented (the tourist traffic may have played an encouraging role here). Now, without unnecessary fanfare, the goal has been achieved within the EU – not exactly in the same way but pretty close to what the Austrian parliament wanted to accomplish in 1922 but was prevented by the allies.

-13-

BEGINNING TO "SEE THE LIGHT"

In the second part of Chapter 6, I described my first years in the Jungvolk and that I joined a singing group just before the war. Now, I have to turn to a different aspect of the war, namely the nightly black-out. It was total: no street lights nor illuminated store windows (soon, there would be nothing to buy anyhow), not a sliver of light from any window. The few cars that were about had their headlights covered, leaving just a little slit. Trains ran on dim lights, and the train stations were lit just enough to keep people from falling onto the tracks. A practically completely dark city is, in a way, frightening. People just hurried home or stayed home in the evening, and in winter, darkness fell early. Aside from the fact that, under these circumstances, adolescent "staying out" was not much of a problem, my singing practice was in the evening once a week and my mother wasn't happy about my traipsing around in the dark. I didn't much care one way or the other.

Right around that time, I was invited to join a different and more local unit, a kind of signal corps and engineering outfit. Strictly speaking, this was a kind of pre- or para-military unit, and undoubtedly was so intended, but all of us who joined were interested in this kind of thing. The leaders of the group were slightly older kids with engineering interests and so, again, no politics were involved. We learned a lot of technical and physics know-how, such as how to make a telephone work and how sound travels in a wire from one end to the other. But we also learned other things, like building tents and other contraptions, with the benefit that we became less clumsy in practical matters. We did, at first, have a lot of fun. After some time, however, particularly in the fall of 1941, things got boring because there wasn't as much material available for us to use, nor did we have the clothing needed for winter. So, the signal corps outfit began reverting to "regular" Jungvolk which, simply through observation, I had already come to thoroughly detest. Thus, I began to stay away from it to an increasing degree.

In the spring of 1942, two things happened in this regard. Not surprisingly, it got warm, and our hopes rose of having fun again with our signal corps stuff, but that didn't materialize. Our age group, however, was then supposed to be transferred to the so-called Hitler Youth, a boys' organization for 14- to 18-year-olds. I remember attending an assembly with some of our old group. Like me, they hoped for more engineering stuff but with better equipment, because we were now older. There, we met a fellow who was supposed to be our leader – I think his title was Gefolgschaftsführer (literally translated: "leader of followers" a not very imaginative title). He was what you may call a super-Nazi; he knew nothing of electrical engineering or the like; he gave a purely political, pep-talk speech, yelling at the top of his voice. Encountering only icy silence, he must have thought that yelling louder would overcome this apparent lack of enthusiasm in the audience, but the silence only became icier. I don't recall how it ended, but I was determined to have nothing further to do with that organization and so stopped going completely. At that time, membership wasn't obligatory, but later in the year when it became obligatory, I just ignored it. Things were beginning to fall apart, and I simply was never caught for not joining. Obviously, I didn't have much enthusiasm for the current political set-up. My antagonism towards military regimentation may have been the root of the aversion, but in 1942, the world around me began to develop in a way which I regarded with an increasingly critical eye.

During the summer of '42, we were supposed to help with the harvest and classes were "drafted" for that purpose. How I managed to avoid that, too, I don't remember, but I did. Was it just laziness on my part? Perhaps it was, but I knew that this harvest effort was, again, to a considerable extent, under the regime of the HJ, which I wanted to avoid. I had to do some other work: packaging stuff in a warehouse of some publishing outfit. It was rather boring, but it was for me the first modicum of a job and thus a rather curious experience. For some strange reason there is a peculiar knowl-edge / remembrance lacuna for the year 1942. I didn't think much of it, but my longtime friend, Wolgang Baecker, recently told me that he experienced the same phenomenon. A coincidence? Perhaps, but could it have something to do with our age? Were we, as adolescents, in fact overloaded with conflicting stimuli? Adolescence is the time of troublesome awareness and experience with the world around you and in a manner that invites participation, so that placid acceptance of earlier childhood is rejected, resulting in rebellion. During exactly that time, our world began to come apart. Oh, yes, the Germans were still winning, but at home, things just began to dissolve.

For example, matters became serious, as far as air raids were concerned. They still weren't heavy; the originally occasional bomb-ing became more frequent and lasted longer, with more anti-aircraft fire to "listen" to. We "older" children – we had reached the ripe age of fourteen – were assigned to spend some nights in the school as a kind of air raid warden; we were supposed to watch the school during attacks. Exactly what we were supposed to do wasn't clear, except that somebody showed us how to deal with small incendiary bombs: you pour sand on them. I don't believe that anybody had the slightest intention of even getting near them but since no bomb ever fell on our school, we defended it valiantly. My mother wasn't happy about this, but we liked it. It was more interesting than sitting in a basement during an air raid. We had some kind of dug-out, and when there was no shooting of AA guns directly above us, we could observe, all over town and in every direction, aimless shooting. At that time, too, there were occasional fires on the horizon, but by and large, our guard duty was quite uneventful.

My memory of the '42 to '43 school year is somewhat blurred; hardly anything sticks out. We had a different math teacher, which didn't change things. Physics and Chemistry became more interesting. We had a number of wartime substitutes who didn't leave any memorable mark, but I do remember that, by and large, they fit into the school.

One thing does stick out from history class (we no longer had Ms. Henrici): we were supposed to cover the late 19th century and continue into this century including WWI, the Weimar Republic, and the beginning of the Third Reich. The teacher was very astute and somehow managed to tone down the beginning of the German Reich and the questionable nature of Bismark's war policy. He managed to dilly-dally about the period after the end of WWI and simply denigrated the Weimar republic and the drooling over the onset of the Third Reich. A cop-out? Perhaps, but the subject matter was dangerous, and to avoid teaching us what he knew or felt to be lies was indeed second best to the truth.

But more important than the school teaching was the increase in discussions among us, notably Wolfgang Baecker and Horst Scheunemann. Increasingly we questioned what was going on. Thus, from 1942 to 1943, I actually became consciously opposed to the Nazi state and to Nazism in general, not just the stupid Hitler Youth. Why? We didn't even know then about gas chambers in concentration camps. I wrote briefly about concentration camps earlier. In my early childhood, I heard about them but didn't know what they were.

As time progressed, my curiosity grew, albeit not that much. As I've said and now most emphatically repeat, as an ever-growing experience of that time: people in Germany were sluiced to an increasing extent through camps of various kinds, but they all had in common excessive, military-style regulation.

Some militaristic regulation already existed in the 1940 KLV[32] camps (see the end of chapter 12), though very mildly. Aside from the forced labor camps for 18- and 19-year-old boys, there were worker camps for innumerable projects, called OT[33] camps. I'll discuss them when we reach the end of the war, because an OT camp in our neighborhoods became quite important. Another reason for an elaborate camp system was that the size of the army organization exceeded its available barracks facilities. However army barracks were, in fact, also camps – just with more solid housing but the same regimentation. As the camp network spread, concentration camps were just a different kind of camp, or so one thought, nothing to get particularly excited about except that, for me, this entire realm was increasingly anathema and outright repugnant. And there were other things.

For example, my widowed great aunt (the one who bought victory garlands in 1940, just to be on the safe side) lived alone in a fairly large apartment, and she was urged (or maybe, ordered) to make a room available for government visitors. The first one had no high position, he was just an ordinary SS officer, a seemingly very cultivated man. I don't know why I met him, but we were very close to that aunt, so it was inevitable that we would meet him, and later, his wife. He was rather quiet and only by accident, I don't recall how, it became apparent that he'd been an officer in what later became known as Sonderkommando (i.e. assassination squads) in Russia.

---

32 Kinder Land Verschickung, children evacuation program

33 Organisation Todt – the Todt organisation, named after its founder who built lots of defense structures, including among others, the Atlantic wall

What he actually did came to our knowledge only very indirectly, but gradually, it became clear that his actions had something to do with partisan warfare and the elimination of its participants. I think a great deal of intuition led me to believe that there was something wrong, but my mind was already set to look for something to bolster my aversion.

As I have mentioned earlier, we always had a roomer in our house, and during this period, Mr. Turetscheck, a physicist-engineer specializing in explosives and the physics of explosions, shock wave propagation etc., stayed with us. He was in his mid 30's, clearly of draft age, but indispensable for the war effort. Occasionally, he went on field missions and was in Poland several times – or the General-government as it was then called. When he returned from one such a trip, he was very disturbed. He talked about the abominable conditions there; he also spoke about Jewish ghettos and about his growing belief, gathered from the local authorities there, that the goal was the extermination of the Polish people. I remember him well and certainly gave more credence to his tales (i.e. to the narrative presented by this quiet, no-nonsense physicist), rather than to the official publications. I also remember that it quite exceeded my understanding. What does that mean, to eliminate an entire people? But I believed Mr. Turetschek's concerns and observations, not because he was our roomer, but his background dovetailed with my growing interest in physics and factual observations. Still, eliminating people was an abstraction and something that couldn't be real.

As a sort of intermediate corollary, 1942 brought to us the disturbing fact that we weren't supposed to have a maid anymore. So, we had to let her go. On the other hand, here or there, people had Russian maids. That is, Russian girls were brought from Russia to serve as maids. To what extent that was involuntary, I don't know. After the war the slave / involuntary nature of this "relation" was assumed. But what was the reality? Possibly, they were "recruited" involuntarily, but living in the land of the vanquished or in the land of the victor is an alluring choice, as history has told us. I saw quite a number of these girls. The people who had such maids included Eberhardt's parents (the super Nazi), who had instructed me on the evilness of Jewish crooked noses. The girl in that household was undoubtedly safe, because Ms. P., the wife of that dumb local chief Nazi, was one of the most decent people I ever met in my life[34].

1942 also brought more victories, oddly though, not near Moscow or Leningrad; but more and more, as the result of the German army's ridiculous intrusion into the Ukraine. I use the term "ridiculous," because you just have to look at the map to see that that move in the south of Russia extended the front line to the point where a rupture became a matter of virtual certainty. It is difficult to recollect how, by bits and pieces, I became aware that the government was just plain lying. To a kid, this revelation is astonishing and hard to believe, cautiously reinforced among us kids by discussions at school. German troops weren't generally regarded as liberators of the Ukrainian people from Bolshevism as was officially claimed, and this became increasingly apparent through rumors and the trickling-down of information, for example about partisan activities such as the blowing up of rail lines, etc. These rumors, in turn, reinforced my suspicion that, indeed, that SS officer had ordered assassinations.

Then the general "climate" changed, ever so gradually, but perceptibly so, that we adolescents particularly became increasingly aware of such matters, namely the growing suspicion that Germany had actual started this war. I began to put things together, starting with the peculiar Polish situation, the overrunning of Holland and Belgium, the apparent attack on the Balkans, then the campaign

---

34 I do not believe that by and large these girls suffered in any way one may seem to believe, at least the ones in our neighborhood. In addition, it must not be forgotten that after the war, a new class of people came into being – displaced persons – they were, for a considerable part, people who had been taken from the east into Germany and who didn't want to go home to the Soviet Union. One wonders why.

against Russia and lastly, the German declaration of war against the US.

There was also the growing awareness that the adults were increasingly afraid to speak out. Occasionally, I was admonished not to say this or that, having nothing to do with foul, teenage language.

A first turning point, though not so perceived, came in late summer of 1942, when the stunning victory in North Africa under Fieldmarshall Rommel turned into a sound defeat at the hands of General Montgomery (to my way of thinking the most able army leader of WWII). This was largely covered up and overshadowed by what seemed to be the impending victory in Russia although people – openly at first, later covertly – began to wonder if Germany was going to permanently occupy all of Russia. What a completely ridiculous undertaking, but what else could they be intending?

Christmas and the pre-Christmas season of 1942 was the last one celebrated in school although of course we didn't realize it then. But clearly now, this was a make-believe world. Nobody dared to speak of impending peace, and life in general became increasingly drab. On the other hand, movies and other entertainment still ran. Occasionally I went to the theater, and to the movies almost every weekend; just the choices dwindled. And then in the middle of winter, as the year turned from '42 to '43, came Stalingrad, probably the largest battle disaster ever[35]. For a long time, it was covered up. Actually, it began when Russian troops began to encircle about half a million German soldiers in November. The official version was that it was a valiant attempt to conquer Stalingrad, but there came a point where it couldn't be denied that the main front was quite far to the west from the army supposedly taking Stalingrad, but actually besieged in a hopeless situation. Also they couldn't hide that Fieldmarshall Paulus had surrendered his army when it

---

35 Verdun in WWI cost more lives, but lasted well over a year and thus was not a single battle.

was obvious that his army wouldn't be relieved. There was no heroic last stand, but as the outside world then learned (and we later), an incredibly pitiful debacle caused by sheer incompetence at the ultimate decision-making level. I don't remember who made the final speech in the matter, Hitler himself or one of his underlings, but I remember the invocation of the Spartans commemorating Leonidas and his stand against the Persians in the Thermopylae pass ("traveler, when you come to Sparta, tell that you saw us lying here as the law commanded"). Well, many of them did; most of them surrendered, but 95% of them died in Russian prison camps.

I don't remember that we discussed this affair in school, though I'm sure that outside of class we talked about it. I positively remember the shock this event created in the adult world: a sign of doom, a foreboding of the beginning of the end overcame them. Am I projecting subsequently gained knowledge into the scenario as we experienced it then? I don't think so, because the emotions of the people around me were a real experience, not a projection or conjecture. After a loss of about half a million men, the high command had to admit that the German army had been driven from the Volga river for quite a significant distance. Earlier, there had been doubt what victory could possibly mean, and comparisons were made with Napoleon's disastrous campaign. Now, the previously victorious German army was flooding back after a staggering loss in manpower. Indeed, the mood was somber and, to some extent, beginning to get desperate.

I hate to say it, but as far as 1943 is concerned, the continued beginning of the end was rather boring. So, there was a difference between the current state of affairs and Napoleon being routed out of Russia within one winter. The summer of 1943 covered it up. The front line was officially defined in a rather confused and imprecise manner, which was, undoubtedly, the intention. The incessant retreat was covered up with language such as "straightening out" or "shortening" the front line. We didn't hear much about the great Battle of Sebastopol and, as for the Russians, liberation of the Crimean peninsula. Nor did we hear about the battle in the Kursk bend of the river Don. Following the disaster of Stalingrad, there was a sense of make believe: it didn't really happen or doesn't matter, all that was so very far away, so, not to worry. But the relentless rout of the German army could only be ignored for so long, as it progressed and progressed.

There was no natural barrier between the Volga River and Germany. In 1941, that had worked in the Germans' favor in their advance against an unorganized foe. Among the Red Army generals and colonels who had survived the 1937 purge, there were apparently a few to whom Stalin may have listened. But now, it was 1942 and from German soldiers on furlough we heard stories about a well-organized but thoroughly ruthless Russian offensive; ruthless, that is, to their own people. We heard story after story about the incredibly ruthless way the Russians conducted the war, of untold numbers of unarmed people driven against German lines until the German troops ran out of ammunition, and then the armed Russians moved in, overwhelming the Germans. Were they horror tales? Propaganda? Possibly, but in a way, all sides came off badly. Even the wildest story had to be given some credence; at least a basic core might be true. The total number of Russian war dead was about ten times that of the German losses. It is usually the loser who has the greater losses, and the Russians had free sailing through their land, but the Germans had their supply lines cut by partisans. That, too, was widely rumored and well known, but not admitted officially.

I had begun to read the newspaper and, more often, I listened to the radio news although a great deal was cleverly contrived lies. I don't recall when I began to suspect that the official versions were lies, but when the German army was flooding back in Russia and the German retreat was time and again described as a "straightening out" of the front lines, I clearly felt that we were lied to. In 1942, particularly, I was increasingly annoyed by the militarization of daily life and separated myself as much as possible which, with the school as a sanctuary, was not that difficult. Now, with my eyes beginning to open in a critical way, I discovered that, indeed, we were lied to. The information I had available were the rather unofficial channels of rumors; but beyond that, I began to listen to Radio Beromünster[36] and the BBC. This was strictly forbidden but that, of course, made it more interesting. All these sources of information cast a picture very different from the official position set forth in the newspapers.

In the course of the developing war scenario, it went relatively unnoticed that in the spring of 1943 the German army was kicked out of Africa and soon thereafter, the Allies landed in Sicily and later in Italy. A mildly interesting side show, but made colorful by Mussolini's deposition, rescue by some German commando unit, and reinstatement, but now as an obvious puppet. I'm sorry, but nobody ever took the Italians seriously anyway. There was the nasty comment that the house of Savoy[37] never ended a war on the same side it began, unless they changed sides twice. Be that as it may, not to worry, the Alps were between the Allies in Italy and Germany; they are, to this day, a formidable obstacle.

So, the public aspects of we who were in our early to mid teens was dominated by a growing tide towards catastrophe, coupled with a growing awareness and understanding of the situation. I must say, however, that we didn't feel helplessness. "We did our own thing," as successfully as possible, sticking to our refugium-sanctuary as long as possible, leaving, so to speak, the final outcome open. There were, nonetheless, upcoming aspects that tied us to events as direct participants or, more accurately, victims.

---

36 Beromünster is a small town in Switzerland, situated between Zurich and Lucerne. During that time, it became a kind of icon in objective reporting.

37 The Italian Royal family.

-14-

THE BEGINNING OF THE BEGINNING OF THE END

Shortly after Stalingrad, the U.S. was ready to throw its war potential into the balance. What I mean is: America was far beyond the Atlantic, but after some time, its bombers arrived in England and the British had their own fleet replenished. So, the bombing began in a rapidly increasing manner, first in the Western part of Germany, but then reaching Berlin, and on a much larger scale than before. At the end of February 1943, I believe, large scale attacks started. If you looked outside during an air raid, you could see what were called "Christmas trees," that is, bundles of light slowly descending and serving as markers for the bombers who just dropped their load in areas delineated by these markers. Precision bombing was not yet invented, and probably not of interest anyway.

Let me be somewhat specific here. At that time (as I found out later from Allied newspapers), just as today, military communiqués speak only of hitting military targets. Of course, nobody ever admitted, at any time, during any war, that civilian centers were systematically targeted. As such, maybe that wasn't always quite accurate. Even today (i.e., more than half a century later, with all the smart-bomb technology), it's very difficult (though it shouldn't be) to hit a definite target from say 10,000 feet in altitude. Certainly, there's little accuracy from an altitude of 30,000 feet. Cities were clusters of intertwined living quarters, commercial areas, industrial complexes, a few barracks, transportation facilities, power stations, luxury villas, sports areas etc. etc. In order to hit an enemy's war-making machinery, you had to hit any area that contained that war-making machinery, which was often mixed with all the other "civilian" stuff. To single it out from a safe altitude (e.g. 30,000 feet), at that time, was impossible.

Even at the time, I understood that the notion of civilian as distinguished from the military is just illusionary or even outright nonsense. I may have come to this conclusion quite intuitively from the general militarization of public life that had been going on for quite some time: many people were running around in one kind of uniform or another. Even then, I felt no anger toward the Allied bombers. Why not? After all, I was kid and hadn't done anything, except occasionally disobeying my mother and my teachers, and surely, that wasn't sufficient to warrant throwing bombs at me. Also, in 1943, I hadn't yet developed an attitude of understanding the justification of these attacks, but I think I understood the notion that war is an all-embracing affair. How did I understand it that way? I don't really know, maybe the pervasive militarization contributed to a mindset all along such a line, clearly not in a way the officialdom intended to, but one senses through the militarization of civilian life that everyone might pay the price for whatever else is being done, no matter how little you have to do with it.

On March 1st, 1943, our area was hit. Hearing bombs roaring down is an unforgettable experience. The closest bomb hit about 100 feet away; it demolished the rear of the house two houses away from ours. In our house, the wall between the dining room and the kitchen collapsed. We thought that the house had collapsed in its entirety from the noise we heard from the basement. Well, it hadn't, and after the raid, we celebrated the fact by making an omelet out of all the eggs we had.

Few windows, however, were left intact. Fortunately, all our windows were double windows, and just after the beginning of the war we had taken one set off. They mostly survived, so that we did have windows after the war ended in 1945. As to the windows in place, not many but just a few panes were unbroken so we boarded them up, leaving the house rather dark. There was some damage to the roof, but that was soon repaired, though not for the last time. The electricity was out for a little while, but nothing else was damaged except for our nerves.

A few streets over, actually in the Lötzenallee where I'd lived right after being born, just a few houses down from ours, there was another four-unit house, just like ours had been. I knew all of the people who lived there including several boys who were a bit older than I; many of them had already been drafted. The people had built a covered dug-out with a fairly heavy top and entrances at both ends. One bomb exploded directly above the shelter, and all but one occupant in this contraption suffocated. Their house was partially demolished, but the un-reinforced basements held: they would have survived had they stayed there. They were the first "civilian" dead I knew about. Our nearby school wasn't damaged; school continued as if nothing had happened.

Before the school year ended in 1943, there were more attacks but nothing as close as the one on March 1st. After every raid, the entire horizon glowed red and yellow, and with the March 1st bombing we encountered for the first – but not the last – time, the phenomenon of a strong wind after such an attack, the so called fire-storm: wind resulting from the strong draft caused by fiercely blowing fires drawing in more oxygen. And as I said, school continued despite the almost nightly interruptions.

-15-

LEAVING BERLIN – SCHOOL IN BUNZLAU

After the 1942 – '43 school year ended, my mother and I hurried to Bunzlau, which was quite out of reach from bombers. At some point during the year, the children evacuations and school began on a large scale. My school, this time including all the students and most of the teachers, was evacuated to a little town on the Baltic Sea, Henkenhagen, in Pomerania. The general spirit of the school, teachers and students living together during the day, proved to be very helpful in these unusual circumstances. Even the not-so-desirable teachers became human. I would have liked to go to Henkenhagen with my school and classmates but it was more practical for me to enter the Bunzlau high school instead, which was obviously more organized than the makeshift school in makeshift quarters.

During the summer, my grandfather died and my grandmother became more human, too. However, for reasons I didn't understand nor appreciate (and still don't), I wasn't supposed to stay with my grandmother, who had been joined by a sister and my aunt – the same one who had bought victory garlands three years earlier. And so I entered a boarding school which was an adjunct and part of the

Bunzlau high school. I felt, to some extent, shunted out of the way by my grandmother, but I wasn't so thin-skinned that I suffered from it. In retrospect I'm glad of the experience because I became better acquainted with a completely different world. My new schoolmates were, shall we say, ardent participants in the new order, including, particularly, the Hitler Youth. My lack of interest in these matters was beyond their comprehension. I covered-up (concealed?) my non-membership in the HJ by asserting that documents had to come from Berlin. Being good Germans, they bought this, because anybody who waits for documents is justified in doing nothing in order not to upset the bureaucratic apple cart.

Of course, the idea that anyone would oppose or take a stand against Nazism, the war effort, the government's say-so, the prevailing doctrines, didn't occur to them. That was true for the kids in the boarding school, as well as those who were just day students. In the boarding school, there was some military-style regulation which I found increasingly annoying. Often, I devised ways to avoid it whenever possible. For example, we were to stand at attention before entering the eating hall. This I circumvented by just being late. I was also bothered, to some extent, by the lack of privacy. There were relatively large, dormitory-like sleeping quarters but there were day rooms, and four or six boys shared such a day room. I remember some of them, but only vaguely. Since I didn't smoke at that time, but others did, I had cigarettes available; that way, I bribed my way into favors so that I avoided duties and other boring aspects. It was quite difficult to hide my political persuasion, but I was helped in this by an overall naïveté. My fellow students didn't question my beliefs, and they let me be, this peculiar guy from the big city (Berliners were suspected of being kooky anyhow). They did wonder, however, why I did not have a Hitler Youth (HJ) uniform, but fortunately they weren't that interested. They were a decent bunch, naïve, but not out to get me; they weren't informers, out to advance themselves by "turning" others in. I would really like to add here that, from my experience, this "Nazi era informer" inferno has been overstated. If people, by and large, had been out to get others as we're told, the German people would not have survived Nazism, and the Russian people, bless their souls, would not have survived Bolshevism.

I spent a good deal of my time at my grandmother's house, reading or listening to BBC radio. In my class, there was another boy from Berlin who was there for the same reason, but we had nothing in common and, hence, had no contact. A little later in boarding school, I shared the day room with a student from Hamburg. He was also one of the evacuees who had experienced the horrible, three-night attack on Hamburg in July 1943 when a large part of the city was wiped out. His home, school, and neighborhood had all been demolished, but that didn't shake his faith in the Führer. To me, his attitude was beyond comprehension.

The teachers in the Bunzlau school were quite different from those in the Berlin Waldschule: the teaching lacked the closeness I was accustomed to and had more of an "us versus them" kind of atmosphere. However, the quality of teaching was equivalent. For German literature, etc., we had a former deputy of the German Parliament, Mr. Ölze, who had been a member of the Conservative Party throughout the republic. That party actually had supported Hitler in 1933, getting him into power; but shortly thereafter, his party was kicked out. I didn't know Mr. Ölze's actual beliefs, but the Conservatives were an arrogant bunch who thought that they could control Hitler. They were naïve but, by and large, had very high integrity. I'm glad that I had the opportunity to meet such a man, and I remember him well as a teacher.

We read Schiller's *Wilhelm Tell* in his class, even though that drama would soon be considered highly suspect by the Nazis, but they didn't (yet) quite know how to deal with one of Germany's literary idols. In any event, Mr. Ölze's lectures were usually quite memorable. In history classes, it was the standard German high school program to start on German / European history again with the 10th grade, but now in an in-depth fashion. We began with ancient history which was fairly neutral, but the teacher fed us the line of Aryan Nordic-derived Greeks (just don't show them pictures with black hair – statues don't show hair color). The idea was that the Greeks supposedly came from the North, where the Aryans lived. At the time, I didn't really care where people came from[38]. One simply knew that people were milling around; plus the lack of indoctrination throughout the previous years about the supposed superiority of the Aryan race prevented me from seeing the Greeks in a distorted light[39]. The Celts somehow didn't exist, and the relation between the Romans (with their great military tradition) and the wild, unruly Teutonic tribes presented some ideological difficulties to the Nazi era. Interestingly, I never felt any affinity to the Teutonic tribes – I wonder who did. What the Romans had done was so much more interesting.

The English teacher was a very intelligent and able lady who didn't teach much English but Nazi propaganda instead. I found this remarkable for two reasons. It was actually the first time I encountered in a teacher a "genuine" Nazi propagandist. The other reason was that she was far from voicing vulgar anti-Semitic / Bolshevik / plutocratic / etc. propaganda. Rather, I remember her as sly and clever even without recollecting many details, except that she tried to convince us that "inaccuracies" (i.e. outright lies) in the press were meant to mislead the Allies; how this was supposed to work was not clear, but I believe that she relied on the assumption that the HJ–infested students were about ready to believe anything as long as

---

38 It took me many years before I realized that it doesn't really matter.

39 Isn't it hilarious? During the Nazi era, we were taught that the Greeks were, of course, of Nordic-Aryan extraction, demonstrating that civilization was of Nordic-Aryan origin. Late in our century, Bacal's Afro-centrism tried to advance as a politically correct point of view that the Greek civilization is the derivative of early African thought. Things haven't changed; Nazism. and postmodernism are apparently engaged in the same kind of deception for political purposes.

it was uttered with authority. I was careful to keep my mouth shut, but the cleverly disguised nonsense had its moments of interest and reinforced my own beliefs. Coming from Berlin, I knew that she was lying. Should I have spoken up?

Perhaps, but I was new in the school and insecure; still, that's no excuse. Aside from those details, nothing else comes to mind, and basically, I had an uninterrupted first half of the 10th grade. I will discuss the second half it in the next chapter.

Once, during late 1943, I went briefly to Berlin, and in spite of the air raids that greeted me and had become an almost daily affair, I loved being back home. Train rides were still possible at that time, and the trains ran punctually – the bombing had hardly any effect on the track system. During that time, my mother was on and off in Bunzlau and in Berlin, growing increasingly scared. I wondered why she didn't stay in Bunzlau, but the attacks came in spurts or bunched together, followed by a lull. The timing, though, was something she couldn't know in advance. So, when things got bad, she came to Bunzlau; then, after a while, the attacks stopped and she went back to Berlin, and soon they started again. It was so regular that there were some people in Berlin who, when they saw my mother, said: "Oh no, now you are back, the attacks will start again."

In any event, she didn't want to stay in the house during an air raid. So, whenever the radio announced a pre-warning condition, she packed a small satchel and hurried off to the Deutschlandhalle, a newly built auditorium which had been bombed but the basement was left intact: it had proved itself! It was about a fifteen-minute walk away, and then, of course, she had to walk back, but she didn't mind; she felt safer that way.

As 1943 drew to a close, the German army still occupied some, but not much, of Russia. The Allied forces were advancing toward Rome, and the western part of Germany sank into rubble. How some people could still believe in a German victory (and my Bunzlau classmates did) was beyond my comprehension. My logic was simple and had nothing to do with military strategy: The German armament industry was within the range of Allied bombers, who had gained superiority over German airspace; the Allied armament industry was beyond the range of the German bombers (whatever that was at the time), so that the German defeat was a mathematical certainty; the only question was when. And eventually, in school, I did become regarded as subversive, lacking faith in the Führer simply because it was apparent that I never joined in the exuberance that accompanied everything related to Hitler. I don't remember ever criticizing the Führer directly, though most likely I contradicted some of the more ludicrous assertions concerning his person. I guess my consistent though quietly hostile attitude just came through, and I still missed my school in Berlin.

Sometime in the fall, the German war effort took a desperate turn. The lack of manpower, staggering losses, and the need to rev up the production and repair bomb damage was a terrible strain on available man / people power. So, they started to draft children born in 1927 – those born in '26 were already in labor camps or in the army somewhere. The sixteen-year-olds were taken *en masse*, that is, by classes, and pressed into service with anti-aircraft units. They were called "airforce helpers" (*Luftwaffenhelfer*). So, what was left of the class above mine (at that point, the 11th grade) and the older half of my class were drafted. This was, of course, also true for my now-evacuated Berlin class. When this drafting was announced in Bunzlau, the reaction among the students was not quite as ridiculous as the opening scenes in the movie *All Quiet on the Western Front* where, under the tutelage of their teacher, the entire class burst into a wild orgy of nationalism, but the mental state of my classmates was close to that. These kids, though, were going to be placed on guns in the upper Silesian coal district. That area, of course, was even farther away from the Allied bombers' range, and the Russians didn't have much of an air force, so no matter the enthusiasm, there was nothing to defend and they were quite safe.

Since Bunzlau was a small town, this impending service call was a major event, and when the time came for these kids, about 20 or 30 of them, to depart, the entire school accompanied them to the railway station. All but a few of the students were in HJ uniform. My grand-mother was horrified because I, the grandson of one of the leading citizens of the town, had no such uniform. The idea that I found that kind of clothing objectionable didn't enter into consideration. The connotation was that only poor people who couldn't afford to buy a uniform didn't have that kind of garb, so I was expected to be duly clothed. Wearing the HJ uniform, in her mind, had nothing to do with politics; it concerned only social status. But I strongly objected and put my foot down; my argument was, in order to buy a uniform, you had to surrender a certain amount of clothes-rationing coupons, and that I was unwilling to do. I needed other stuff for the coming winter, having outgrown my previous winter clothes, etc. etc. So I, together with some others (who, I suppose were motivated like I was; I simply do not remember anybody dressed like a pauper) marched (sauntered, really) at the end of the uniformed column; I think I ditched the "procession" at some point, and it was all forgotten. I still had my clothing coupons, which I used to buy a nice, dark blazer and some elegant, light gray slacks.

Afterward, the school scenario actually improved because the class was smaller. How this disgusting endeavor of putting children on guns affected our teachers I don't remember; were they ashamed? I do remember, however, that teaching became, in a manner of speaking, a more urgent affair on their part; mental stress on them generally increased gradually. And in Bunzlau, I enjoyed uninter-rupted sleep. Since I was now among the oldest in the boarding school, I was put in charge of a day room for some kids who were a few years younger. I think I was quite popular because I abhorred military discipline, which the younger kids readily sensed.

In Bunzlau, then, I still enjoyed something resembling a normal life; there remained even a few cafés and movies. The HJ was in total disarray and left me in peace; they had enough to do with keeping organized those "willing" to be part of it. And so 1943 drew to a close. Would the war end next year? Would I be caught up in it?

-16-

LUFTWAFFENHELFER

In January of 1944, boys born in 1928 were drafted into the service to serve as Luftwaffenhelfer (LwH). This, of course, included me. A medical check-up was conducted in a clumsy and obviously ineffective fashion. I tried to get out of it but didn't really know how to go about it. One of my classmates was rejected as too small. He was devastated and felt disgraced and dejected. I didn't hide my envy; to some extent, he understood me, but not really, though he was too bright not to see my point of view. I probably confused him; he was too much enthralled by years of unrelenting propaganda extolling faith in the Führer to see things realistically. This was, of course, true for so many of my generation who had no alternative source of information.

I learned that my Berlin classmates were pulled out of their evacuation quarters in Henkenhagen, Pomerania (now Poland) and had to return to Berlin to report for duty, and I was able to join them there. I liked the kids in Bunzlau a lot but had almost nothing in common with them. I really got sick of them in a general way when it turned out that one of them – actually he was about the tallest one in our class – was "deferred" because he was deemed indispensable as a HJ leader. Just as in the Soviet Union, you save and take care of the apparatchik – the commissars first – and sacrifice the others.

In retrospect, I was glad that I returned to join my Berlin class-mates. The cohesion that had developed in the Waldschule over the years was a very strong bond for weathering the new situation and ambience, so totally alien to us. In *Vom Krieg ein Leben lang geprägt*, "Marked for Life by War," a book about the experience of a number of former *Luftwaffenhelfer* and to which I will occasionally refer for reasons of comparison, the author seemed to suggest that there was a seamless transition from HJ experience to the military. For the Bunzlau bunch, that may have been true, but it was far from the truth as far as we from Berlin were concerned. What some of the contributors to the book may have unintentionally implied was that the HJ had subdued that generation sufficiently to accept the moroseness and monotony of military discipline as normal. That had not been case with us; we hadn't been subdued and didn't really know what to expect. The HJ, to varying degrees, had played very little part in our lives; most of the boys had very little connection to the Hitler Youth.

One may object here: how did I know that? From 1942 onward, a general confusion began to rise and I simply don't remember any of my classmates going into some form of HJ activity. But much more important is this. The KLV – children evacuation – was, by orders of the official world, to be run to a great extent by the Hitler Youth, who actually controlled many of these army preparatory-style camps (I learned this from others after the war). The Nazis created an infamous group of people called "camp troop leader" [40] who often took over, that is, even over the head of the school authorities.

In Henkenhagen, however, with Chef Krause in charge, the HJ had no say in anything. So, for those of us with this background, there was no seamless transition. I distinctly remember that I looked

---

40 *Lagermannschaftsführer*

at the military scenario as a kind of curiosity, akin to investigating a peculiar species of insect.

An even more important aspect was this: Ordinarily, when people were inducted into the military, none of the inductees knows anybody else. In the beginning, they're not really a group but a completely incoherent bunch of guys; they're isolated from each other and thus fairly easily dehumanized and rendered defenseless against the militarizing process. That process is based on making anonymity, lack of cohesion and an amorphous frame the basis for controlling them. Am I unduly generalizing? No, not at all. We / I was sufficiently long exposed to the workings of the militarizing efforts to extract their method directly from that experience.

We Waldschule students, on the other hand, faced them as a bloc; not a conscious conspiracy, but an unconscious ganging up on "them." In our past, I dare to say, it was hardly ever us against them (them being teachers, parents, grown-ups; well, occasionally, maybe a little bit, I don't want to paint us better than we were). Now, it was exactly that, us against them, and right from the beginning. There were a few outsiders among us who purported to love the military; apparently, it made them feel grown up. To the bulk of us, "they" were nothing but a pain in the neck. Without having taken Psychology 101 and often being just dumb kids, we subconsciously tried to remain human. We were arrogant middle and upper-middle class brats and let the non-com officers feel and know our contempt. That didn't endear us to them, but of course, these soldiers, almost all of them, quite lower class on one hand and also the officers, on the other hand, didn't really know what to make of us. It turned out that, after a while, at least some of them came to us rather than us kowtowing to them. That, of course, developed rather slowly.

In the first two months or so after the induction, we were to serve in Berlin on 20 mm antiaircraft guns, four barrels mounted together in a two by two array. The purpose of these guns is to defend a position against low flying attack aircraft. Whenever you see a movie in which, say, a battleship or aircraft carrier defends itself against attacking aircraft, that's the kind of guns that are used. In the multiplicity, they exhibit a very photogenic display. Well, the purpose of these guns at that location was obscure, because the Allied bombers attacking Berlin flew about five miles high, well outside the reach of these guns. Supposedly, low-flying aircraft attacks were expected to hit specific, industrial targets. But in our case, there was a large industrial complex of the Siemens company; obviously, there was no need for low level attacks and there were none. That complex could have been demolished in its entirety from high-level carpet bombing. Well, it wasn't then and amazingly, it never was.

The first few weeks as LwH brought to us several interesting novelties. One was, for example, the discovery that my bed was inhabited by creatures I had never seen before – bed bugs. My request that something be done about them was greeted by the 'higher-ups' as a kind of insolence on my part. That was, of course, part of the first exposure to the military realm. The idea outlined above, that there was a seemingly readily-accepted transition from HJ to the military, in the sense that one knew what was expected etc., is certainly not true. Another novelty was this: it certainly was a different experience to stand on top of a factory tower and next to a gun, that is, on an elevated vista point, seeing all around you a panorama unfold: a large scale bomb attack with its explosions and a lot of fire on the ground, a display of Allied might and the complete defenselessness on the German side. The Allies were never hit with anti-aircraft guns nor intercepted by German fighter planes. It was quite a different experience from sitting in a basement or even just sleeping, and of course far from anything I had experienced in Bunzlau (and the others in Henkenhagen), or earlier when we still were in school in Berlin.

Our living on the factory grounds also brought us into contact with the factory's forced foreign labor, who lived in some quarters nearby. Very frequently, some of us went to a particular area in the factory to procure some flavored carbonated water (Brause) and that brought us very close to these workers. Thus, some of us saw them daily. While, undoubtedly, they were clearly all cases of involuntary servitude, it was also quite clear to us that these people, men and women alike, were treated decently. They were well-fed and in fact, they suffered less regulation than we did. We had some minor, quite friendly contact with them. Technically, they were the enemy, a notion we found quite ridiculous. For them, it must have been amazing to see us children in uniform; what better way was there to show them that their victory must have been close at hand!

The German habit of excessively organizing everything proved fortunate in our case. Luftwaffenhelfer were supposed to continue with their schooling, so we were combined with those guys who had been in our class but were older (i.e. born in 1927, and had been drafted half a year earlier). They were someplace else in or around Berlin. We were all transferred to Wittenberge, a small town to the west of Berlin on the river Elbe, this group of about 40: our class (i.e. the boys in the 10th grade) and those of the 9th grade. In Wittenberge, we were "manning" three such four barrel – 2 cm guns, near a major railroad bridge across the river. Now, that made more sense – defending a bridge against low-level bomb attacks. Smart bombs hadn't been invented yet. The bridge was quite important; many freight trains crossed it.

Long after the war, when I was already in the US, I met a high-ranking Air Force officer who flew in the Pacific, and I told him that, obviously, I was only alive because the Pentagon men goofed. If they had consistently attacked and destroyed *all* of the few bridges across the Elbe River (I guess there were less than a dozen) and kept them down, the entire transportation system in Germany would have collapsed. This could have been done already in '43, shortening the war considerably.

Lucky for us, the Pentagon men were not that astute, so we

embarked upon a very peaceful existence; no attacks on the bridge ever came, from any altitude. Later in the summer, there was one attack on a factory in the town nearby, but that was a safe distance from us. Otherwise, we saw only high-altitude bombers in large numbers flying to Berlin, and sometime later, they came back. But occasionally, the routes were different coming and going. We had an airfield fairly close by, but I can readily say that never, absolutely never, did we see any German air attack by fighter planes on Allied bombers. The Allied air supremacy was paraded in front of our eyes several times a week. Previously, the air attacks were conducted only during the night, as we had seen in Berlin. But by 1944, the German air defense seemed to have no longer posed any significant threat to the Allies, so day raids were added. We saw the might of the Allied air force, but we were spared any harm from them. In fact, given the circumstances, and that the air war was steadily increasing, we had a rather pleasant summer.

We occupied a fairly spacious boat club, on a dike extending between the river proper and a harbor bay. The guns were on sites on the dike, next to the clubhouse, and there were additional quarters, not luxury facilities but not shabby either. Aside from uneventful air raid warnings during the day and often in the night, we had a peaceful existence. There was, of course, the scenario of military boredom but only to some extent, as there were activities to relieve us from that boredom. One benefit, of course, was the location of our quarters. As I said, they were simple, but the location had almost a bit of a resort quality: boats, swimming in the harbor, even loafing on the dike. On the other hand, and in a way more important, was our continued schooling. Teachers came to us, and we had regular classes; well, charitably, you could call it that, but we did actually learn a lot.

As to me, I put into play my "experience" in the signal corps Jungvolk; I bargained myself into a position at the telephone exchange. This exchange was located in the office of our "organization" and connected various phones in our quarters etc. together, to the office of the commanding officer, and to the public exchange system as well as to the airfield nearby. From them, we received position information on non-German planes (there weren't any German planes anyhow) flying around; that information was posted as markers on a pane of glass covering a map. On the basis of such posted and marked information, alarm was given if the planes came too close. Basically, this was a nice, cushy job and sure beat standing at those guns, particularly during the night or when it was raining. The occasional drawback was that some nights, I had to get up before the others to plot the airplanes coming. That was a minor drawback; for me the name of the game was to keep warm and dry, to do as little as possible, and not to become mentally deconstructed. If I had to get up earlier, I could sleep in a bit longer.

I have dwelled extensively on the importance of my high school in my life, particularly during my pre- and early teens and how indirectly it carried me over to the half-year-plus of boarding school in Bunzlau. Also, this carried me into my time in the LwH. As I have said, it was us against them. That, of course, can easily be written of as related to "the generation gap." But there's more to it than that, and that's why I'll dwell on this period a little longer. It covers the time towards the end of the war, and in a kind of blend of a war scenario and of continued school, combined with other personal experience. As I have said, I'll occasionally allude to observations made by the author-editor of the contributions made to the book, *Marked For Life by the War.* In that book, the author asserts that, by and large, the LwH's were proud to be able to contribute to the war effort and to the defense of the fatherland etc. etc. Nothing could be further from the truth, as far as our bunch was concerned. Being a LwH was nothing but a pain in the neck. Well, admittedly, there may have been a few among us who felt differently, even elated, but if so, they kept their mouths shut. They intuitively sensed the general mood; the bulk of us wanted nothing but to go home and back to our school.

We wore a kind of blue-gray uniform, the air-force colors, but the style was tailored after the HJ uniform. Apparently, it had been specially designed for us. For ordinary duties, we had regular army service attire, except that they didn't have children sizes. The HJ-style tailored uniform was in addition to be adorned by the HJ red-white swastika armband. We were supposed to be Hitler Youth boys, and not children flagrantly attired in army uniform. Intuitively, we felt that, if we were treated like soldiers, then that's what we were. So, we flatly refused to wear these armbands. Even the Nazis among us didn't like them; in fact, our refusal almost amounted to a kind of insurrection, and our superiors backed down; was this evidence of the tacit decay of Nazism?

We were entitled to two leaves per year of two weeks each, some weekend furloughs, and occasional afternoon outings into the city. Being close to the company office (i.e., the "powers that be"), when sitting next to the telephone and the all-important chart for plotting airplanes, I managed to get my first two-week leave quite early, after a month or so in Wittenberge. I just went to Bunzlau and enjoyed the peace and quiet. Of course, one of the first things I did was dump my uniform and wear civilian clothes, which we were allowed to do. Thus attired, I visited my former boarding school. Some of my former classmates were there, and some were, "of course," in uniform, with the HJ armband adorning them. They were astonished to see me in civilian clothes and not in uniform, and I was astonished to see them in uniform and not in civilian clothes. I told them that we refused to wear the HJ armband, and they just looked at me in total amazement. Well, obviously, nothing had really changed in terms of attitude, and I was certainly glad that I had joined my old schoolmates from Berlin. Even though Wittenberge was less restful than upper Silesia, where the Bunzlau guys were, it was very clear to me that they were more "in the military" than I was. Our Berlin group was bent on out-smarting "them," but my former classmates of Bunzlau simply didn't know what that meant.

I spent the weekend furloughs in Berlin, going to movies and just sitting in the garden; even air-raids could not spoil such simple pleasures.

The "Marked for Life" book about the LwHs refers to the experiences we were supposed to have learned as valuable life lessons. I dispute that vehemently. What we "learned" was conniving, evasion, trying to get away with doing as little as possible, effective lying, cheating, even stealing. In one form or another, we became what is today described as "street smart." Being the spoiled middle-class brats we were, one might consider this a life lesson! Well, I don't. It helped, of course, to survive these conditions mentally-spiritually, as well as physically, but that wasn't an enrichment for a normal life. For us, normal life was represented to us by the schooling we received, even under these strenuous circumstances.

As I said, three or four times a week, teachers came from Berlin. Some were our old teachers; others were "new." In general, that worked quite well. It brought a kind of normalcy to our lives; possibly it was a kind of illusion, but at least we were engaged in something that had nothing to do with war, the guns, the military. Of course, most of it was makeshift, but I believe that we learned something, and even if it that didn't amount to much in terms of substance, it was a steady reminder that there was something else in the world.

The same book "Marked for Life..." elicited from some former LwHs another interesting aspect, also not applicable to us. The author raised the question whether we (i.e. the LwHs generally) felt cheated by this experience. He actually posed the question in an unduly 'loaded' way, namely, did we feel cheated at a time well after the war, that is, in retrospect. He didn't ask the people whether they felt cheated in their lives right after the war. Why didn't he? I believe he assumed that, to pose the question how we remember having felt in this regard at that time, may have invited a near-100% negative response; and even 50 years later, only 60% of his respondents felt cheated. While I don't question the accuracy of this result, as far as statistical evaluation is concerned, I still find it astonishing. Most certainly, I felt cheated at that time, and I don't believe that most of my classmates/fellow victims felt differently. We wanted to go home, finish a normal upbringing, and go back to our school. Yes, we were cheated by the powers that be.

Let me talk a bit about the people who were supposed to or believed to run our lives. There was, of course, the "usual" assortment of uneducated, lower class, proletarian, non-com officers as our immediate superiors. Do I sound snobbish? Of course, I do, and that was intended. They were the "them" to which the "us against them" syndrome applied. We had fun in a way, outwitting them as much as we could, and here again, we stuck together right from the beginning. For example, occasionally we spoke English among ourselves, which they didn't understand. Since we were supposed to receive schooling, there was nothing they could do. We were supposed to clean our own quarters (how dare they!), and so we were assigned on a rotating basis to sweep the floor. One day, it was my duty, and in a sullen way, I attended to it. The floor was bare wood and I attacked it with a kind of whisk broom, something I'd never encountered before. As I was going about this business, one of the non-coms accosted me because I had "forgotten" to water down the floor, a suggestion I found perfectly ridiculous. He screamed at me, "How does your mother sweep the floor with a broom?" With all the arrogance of a 15-year-old, I countered him, "We have carpet at home, and the maid cleans it with a vacuum cleaner." He didn't like that response very much, I should have learned not to flagrantly play the class issue "card," but I was too young for that. To me, it was a notable victory I could wallow in.

On the other hand, for most of the time in Wittenberge, we were quite lucky with officers and higher ranked sergeants. For reasons of organization, we constituted a kind of company, even though we weren't much more than a large platoon. But we had the organizational structure of a larger unit. In any event, there was a kind of master sergeant, a very nice, elderly man (remember, we were on the average 15 years old, so everybody over 35 was old). He was very congenial, even convivial, always helpful and never bothered us. Since we were a company in structure, we had a captain as company commander. Here again, we were quite lucky, because Captain Anton was a Lutheran minister. He clearly understood the difficulties of the situation and the problems we were in. In retrospect, I believe he fully understood that we were nothing but a bunch of children, and that he was nothing but a glorified babysitter. He also understood that, on the surface, we wanted to be men, but he had enough wisdom to realize that what we really wanted was to stay kids. In retrospect, he was to us a kind of analog to Chef Krause at our Waldschule; namely, he, too, shielded us from the "unpleasantness" of the ambience. Of course, he was different from Chef Krause, and I've given Captain Anton credit as far as our life was concerned. He had nothing of the pomposity of Chef Krause, and in that regard, I hold him in higher esteem than Chef Krause. In a somewhat more muted fashion, Anton shielded us from the Nazi environment, even more than Krause did. This is very important, because much more than Krause, Anton stood really between us and the barbarism of the Nazi-dominated, military milieu.

In between the company commander Anton and the non-com bunch was another guy, some of the time a master sergeant or less; at other times, it was a lieutenant, the only one I remember. The lieutenant was just a few years older than we were. He really wanted to be our friend and he never did any of the chicanery the military is famous for. Often, he came into our quarters just to sit and talk with us. He was a high school graduate and I think he felt closer to us than to the Captain or the non-coms. I don't remember exactly what we talked about. It wasn't politics or anything dangerous, and it really does not matter. At that time, people were just grateful for even brief periods of time when they could be human.

In the LwHs book, the author examined the relationships between LwHs and their superiors through surveys. He found that, quite often, the LwHs were lucky to have understanding superiors; thus, our experience was not a rarity. As a subordinate issue, the author of that book tried to find out whether former LwHs believed that these superiors were role models in later life (e.g. in professional or job situations). Interestingly, his findings are rather ambivalent; my conclusions are not. It was a good experience to learn how to find out who was decent and who was not, what kind of person can be trusted and who cannot. We all grew up in a sheltered environment, and now we learned how to find who was scum. Previously, I derided my experience as LwH as one to make you unnecessarily "street smart". This, then, is an exception. It was indeed helpful in later life to be able to separate the chaff from the grain, as far as people were concerned.

I have a confession to share about Reverend-Captain Anton. Even though I appreciated, to some extent, his moderating role at that time, a few years later (i.e. shortly after the war) I came across him in some matter and I treated him with contempt and cold indifference. My anger towards all those connected with the Nazi power structure in one form or another was at that time still unabated and uncompromising (I was 20 or 21 years of age). In retrospect, I feel quite ashamed of my reaction and attitude. No doubt, he was a good man, the best we could have asked for under the circumstances; I want to use this occasion to apologize for my behavior.

-17-

GUNS – NOTHING BUT TOYS?

In between school, some alarms, some duties, and training at the guns, we really had, relatively speaking, a good time being stationed along the green river embankment, with views towards the other side of the river. In the opposite direction, we saw the harbor front with its usual, messy picturesque-ness. Occasionally, we had the afternoon off, went to movies or a café, a bit of a make-believe world of peace; we were, after all, still children. Let me share some different aspects and very different scenarios, one childishly funny, one horrible. First the relaxed one.

As I mentioned, I was staffing at times the telephone exchange, including the connection to an airfield where we got information about incoming planes. Whoever staffed the phone had, in effect, exclusive control about the alarm conditions in our station. The officers, as well as the non-coms, never bothered to listen in or check the correctness of what we plotted. They mistook my and others attempts to hold on to this cushy job as responsible enthusiasm.

Well, on several occasions, when I had night duty and when planes were approaching, I just ignored them and let the guys sleep, hoping that these planes weren't destined to come to us. I reasoned that attacks on the bridge were only expected during the daytime. I hadn't heard of infrared bomb sightings, and I guess that didn't exist then. I was never caught. But that's not all. I remember that, one day, we had been caught by the noncom officers in what they considered an infraction of military discipline and they imposed regulatory exercises as a penalty. Well, not to worry, I faked an incoming bomber stream, plotted numerous planes on the chart, and rang the alarm. My superiors never checked the validity of this fake. So everybody attended to his duty on the guns; the penalty exercise, of course, had to be called off. When the time came for the exercise to be over, guess what? The "enemy bombers" flew away. The penalty exercise we never rescheduled. Did they realize that maybe, upon rescheduling, the "enemy bombers" might return? All this may sound silly, but it was a part of a scheme of fighting back, and it worked. We remained human; they didn't get us.

Occasionally I had to be at the guns when somebody else staffed the phone. But let me say that, particularly during the night, and most particularly when it was raining, we convinced "them" that the phones "really" required two, three, or even more of us, in order to make sure there was adequate service. Let me tell you, the scheming of teenagers is nothing new! The teenagers of the world will always survive. In this case, it was all about mental survival.

Now a serious remark. At some point during 1944, my attitude changed. I had always been prone to posing radical ideas. But in this case, my classmates didn't follow me, at least not initially – later, of course, they did. But now, I shifted from the certainty in the belief that Germany *would* lose the war, to the notion that Germany *should* lose the war – a rather drastic shift toward wishing that your own fatherland should lose the war. The reasons underlying my change in attitude are difficult to delineate, but I think that the following aspects may be illuminating.

The four-barrel guns we were to "man" were a single unit to be operated by a person (one of us kids), who sat in an operator seat. His function was to look through a sight and operate the guns by pressing the foot-pedals. In order to get out of his seat, he had to wiggle himself out in a somewhat inconvenient fashion. To his left and to his right were seated other kids who had put into the barrels cartridges of ammunition, twenty apiece. These cartridges were put into place, but there was supposed to be a safety latch on. However, in order to disengage the cartridge, you had to release the safety latch. The tips of the barrels were normally covered by a leather sleeve. The sleeve was removed when the guns were made ready for operation, and they were replaced whenever the time had come for terminating any alarm. There was a strict rule never to stand in front of the barrels. You were to put the cover onto the barrel tip from the side, but never, as was more convenient, from the front.

One day, we had an alarm. I remember it was a balmy, summer day, where nothing was to be taken seriously. I wasn't at the phones but stood right next to one of the guns, next to one of the guys who was handling the cartridges.

At that time, he was fooling around getting the cartridges out of their positions. He was just to my left, and on my right was Jürgen Potz, taking the barrel covers and putting them onto the tip of these barrels, standing in front of them. The guy in the operator's seat got out of his seat—the easy way—but slipped and stepped on the foot pedal. Since the cartridge was still in the barrel, but the safety latch was released (Why hurry?), the operator actually released / triggered a number of shots, that is, 20 mm bullets. I saw Jürgen Potz, right next to me, collapse. He didn't even cry out, so at first, nobody thought that there was anything wrong. However, I very vividly remember how he collapsed, with his chest cavity breaking open and a rush of blood pouring out. It won't surprise anybody that, to this day, I remember even the minutest detail of the event. Jürgen Potz was killed. Well, how come?

Of course, we weren't privy to everything that ensued subsequently surrounding this event. It is, however, not too difficult to reconstruct what happened afterwards. The higher-ups (that is, well beyond our local unit, but including them) were horrified by this event. Through our parents and the school, it spread like wildfire that a kid was killed through some form of carelessness. This wasn't enemy fire which you can always brush aside with some heroic nonsense. Here was something beyond heroism; right from the beginning, it was dealt with as an infraction. Things haven't changed; when something drastic happens, you need a scapegoat, somebody to pin the fault on. So let me be very precise here. The idea of placing the real criminals on trial, that is, those responsible for placing children on guns, didn't occur to those in power, because that would have meant putting Hitler and the High Command on trial. The idea of placing the glorious Führer and his henchmen on trial was, at that time, still inconceivable, but obviously that should have been done as the fault lay with them.

I well remember that a bunch of pompous and important looking officials (*Kriegs-gerichtsräte*) presided over the proceedings. They may have believed that they served the administration of the law, but I doubt they had any idea of what justice really meant. I am trying to reconstruct what really happened then. To hold Captain Anton responsible would have been difficult. He was in his office at the time, so no immediate command could be attributed to him that could have led to this disaster. Also, to hold a member of the clergy responsible may have intrigued some of the Nazis, but this was the military and they were not yet completely subverted. I really believe that at least some of the military didn't want to be a part of that kind of scheme. So, in a class-oriented society, the goal was to pin the guilt-responsibility-fault on the noncom officers.

I remember very vividly how scared these sergeants were. Intuitively, they must have sensed that they were to be the scapegoats. And here, I must give us students credit for decency. We didn't like them at all, but in a naïve, honest and decent way, we didn't want them to be the sacrificial lambs for something they didn't do. They were, from our point of view, stupid soldiers, but they didn't sign up nor were they drafted to be babysitters. I want to dwell on this a bit, because it was quite obvious that we, the children, knew very well what made these guns work; we had learned physics and knew the basics involved. They, the non-coms, had no idea at all; these chaps had been told something about these guns, and they most likely, quite dutifully, conveyed their "knowledge" upon us. This event very clearly demonstrated the thin line of what was involved. We knew what had happened; they didn't.

In any event, and even though we hated them, we didn't sacrifice them. It would have been very easy for us to crucify them. Because of my position at the time of the incident, I was called to testify in court, as were others. We truthfully testified that these noncoms, and possibly others, had time and again instructed us never to step in front of the gun barrels. Of course, why didn't the non-com in charge of our gun yell at Jürgen to get away from in front of the barrels? The military "Justices" were clearly looking for scapegoats, and we could have presented them. We could have denied having been taught anything ever concerning the safety aspect involved. We could have denied that we were ever told not to stand in front of these guns. Maybe we should have put, on record, the irresponsibility of putting children onto guns in some form. Perhaps the justices would have done something, but I really don't know. Intuitively, I believe that we were right not to throw the non-coms into the gutter. These justices wanted to have their scapegoats but, in all honesty, we didn't and couldn't give them their culprits.

The fact that the operator didn't get out of his seat, as he was supposed to, wasn't discussed. Well, it wasn't really clear, nor was the fact that one guy left the cartridge in an unsecured position just a little bit too long. After all, how long is too long? The final verdict was that Jürgen Potz was killed by his own fault. He shouldn't have stepped in front of the guns. Considering the scope of the people involved directly, I believe that the verdict was correct. None of our noncoms, nor any of the local power structure, could possibly be held accountable. The real criminals weren't tried at that time, namely, the people who put children on guns. It was about that time I became convinced that Germany not only would, but should, lose this war.

-18-

GREAT EVENTS AND SOME IDEAS ABOUT PHONINESS

I will now turn to three rather important events, though I don't remember whether the Jürgen Potz affair occurred earlier. As to the *first* event, I remember very clearly when, on the radio, it was announced that the Allied forces had landed in Normandy. There was great fanfare about the German troops driving the Allied forces into the sea. However, after several days, such a thing wasn't announced as having occurred. I distinctly remember, however, a general feeling (not had since Stalingrad) that this was really the (second) beginning of the end. After a month or so of consolidation, the Allied forces advanced deep into France, and the German radio admitted it.

The *second* event of interest, in the summer of 1944, was the announcement of the deployment of the German V-weapons, which were hailed as miracle weapons. To call them that represents a very interesting cultural-social phenomenon. Nazism was built, as I was beginning tacitly to understand, on some kind of supernatural belief in the powers of the Führer. He openly claimed that he had been ordained by Providence. His power was, therefore, rooted in the mystical realm. This helped explain the early victories, the kind of which eluded normal, professional soldiers. So, sensing that the people must have "felt" a downturn in the political-military events, they seemed to need a reinforcement in the belief that "he" had supernatural powers. For some years, allusion to Hitler as the prov-identially-ordained savior served well to cover any probing questions about reality. But now, in summer 1944, the Russians had liberated (well, whatever that means) their country and were advancing toward Poland. The Allied forces were well to the north of Rome. Nothing was said about the Balkans, and the Western Allies were not only firmly entrenched in their Normandy landing sites, but they had begun to pour into France. Obviously, this was a hopeless situation for Germany and only a miracle could reverse the situation. And so the pouring of miracle weapons onto England was announced with great fanfare.

I want to dwell on this a bit because it confused me greatly. It seemed to negate my calculations and deductions about the destruction of German armament. Of course, we weren't told what these miracle weapons were. That was a great secret, in a way under-standable, but the secrecy served to conveniently cover up the gross ineffectiveness of these weapons. We didn't know that one kind (the V-1) were nothing but pilot-less, rocket engine-driven, very slow-fly-ing airplanes, with a miniscule amount of explosives on board. This "weapon" couldn't be aimed at anything, and at some point in time, these flying bombs just fell, made a little boom, and that was it[41].

The other kind, the V-2, was the forerunner of all modern rockets. Rather small, they had a fairly large range but a very small payload, no aiming facility, and just made a little louder boom. They

---

41 The British pilots engaged in the sport of kicking the planes around to fly back, or at least that is what I learned later, as well as admissions by people in England that the V-1 weapons were psychologically disturbing. People heard them coming and then the rocket engine would stop and everybody knew that it was now falling with no idea where it would hit, as it took quite a while before it hit ground.

seemed to have no influence on the outcome of the war. After some time, and still not knowing about their ineffectiveness, we heard little more about them. Most importantly and noticeably, they had no attenuating effect on the air war generally and the bombing of Germany in particular, nor did it slow the Allied advance through France. At that time, the Russians seemed to have stopped for a while in Eastern Poland, perhaps inviting a kind of lull, which was of course deceptive. Whenever German doom seemed to have incurred a delay, you relax; a stupid response, isn't it? But that's the way it is.

And now I turn to the third event of major importance, the foiled assassination attempt on Hitler on July 20, 1944[42]. Since I was staffing the phone, I remember that it began with a barrage of confused telephone calls between peripheral military outfits and units such as ours, and "higher ups." There was, of course, the danger of the revolutionaries giving orders that may have affected the stability of the Third Reich. Indeed, the military took over Paris and issued a barrage of orders, but the people supposedly running the revolution in Berlin were a bunch of incompetent bunglers. Admittedly, this goes beyond my own observations although with a properly prepared revolution, we should have been subjected to significantly more extensive revolutionary activity, i.e. confusion, activity, conflicting orders etc. In addition, almost every account of the 20 July uprising, implicitly at least, demonstrates an underlying incompetence. In retrospect, it clearly demonstrated that Germans were incapable of staging a revolution.

Lenin once said that if Germans wanted to storm a railway station, they would first line up to buy tickets. The orderly military wanted to take over from the existing order in an orderly fashion. Obviously, that is not how things work in history. If they had not

---

42 [A cadre of German high officials had crafted a plot to assassinate Hitler, then take over the government. Colonel Claus von Stauffenberg was able to plant the explosive-filled suitcase but the explosion did only a fraction of the intended damage and only injured Hitler. The rest of the plot fell apart – KS]

bungled things so badly, if at least for a day or two they had held onto some kind of preliminary government announcing the take-over and promising democratic elections, my reaction would have been very positive I am sure, but that mess caused a great deal of confusion. Why? I will dwell on that a bit longer.

To what extent this was typical, I cannot say, but I plead for some element of understanding concerning my ambivalence. Nazism as such, and the domineering effect it had on us, fueled the opposition many of my classmates and I felt, an opposition I found increasingly growing with each visit and furlough home, with each separation from the military environment. So, why did I find the assassination attempt on Hitler unnerving rather than elating?

I know now that I, as well as many, many others, had become a victim of something I call a bifurcated focus. One of the forces underlying the focus was the very clever, possibly not even consciously conceived, elevation of Hitler by himself to a stature of semi/pseudo/near divinity. That dictators focus on their person is nothing new, but focusing on a role as a prophet, not just in the abstract, but with definite allusion to reality, is very different. You may not believe abstract concoctions, but reality stares you in the face. Reality was the rapid conquest of France in 1940, of the Balkans, the occupation of Norway and Denmark – literally in a few days. And then the unbelievable advances into Russia, for years and years, that was proclaimed as being the result of providence having chosen Adolf Hitler as the savior of Germany etc. etc. These were aspects of public reality. That, in turn, had nothing to do with the opposition I felt against the regime, the militarism, the pomposity of Nazism, the dishonesty all around me. What I'm saying is this: in spite of all the personal, emotional adversity I felt towards all of the Nazism and in spite of the intellectual opposition I'd mustered, I believe that I, too, was under some kind of spell of that individual. How come?

We need to consider people like Lindbergh, brought up in a solid, democratic tradition, or Mussolini, who was a dictator in his own right and who detested Hitler before he met him, but fell under his spell as soon as he met him. Take Chamberlain, a very able and conscientious man, who announced "peace for our time" after he met Hitler. And there may have been the memory (persisting even today) of the seemingly stoic, majestic figure standing in the front of his automobile, riding along the major boulevard. So, may I be excused for being confused about the failed attempt which is really an inconsistent attitude? Among us, there were only very few who were not. Most of us clearly took a "don't care" attitude. There were no services held to kowtow to the miraculous saving of the Führer. Maybe it was some kind of manifestation of a generational conflict. Maybe we took basically an *en bloc* position vis-à-vis this event in the grown-ups' world: who cares?

In later years, this peculiar attitude towards Hitler in a kind of shielding fashion found its corollary in the belief by many that the Nazi atrocities were committed by his underlings. That, undoubtedly, was true; he personally didn't kill anybody. He may not even have ordered the killing of anybody, with the possible exception of personally ordering the killing of his archrival Rhöm in 1934. However, as the years went by, the belief grew that he had nothing to do with the atrocities committed by the regime. This belief was reinforced by the lack of written documentation linking him to any specific murders. Hitler, undoubtedly, was a master in availing himself of the "Becket method"; the famous incident when King Henry II of England didn't have to give any order to assassinate Thomas a Becket. All he had to do was to moan that he would like to be rid of this meddlesome priest. His underlings understood and acted. I believe that the situation was very similar in Germany; Hitler did not have to give explicit orders to eliminate the Polish intelligentsia, Jews, Gypsies, mentally ill people, etc. etc. A hint to his underlings may have sufficed, and that set into motion many terrible sequences of events, of actions clearly perpetrated by these underlings.

So there may have been a seemingly clear-cut dichotomy between Hitler, as an ever-elevated leader who could do no wrong, and the ever-increasing scope of henchmen doing his tacitly-invited bidding. After the war these underlings, in various capacities, referred time and again to Hitler's orders – except there were none. If there ever was a culmination of evil, he represented it. He didn't give orders; he let his underlings know what he wanted. He made them, without any doubt, subservient to his bidding; without issuing formal orders, he indirectly let them know that they were as rotten as he was, they just needed his superiority to implement what they, too, wanted to be done. They had him to lead them. He was their leader of divine providence.

Admittedly, the foregoing is a kind of psychological speculation. It isn't a political theory, just a result of what I believe the effect Hitler had on others was all about. And somewhere there was me, feeling then and in retrospect that I was confused about him. I don't know how I would have reacted if I ever had been confronted with him; would I have been able to evade his influence, would I have been able to resist his spell towards doing wrong? I'm honest enough to say that I don't know, and I defy anybody who thinks he could. But I do know that in 1944, I intuitively sensed the evil of this man but didn't understand it sufficiently or explicitly. All this is a mouthful just to cover my ambivalent feelings concerning Hitler's escaping the attempt on his life. I hope I've been able to separate this aspect of the peculiar aura that enveloped Hitler from the disgust at how it was so terribly bungled.

Present history elevated this attempt on Hitler's life, on July 20, 1944, to a major effort of German resistance. etc. etc. I disagree. The German resistance is largely a myth, with very little root in reality. On the other hand, there was moderately widespread resistance among the military against Hitler, not just before he started to lose the war, but for his attempts to start it[43]. This isn't the occasion to narrate historically about this. I just want to convey these points. I was confused on the matter, and the fact that the coup was bungled became obvious day after day after day. There simply is no excuse that this revolt didn't succeed, and I might be excused that I too was confused but also disheartened in a diffuse way. Why wasn't there a way out?

After these three major events the summer continued, and little happened in Wittenberge that concerned me directly. At some point, I got my second, two-week furlough, and my mother and I went to the mountains in Silesia, to Spindelmühle, enjoying a thoroughly peaceful environment. We'd been there a few years earlier and enjoyed the return visit. I remember a very peculiar atmosphere in the inn where we stayed, a general aura of impending doom, but not in foreboding way, rather, in a matter of fact way, recognizing its inevitability but as if it was nothing to be concerned about. For me, it was a very intense study of what people expected was coming.

Back in Wittenberge, the older boys of our class were, one by one, drafted. Some of them were probably inducted into the slave labor service first. Let me be more specific. I've talked about three major events in the summer of 1944. But there was actually this *fourth* one, that the 17-year-old boys from among us were called up to be stoked into the war furnace of oblivion, to serve silently as cannon fodder. I'm relieved to tell you that only one from our group died as a result of this insanity. As they left, they were replaced, *en bloc*, by a bunch of interesting boys. I never really found out what their ethnic background was. Were they Germans or were they Poles? Actually, the very fact that this could be a factor is interesting in its own right. They were quite young, a bit younger than we were, which made it somewhat difficult to pinpoint them. Were they Germans when that was the thing to be, but Poles when that was more advantageous?

---

43 The Halder coup, foiled by Chamberlain's cave-in

They spoke German as if it were a foreign language to them, while, among themselves, they spoke Polish. It was interesting, and we didn't fully appreciate it. They demonstrated that multiple culture exposures can conveniently serve as a tool for survival. Genetically, you can be anything in a border region; culturally, you're whatever is required or convenient. Opportunistic? Of course, that was how border people and minorities managed. Cultural pluralism serves adequately as a font or fund from which to select whatever you need to survive.

They didn't have any school (we didn't envy them for that! School was, for us, the last vestige of normalcy). These guys were very friendly, and we got along well. They were – in our eyes – on the same social level as our non-coms, with whom they had no problems even though they were anything but disciplined, in the military sense. Some were amenable to homosexual advances by at least one of the non-com officers; he hadn't dared to approach any of us, since all that occurred after the Potz affair which established our peaceful co-existence with the non-coms.

Another facet to the mosaic of our scenario was the so-called Hiwis: Russian prisoners of war who had either volunteered or been selected otherwise to help. What they were supposed to do, I don't remember; in fact I do not even know whether I ever knew. I do know that we were not to fraternize with them; as we were teenagers, of course, this had the opposite effect and we sought out contact with them. Among them were several who were well-educated and spoke some, even a passable amount of, German. This was our first exposure to, and even a kind of indoctrination of, Communism and about life in Russia. Likewise, these Russians were now exposed to bourgeois Germany and may have had second thoughts about the supposed rottenness of the Western world. But they were far from home and held onto whatever pleasant memories they could, even though their lives had been (presumably) very miserable. I'll never forget how often one very friendly Russian, who apparently travelled fairly frequently, mentioned to us that in the railway stations you could get tea with sugar. To him, this was like somebody reminiscing about a $200 bottle of Champagne. As to communism, I remember them talking about workers owning everything, but for us middle class brats, this didn't mean anything.

-19-

NOW THE END IS OBVIOUS

This chapter concerns the last phases of the war, but before the beginning of the actual end. This is somewhat difficult to delineate; when did that last phase actually start? Clearly, in general terms, the beginning of the end was the battle of Stalingrad in 1942 and '43. I've chosen here, quite consistently, my own experience. To me, the end phase began around the same time we were moved out of Wittenberge and back to the outskirts of Berlin. Whether we left the poor bridge defenseless, I don't recall; but the new position resembled an all-around, Berlin defense position. We'd been in Wittenberge for about three-quarters of a year, and in a ridiculous way, it had become a kind of home. No doubt, our then-superior, Captain- Reverend Anton's decency had a lot to do with this. As I said, after the Potz incident, the non-coms became quite human.

The unit command changed at some time, but not for the better. In the first part of the winter of '44 to '45, we were stationed near an airfield, defending it against who knows what. Things began to deteriorate. First of all, I lost my cushy telephone job, since where we were stationed, there was already an existing "infrastructure"; I tried to get in but didn't succeed. Whoever held a cushy job held onto it for dear life. The food got poorer, our quarters were fairly cold, but our spirits were not broken. That sounds a bit pompous and, of course, had nothing to do with any will to resist the enemies of the Third Reich. It had to do with our will to resist our military power structure. For example, we were supposed to guard our guns throughout the night, each shift for an hour or so, then waking up the next shift to trot out into the cold. Well, we beat the system. The guys coming in at 10 didn't wake the next shift, but some of us had to wake up at about five in the morning to then wake up the next shift. Believe it or not, the system worked consistently. So, to some extent we still had the upper hand.

The airfield we were supposed to defend was an interesting site. There were some odd-looking airplanes: they didn't have any propellers but peculiar looking tubes – these were some of the first jet planes. One day I saw one of them running – that is, expelling who knows what with an infernal noise – but these planes never flew: there was no fuel. What these planes could do was, of course, unknown to us. What was known and seen was that they were useless. We heard about their phenomenal speed, and that they could easily attack bombers without danger of being shot down. Another miracle weapon. But this one was clearly of no use, in the absence of sufficient gasoline.

Our lives became increasingly miserable and cold. Dealing with creature comforts became increasingly important, including procurement of food. Acki, my early childhood neighbor from whom I had sort of separated, but restored friendship with in the LwH service, planned a break-in into a food storage facility. I learned that artificial honey (some kind of sugary mess) was easily spread on paper and, when pressed against a window, it quietly broke it and caught the splinters. But I guess we chickened out. I must add that moral consideration didn't enter into it. We were beyond that; we were beginning to be hungry on a regular basis. With the end of the war looming ahead, survival became the dominant theme. Of course, we would never have stolen from other people, but government property was fair game. I think that if you live in a country that's about to lose a war, morality becomes somewhat relative.

At some point, a roller went over my right index finger and popped it open, which wasn't much fun; but things were looked at differently: Because of my wound, I was excused from the regular tedium. I still have the scar.

We didn't hear much regarding the goings-on in the outside world and how the war was going. I don't think we had access to radio. In fact, what we experienced during the winter of '44 to '45 was, in a way, rather difficult to understand. We all entered an era of seeming oblivion and ignorance. Many years later, much has been written about what happened in the last months of the war. No doubt, many accounts were accurate or may have been remembered differently. For me and many others, it was a time of information isolation: We just didn't know, on a day-by-day basis, what was going on, aside from rumors.

Our furloughs and long vacations were cancelled except that, for a while, we could go home to Berlin for a weekend since we were stationed within local commuter train distance away. Going home became a kind of recuperative exercise, during which I would "fill up" emotionally, and then, of course, there was Christmas. I was home either Christmas or New Year, I don't remember, but we all knew that this would be the last Christmas of the war. Just spending time at home was wonderful. But I also had some time to intellectually engage in what was happening. Not just local radio, but the BBC and Beromünster. During these home visits, it became increasingly clear that the "miracle weapons" were a bunch of phony bologna items. From the average advance of the Allies in France, one could project that the war would end by early spring '45. Before Christmas, the Russians had reached the eastern German border; the Western

Allies' temporary setback in the so-called Battle of the Bulge had no influence on us at all. No one was debating about whether the war was lost, it simply wasn't an issue any longer, it was only a matter when in terms of months.

During the winter of 1945, two changes occurred in my life. My mother went back to Bunzlau to help my grandmother and aunts flee from the Russian forces. Why they fled, I didn't really understand. Why not wait for the end of the war at home? But, at that time, that was the thing to do, possibly fueled by the subconscious belief or hope that even though the war was lost, maybe there would be an armistice like 1918, without full occupation, and if you were in the unoccupied territory at the time of the armistice, you may be better off.

In retrospect, that was naïve, but at the time, not yet completely idiotic, considering the lack of information people had about the Allies' goal. Our access to Allied radio had stopped. Up to that time, the mail was still functioning (i.e. they accepted, transported, and delivered it). So, I learned that my mother reached Bunzlau (trains were still running). From there, in February, she took her mother and aunts on one of the last trains to leave Bunzlau. One evening, some Nazi official declared that there was no danger for Bunzlau; the town was occupied by the Russians by the next morning.

The refugee train ran rather slowly; it was very cold outside, and several windows were broken. My grandmother caught pneumonia and died a few days later. My mother got an ear infection and ended up in a hospital in a small town in Saxony. But one of the aunts, who had been ailing all her life, survived the ordeal quite healthily and died only many years later. Then, by the end of March, I lost contact with my mother. Later, people asked me whether I worried about her, but given the circumstances, I didn't. Knowing my mother, I assumed she would somehow manage to stay in that hospital as long as possible; that was, relatively speaking, by far the safest place, and that is exactly what she did.

The other change that occurred in early 1945 was that our unit was relocated to the north of Berlin. Little did we know that units like ours were supposed to be sacrificed as cannon fodder. There were no planes to shoot down, there were no longer any specific targets expected to be attacked by low-level aircraft. But these 2-cm quadruple barrel guns were actually high caliber, rapid-fire machine guns of a rather devastating nature. I conjecture that the plan was to hold us in the rear of the Oder River, and when the Russians reached the East bank of the river, to deploy units like ours on the West bank to stop the Russians' advance. How do I know this? We were actually told something to the effect that, in time, we would be moved to the Oder River. Well, if that had happened, you wouldn't be reading this. Still, I want to dwell a bit on this period between the final Russian assault and our being relocated to some inconsequential holding position.

Here in the countryside, we were fully exposed to the dissolution of organized society through the ever-growing avalanche of refugees. In later years, these streams of refugees became a staple item in movies and documentaries about WWII. This was the first time I saw refugees as a reality. They were like large herds of cattle, an endless flow of people on wagons, others walking. Something that had happened in the last five years elsewhere, throughout Europe, was now our turn. There were also American and British prisoners of war, in good health, well-fed and well-treated. We actually met some of them and found them interesting to talk to; obviously, they felt pity that the Nazis were hiding behind children. By the end of March, the Russians had stopped at the Oder and consolidated their forces for the final assault. We knew that; how we learned about it, I don't remember. That was the time, however, when our planned sacrifice was to begin. Fortunately, things turned out differently.

-20-

BERLIN APRIL 1945 – NO RESISTANCE

In the beginning of April, a few of us from our and some other units, were ordered to travel to Berlin and to report to barracks in Potsdam on the southeast outskirts of Berlin. Was I included as a kind of punishment for my big mouth? The other boy from our unit, Heinz Witte, had fairly strong Communist leanings. In any event, the two of us and several others from other units were put onto a train to Berlin, and thus we entered the last phase of the drama called World War II. Later, I learned that our unit wasn't put on the Oder since responsible higher-ups had only one goal: to get their units out of Russians' reach. So, the unit with my schoolmates was "evacuated" west, ending up for a very brief period as POWs of the British who had no intention of playing babysitter and promptly discharged them and many other kids.

The Nazis had infiltrated the military on a wide scale – just like the Nazis, the military didn't trust anybody. So, I was on the same travel papers with a boy I hadn't met before. He was an officer candidate and was also to report to these barracks. Because of his position as a candidate, he was most likely deemed politically reliable; I soon found out that he still believed in the Führer and some miracle myth. Likely, I was on his papers so he could keep an eye on me. It would have been simpler to put me and Heinz Witte, the other guy from my outfit, on the same travel papers, but Witte had a separate "guardian;" together, we would have been on our own, as will be seen shortly. Was all that a mere coincidence? Perhaps, but I don't think so.

As we arrived in Berlin after a rather rocky ride, I persuaded my companion to join me and come to my home to recuperate. There was fortunately no date on our travel orders for us to report, and so a few days' delay was well within the realm of what was permitted, at least to my way of thinking. After all, trains were no longer running on any schedule. Fortunately, he agreed. Of course, my mother wasn't home; she was in a Saxony hospital. But, there was the latest of our roomers, Mr. Kaufmann, whom I didn't like, but that didn't matter. Also in our house was an elderly couple, Oma and Opa Krause. We weren't related; everybody just affectionately called them that. We had known them for quite some time; they were Lotte Ide's parents, who'd fled from somewhere in the east. I have mentioned Lotte Ide already – she and her husband were the ones who had hidden a Jewish girl in their apartment. And so with Oma and Opa Krause at home we found a very hospitable atmosphere. Spring of 1945 was lovely; the lilacs were already blooming in our garden, and so were the bright yellow forsythias. We enjoyed the peace, there were hardly any air-raids, and for a brief period I lulled myself into another belief of unreality.

What were the realities?

Berlin, April 1945. How do you convey the experience of a city awaiting doom? How do you explain that here was a city which was about to be over-run, conquered, and in danger of being completely destroyed, but wasn't, at least not completely. Fifty-plus years later, it's easy to conjecture that, indeed, the inevitable doom didn't happen. However, at that time, nobody knew what might actually happen.

The worst of the air attacks were over. Downtown Berlin had, for all practical purposes, ceased to exist. Many other parts of the city were destroyed, but the telephone system, electricity, and water supply were functioning perfectly, and even gas was available although not all of the time. The extensive train system was running. I didn't know then that the authorities were forcing work crews, at gunpoint, to keep the trains running, even during air raids.

In my neighborhood, right at the bridge of the Heerstraße overpass across the railway (remember, that was the way into the city where Mussolini had arrived and been triumphantly escorted by Hitler into the new seat of power, Berlin, just a few years prior), a barrier was built to prevent Russian tanks from entering the city. I wasn't too enthusiastic about this, but my companion, to whom I was tied by bureaucratic paraphernalia, was highly impressed by all that: "we" would ultimately defeat the Russians. At least I got him to come home with me, to my house and our garden, and I encouraged him to enjoy the flowers and we slept in real beds. We visited people including the folks of the fellow Witte, whom I had hoped would be on my train ticket. I don't remember what had happened to his "watchdog." I still remember the general feeling of desperation that emanated from everywhere, combined with the hope that it would soon be over. Unfortunately, my companion was oblivious to this development and insisted that we report to the barracks in Potsdam. Remember: I was just 17 years old; what I experienced was, as we say today, the result of raw data. There was no ameliorating or mediating frame of reference. Whatever you experience sticks, and even at that age, you're already well aware of peoples' feelings and emotions, their fears of the present (don't open your mouth too much) and of the future. The very absence of the "gold-pheasants," the mustard colored medal-bedecked functionaries of the Nazi era, was noticeable. These people, to the extent they had some decency left, were about to commit suicide, like our local Nazi-party chief. Many more, however, had already fled the city awaiting its doom, or were hiding somewhere. The Nazi party bunch wasn't exactly characterized by a high degree of intelligence, but they had the survival instinct of rats.

It's difficult afterwards to criticize one's own actions. However, in the middle of April, after having loafed around for several days at home, my travel document companion insisted that we report to the Potsdam barracks. I tried to delay this, hoping that the Russians would stop dilly-dallying on the Oder and launch their final assault – in which case, I would have stayed home, offering my companion either a place to stay or to go fly a kite. Lack of information is always a problem, and while there was no change in frontline patterns, my companion became increasingly restless and so I was cowardly stupid enough to accompany him to Potsdam. On arrival, I became immediately aware of my stupidity, because they had no record of my travel companion and me. I think a part of the military facilities had been damaged by bombs, so they didn't know why we were reporting. Obviously, we should have stayed home.

This is a good example for the following analysis: If you are brought up in world run on order, it's difficult to understand why, when, where, and how such order ceases to exist. Order, as such, has nothing to do with Nazism, with injustice, or even cruelty. It has to do with the reason Germans will stand at a street corner, waiting for a red light to turn, with rain pouring down on them and no car coming; still, they don't budge until the light turns green[44]. It has to do with the belief that order is represented by bureaucracy and neatness of record-keeping, and that, sooner or later, that order will catch up with you; after all, the trains were still running, electricity was available!

---

44 This being still generally true, I'm glad to report, however, that by the end of the millennium, Germans are beginning to comprehend that their order won't collapse if you cross the street at a red light with no car in sight. Sooner or later, in all big cities, people become as blasé as New Yorkers; although I was told that jaywalking has declined in New York.

I did not defect, didn't stay home, didn't run away from the Potsdam barracks when they didn't know what we were doing there, because of the ingrained belief in the power of order that inevitably catches up with anybody who attempts to defy it. This is, by and large, true in many societies; I simply didn't fully comprehend at which point order becomes dysfunctional and that we were surrounded by a mere charade. But to a great extent, order persisted. When the Russians stormed Berlin, people were still talking, so to speak, across front lines. "Hey, the Russians are here already"—"not yet here"—"well, wait – they will be there soon enough." The city trains were running, while fighting around them was going on. Of course, that was simply the inertia of a once-functioning system, which had begun to break down much earlier. But people just kept it going.

In any event, I found myself in the Potsdam barracks, together with a bunch of other guys, some even in civilian clothes, others like myself in Luftwaffenhelfer uniform. My travel companion, apparently, had reported to some officer training or whatever. I never saw him again. They had no uniforms for any of us, no weapons, nothing. When you read accounts from the last days of Berlin as the Capital of the Third Reich, you'll probably never discover that such appurtenances were actually irrelevant. No preparations were made for an organized defense of the city, just an amassing of cannon fodder for the Nazi era's upper crust, to cover them as they tried to get out, or to just delay the inevitable doom at any price. Berlin should or could have surrendered in the middle of April, but that would have been an admission of defeat. My own experience is, of course, limited to Berlin, but to the honor of many German officers, it's become clear to me since then that many of them had only one goal in mind: to get as many of their men away from the Russian clutches and to deliver them to the British / American forces. This prospect doesn't apply to Berlin itself, because once the Russians had pushed across the Oder, the city was encircled in a few days.

A situation developed which I haven't found adequately reported in so-called historical accounts, reports, writings, etc. To explain: In the late nineties, a movie about the steamer Titanic captured the imagination of many. The movie attempts, valiantly, to recapture what went on in the last tremors of Titanic's sinking. In the beginning of the movie, a hypothetical survivor of the catastrophe is shown a computerized simulation of a sequence of events leading to the tragedy. The survivor counters by politely acknowledging the efforts that went into the simulation, but then states: "The reality of it was somewhat different." I somehow feel the same way when reading post-whatever accounts of the last days of the Third Reich, then recollecting what really happened in the last days of April 1945.

Following my arrival in the Potsdam barracks, you'd assume that there was some sort of training. But I didn't get any training at all; they didn't even give me a rifle, not that I was eager for one. Chaos was spreading; there was no intention of training anybody in any manner whatever. I think that, at one point, I was shown how to shoot with a machine gun; a minute or two of instruction was supposed to turn me into a machine gunner. Interestingly enough, though, I did learn, and so reported, that the gun seemed to be defective. Fortunately, I didn't get close to any more of these contraptions for the rest of the war. After a few days of such "training," we learned that Berlin was indeed encircled; we were then "moved out." What happened next, I can only describe in blotches and sketches. What unfolded before me was very clear. There was no organized attempt made to provide something worthy of the label "resistance." There was no organized resistance against the Russian advance.

We, whoever that was, were told to go that-a-way, and so we went that-a-way; "that-a-way" was always away from any shooting, from where the Russians were supposed to be. In other words, we moved gradually, and in a meandering way, toward downtown.

We were hardly armed. At some point, somebody gave me a kind of bazooka, which I promptly deposited in a corner. You followed basically a herding instinct; you stuck with others and very quickly, you knew intuitively who was trustworthy (i.e. who had only one goal: survival). But most importantly, nobody ever took up any position, ordered us to man a defense line, or any such thing.

Near the River Spree or one of the shipping canals, there was a storage space for steel plates and some of us just stayed and built ourselves some shelter, feeling relatively safe, until somebody said that the Russians were approaching the other side of the waterway and we moved out. Next, we stopped at a food storehouse, which seemed to be a good place to be. We stayed there, loading up with bread, a bologna kind of sausage, butter, cheese, and booze. We were, of course, under nobody's command, although occasionally somebody appeared and gave a command, usually to move out. We were a kind of marauding soldateska, except that we didn't harm anybody. I remember walking, on several nights, through streets lined with burning houses, nobody doing anything about it. There just was nobody around; nobody looting or plundering either, just nothing, just a burning city without any commotion. In the background, there was, of course, constant artillery fire, which you get used to.

How do you describe a dying city, rubble, artillery fire, no people, dust, dirt, smoke, but sunshine during the day; not even a remnant of order, no enforcement of anything, just nothing? Of course, there were no bomb attacks, just occasionally, groups of soldiers like us. When I say "us," that wasn't a fixed group, but a kind of fluid or "dynamic" situation; people joining and others leaving. I remember that we came close to a spot where one fellow announced that this was where he had been living. In a short time, he was gone. I sure hope he made it. I should add here that, unfortunately, we didn't come close enough to my home for me to make the necessary bee-line.

So, always walking in the direction opposite from where the Russians were supposed to be, we approached downtown. Occasion-ally, there was some noise indicative of fighting (you assumed that there were some German soldiers doing some shooting), and that was of course sufficient cover for us to be able to get away quickly. At times we must have slept, I simply don't recall. At some point, we reached the Brandenburg Gate and the Pariser Plaza. While seeking shelter, we ended up in the ruins of a building but somebody came and advised us that this was neutral territory, the Swiss embassy or what was left of it, and that was not much. Of course, this was utterly ridiculous, though, technically possibly true; and we, being Germans accustomed to order, duly left.

We must have entered the underground system at one point; this can be understood literally, as well as figuratively. Literally, because of the general darkness (some emergency lights were on, who knows what powered them); figuratively, because my uniformed status became, let me say, obscured. Walking around, some others and I ended up near Anhalter Bahnhof, one of the many Berlin railway stations where we were above ground for a short while. It must have been April 28 or 29 or thereabouts. I still had some food left, I believe a large loaf of bread. I try to remember what I drank; booze comes to mind, but that wasn't sufficient. The underground railway, or any other railway, had ceased to run. Earlier, I mentioned that I'd been wondering where the people were. Now I knew: they filled the underground stations and part of the tunnel system. This proved to be very advantageous; we didn't realize this immediately, but in fact we became gradually isolated from any military order and hid in relative safety in the crowd, in the dark. Not completely, though, because occasionally SS units would pass through the tunnel; we had to completely avoid them. They spelled trouble.

The subway was really a marvel of engineering; we and thousands upon thousands of people were in these safe places. Otherwise, though, you might describe this as the epitome of being in the wrong place: we were about a quarter mile or so away from Hitler's bunker. Later, I read that the Russian army had about 2,000 pieces of artillery trained on that area. Now, I find this an interesting note on "history."

I'm not denying that there was a lot of "boom-boom," but not from 2,000 pieces of artillery! Either it's outright wrong (i.e. that number is an assertion to over-emphasize the Soviet army's might), or else, it reflects the dilapidated state of Soviet industry in that many, even most, of the projectiles were duds. If that's so, then the center of Berlin would still be studded with duds. However, in the building boom that has been in progress since German re-unification, hardly any have been found. Possibly, they've all rusted away. While most certainly, the state of the Russian industry has always been characterized by poor quality, they produced a large number of tanks, artillery, and primitive but effective machine guns; so, maybe there weren't that many guns and not that many duds.

In any event, it was quite noisy. I've described to my California friends an artillery bombardment as a kind of continuing earthquake of the magnitude between 4 and 5, possibly occasionally 6 on the Richter scale. Earthquakes of course last only seconds, long ones, a minute or so; this barrage went on for days, with only occasional lulls in between periods of incessant, waxing and waning bombardments. Believe it or not, you get used the constant rumble and shaking; because you get used to the experience, that no matter how long the rumble and even how loud, the tunnels held. Also, after more than five years of war – four years of bombings – people did get used to a lot; if not, they went crazy. There was chaos all around, but people can get used to that, too.

And now, I faced the third, underground problem / situation – namely: how to escape capture by the Russians as a prisoner of war. I must admit that somehow, but really incomprehensibly, I wasn't consciously aware of that danger. Clearly, one can interpret this to be an unbelievably stupid aspect of ignorance and naiveté. But, in my own defense, I have to say that, up to that point, I worked actively on my survival. Having failed (and I realized that keenly) to stay home when there was opportunity before the Russians came, I continued to concentrate on my safety, of course, together with others. That led all of us, and of course me, gradually to the retreat position in the center of Berlin, right under the guns trained on Hitler. I wasn't stupid enough to face the danger above ground, but believed (justifiably so) in the solidity of German subway engineering. Now, most importantly, we had literally reached the end of the line! I must confess, however, that I wasn't really – consciously, intellectually – aware of that until an older guy, with whom I had roamed the underground for the last few days, said that we should get ourselves some civilian clothes.

I'll never forget the impact this had on me. We were in the underground station right at the Brandenburg Gate called Unter den Linden. Adolf Hitler was somewhere fairly close by and the Russians were closing in. That's when I realized there was nowhere else to retreat to. We were surrounded by thousands of frightened people. They, of course, wouldn't harm us although I won't forget a lady who openly displayed her unrelenting faith in the Führer. No one voiced agreement, so we felt safe – away from that lady. My companion and I stuck together and didn't "fraternize" with others, nor they with us, at least not the other, questionable civilians. Nobody wanted to incriminate others, nor to be incriminated by them. And the "real" civilians were undoubtedly afraid to associate with us. And there were still SS units occasionally coming through the tunnel, though not often.

Earlier, when we were roaming the streets during the day, I don't remember seeing the SS at all. They were supposed to protect the Nazis; the SS role was well known at that time although not all of its infamous details. So, in order to convert into civilians, we had to find, in modern parlance, a "window" between the departure of any SS unit from the station and into the tunnel, and the arrival of the Russians. Finding civilian clothes was no problem. We didn't have to steal any, as there was so much abandoned stuff around. So the problem was when to doff the uniform and put the civilian clothes on. We found, in time, the appropriate window; in the early morning hours of May 2nd there was a lull, and my companion and I became civilians. For me, there were some kind of pants – not too well-fitting – and a sweater. As I later found out, it was full of lice. I wondered, being by upbringing a neat German, if I would have rejected that sweater had I known of its lice content, thus possibly endangering myself and becoming a prisoner of war. Of course, there was so much stuff around, but possibly, that too was all full of lice; ah well, I wasn't confronted with that "problem." We did become civilians, and now mixed with the others.

Shortly after our conversion to civilian status, someone came down the stairs of the subway station – the Russians hadn't arrived yet – and announced that Adolf Hitler was dead. That was certainly believable and was greeted with something close to indifference, but he also announced that Hitler had gotten married. Now, that was totally unbelievable, so maybe, people believed none of it to be true.

Shortly thereafter, the first Russian appeared.

I'll never forget the appearance. He didn't brandish a gun, he didn't threaten anybody, but he had over his shoulder a big sack in which he collected and gathered watches, and he called "uri." He seemed very jovial, and in hindsight, this represented to me an interesting blend of looting and capitalism, and the survival of the latter in Soviet Russia. He, in effect, preceded the armed forces to loot from the vanquished, before the vanquished were really vanquished. How did he know that he wouldn't be greeted by SS snipers? After all, not too long before, the SS had been coming through. He didn't seem to be scared one bit. Somehow, he knew exactly when to make his appearance, just as we had timed to become civilians. Of course, at that time, this was taken as a hopeful sign for the future. We just didn't know what to expect. Actually, we had expected a bunch of soldiers, brandishing and possibly using Tommy guns. I didn't have a watch to contribute to his fortune, but many did. Soon, some official-looking Russian soldier or officer entered and suggested (no, he did not force us!) to get out and go home – whatever that may have meant to many of us. This was, as it turned out, a very important phase in the turn of events.

Just about that time, early morning May 2nd, the SS exploded some bombs or whatever charges they had placed on the bottom of the river Spree, right where the river actually crossed above the subway. Obviously, the subway was deeper than the river bed, and all the subway tunnels rapidly filled with water until, within a few hours, the entire subway system of Berlin was drowned. This subway system, and particularly the stations, was occupied by many thousands of people. The calamity occurred a few hours after the war in Berlin had actually ended, so many people – myself included – were already out. Actually, I learned about this flooding many days later. Nobody can even begin to guess how many people may have drowned. It is possible that those still in the stations may have seen the water coming; I doubt that it was a vast wall of flowing water, because there was a single source – where the Spree crossed over the subway. The subway system had many branches into which the water was distributed. Still, I believe that many thousands died.

-21-

MAY 2ND – GETTING HOME
(WITH A DETOUR)

Before the water reached the subway station, my companion and I and some others emerged from our tunnel existence with no clue what to expect. And what a sight it was. The station opened up onto the Pariser Plaza, near the Swiss embassy. The Brandenburg Gate was still standing, a monumental sight, but to some extent, typical, frugal Prussian and not too imaginative architecture. There was a red flag flying from the top, but it wasn't the famous (staged) picture of the red flag over the Reichstag, the partially burned out Parliament. The Brandenburg Gate was, of course, damaged but hadn't collapsed (that is where I got my first inkling on the inefficiency of Russian artillery). There was some smoke, but no fire (there was little left to burn); and the noise of the artillery barrage of past days had given way to a cacophony of oriental proportions.

Cars, trucks, tanks, armored vehicles, horse-driven wagons, motorcycles, soldiers marching, walking, standing in groups talking, almost like a sightseeing scene (and to some of them, it probably was), right in the middle of the former seat of power from which the devastation of a great part of their country had originated. Having been used to the crispness and uniformity in the German military, including the Nordic look, I was immediately fascinated by the variety of uniform and attire that passed as uniform, but even more fascinating was the ethnic and racial variety. Slavic faces, of course, dominated, but then there was the enormous variety of oriental – Mongol, Central Asian, etc. etc. – people. In the middle of it, several very resolute-looking female soldiers directed traffic in the typical chaotic fashion such a scene almost inevitably invites. But no matter what chaos there was – it was very obvious – they had won, Berlin was conquered and it was all over.

I remember being fascinated to the point of forgetting that, with impunity, any of them could have taken a gun and shot at us, for target practice or no reason at all. But reality soon overtook us. My companion and I, and possibly a few others, blended as much as we could into the background – meaning the rubble alongside buildings and what was left of them – and gradually we walked away from downtown. We would have to part anyway, because my companion was heading for the northern part of the city and I for the west. However, very soon, we were captured by some patrol. There were other civilians like us of dubious status, but there were also obviously genuine ones, as one could see from their clothing.

We were all herded towards the downtown airport which served as the principle gathering / collecting point for German soldiers from the Berlin war theater. This didn't look very promising, but I'd declared myself a civilian. I was still a kid and carried no paraphernalia that proved otherwise. My companion and others were in the same boat, and that helped to keep up morale. That may have meant nothing to the Russians but what did I care. After a while, we were marched out of Tempelhof airfield, but we civilians were kept together – a promising sign. It was a slow process; the streets were lined with people in various stages of shock.

So, we marched and marched along city streets in an easterly direction. As evening came, we civilians were separated from the rest, again a hopeful sign (how selfish one becomes in such circumstances), and we were led to a camp with foreign workers – I think they were Dutch, waiting to be transported home. They had obviously not been badly treated by the German authorities; they didn't look famished. In fact, I remember that they looked quite well-fed; and to their everlasting honor, they didn't feel or act vengeful towards us German civilians. After all, it would have been an opportunity for them to let these damn Germans have it. Well, they didn't. In fact, they even gave us something to eat, and we even slept a little.

In the morning of May 3rd about 20 or so of us were led out and walked back again – that is, toward the west, while the rest continued towards the east. Another hopeful sign. We were led to a Rathaus – town-hall – that had become a Russian "Kommandantura." It was the local town hall of Köpenik, a southeastern district of Berlin. The district and the town hall had become famous for the incident of the so-called Captain of Köpenik. He was a shoemaker who, as the story goes, got ahold of the Prussian Captain's uniform, and then, duly attired and solely on the strength of the uniform, he had recruited some soldiers and impounded whatever cash was in the town hall. He gave the money back; he just wanted to demonstrate how easy it was, in imperial Prussia, to make people obey orders just on the "strength" of the uniform. The German playwright, K. Zuckmeyer, wrote a wonderful play about this 1906 incident which was made into a movie a few years later. At that point, I didn't know that, but it's curious that, in a way, there was a kind of repetition. Most of us "civilians" were civilians just on the strength of our attire! Would that fool the Russians, as it had the Prussians half a century earlier?

We were left outside to wait. I believe whoever was in charge in the Rathaus couldn't care less. Maybe he enjoyed the appurtenances of a neat German office. Well, whatever his motivations were, we 20 or so were soon told to go home. So, we all split and my companion and I separated. I think he gave me his name and address, and I gave him mine, but I lost it and never heard from him again. I hope he made it though his route home may have led him, again, dangerously close to downtown; my route was west and way to the south of downtown. As I soon observed, that part of the city had been conquered a little while before. And so on May 3rd, I started to walk home from the southeastern part of the city.

It was almost spooky, because that part of the city hadn't seen much damage–hardly any bomb damage and not much artillery damage, either. It had been occupied by the Russians quite rapidly, with little fighting; otherwise, there would have been more visible damage. Apparently, the Russians hadn't used their artillery to aid the advance of their troops – a pattern I found repeated elsewhere, which suggests an interesting side issue.

The West uses artillery and aircraft bombing to demolish enemy defense lines so that ground soldiers will encounter little resistance and keep your own losses low. The Russians couldn't care less, and dictators generally have other priorities. Soldiers are expendable commodities; artillery is a demonstration of power. The ridiculous artillery bombardment of downtown Berlin served no military purpose whatever; Hitler was deep down somewhere and couldn't have cared less about people being hurt up on the surface.

As I began my long walk home – 40 kilometers or thereabouts – two episodes stand out. In one of the districts on the outskirts, actually not far from Köpenik, I got thirsty, and believe it or not, there was a pub with customers drinking beer, an almost unbelievably peaceful scenario. That district, however, had in the past been heavily Communist; the talk of the people in the pub I overheard sounded like a subdued victory party. I must have had money to pay for my beer. For them, apparently, the war was over. At that point, though, it hadn't sunk in for me. Later in the day, I got thirsty again, no pub there, and the area I walked through was quite different. Lots of damage, but not complete demolition; many people still lived there but no peaceful milling around.

Here I want to interject something I'll refer to again, but I encountered it for the first time on my walk home.

Let me pose a general question: what do you do for water in a war-ravaged area? How do people survive the lack of an organized water supply? Well, often you can rely on rainwater and snow in the winter. But the spring of 1945 was warm and very dry; day after day, not a cloud in the sky. As it happened, Berlin, as the capital of Germany and earlier of Prussia, had a system of manually operated water pumps for watering horses. These pumps were all over the city, because there had been many horses, and the water table was not deep at all. Those pumps saved the city, not just from death for lack of water, but because the water was good and fresh, and not contaminated. You can die from thirst but also from typhoid. In that regard, the Emperor's horse pumps saved Berlin.

So, I came across such a pump, but there was a long line of bedraggled-looking people, mostly women; they all looked dirty and wore ugly, unkempt rags. I soon learned that many women in Berlin made themselves as unattractive as possible to keep the Russian soldiers away. How often it worked, I don't know, but it must have been successful for some, or these women wouldn't have been on the street. They sure did a good job of it; there were long lines of filthy, ugly, and bedraggled-looking women. Also at the pumps were a few, male volunteers working with them, I volunteered, too, and this way got served earlier. A hard way to get a drink of water, but it worked.

As I walked on, I became increasingly exhausted and wondered whether I would make it home that day, so decided to walk towards the house of friends of the family. It wasn't much of a detour, as I walked toward the home of the Ide family. I mentioned that Mrs. Ide's parents (Oma and Opa Krause) stayed in our house. So, as I started to walk in that direction, actually quite close, I passed what would become a historic site, the town hall – Rathaus – of Schöne-berg. In a few years' time, it would become the City Hall of West Berlin. President Kennedy delivered his famous "Ich bin ein Berliner" speech from that building's front steps.

I was lucky enough to find the Ide's house fairly quickly. Of course, life at that time was never that easy. I remembered where they'd been living, but upon getting there, I found that the Russians had burned the house down. Later, I learned that there had been gun-fire from one of the windows; at that time, that was reason enough to let the structure go up in flames. But Lotte and Walter Ide had found shelter nearby and that's where I found them. Now, I want to dwell on this a bit, because from the point of emotions – despair, hope, exuberance – my discovering them was the first event like this, that would repeat itself in coming weeks and months, fortunately quite often, and which controlled many peoples' emotion to a great extent.

The war was over, you'd survived, and now you find friends who, too, had made it. But not necessarily just friends; other people who had been a part of your life, or, in some cases, even those you just knew and with whom you had lost contact for quite some time, or even people you didn't like who surfaced, and to find them alive is one of my most precious memories of the entire period. Never mind the rubble and the non-functioning technical civilization. How I found Lotte and Walter Ide, I don't recall. Lotte told me afterwards that they'd been busy getting corpses out from under rubble, and that I'd actually helped. Well, I don't recall; they just took me to their current shelter / place of abode and put me to bed. It was May 3rd in the afternoon, and I slept for about 30-plus hours; the entirety of May 4th is unaccounted for.

On May 5th, one of the Ides accompanied me home to check on Lotte Ide's parents and their daughter, Christel, whom they had brought to our house earlier. As one can see, who stayed where, when, and for how long was very flexible. All this may sound crazy and confusing, but it wasn't. It was an attempt, on a day by day basis, sometimes on an hour by hour basis, to cope with confusion – and it worked, to some extent at least. In any event, in the afternoon of May 5th, I was home again, really and for good.

-22-

HOME AT LAST AND THE VERY EARLY DAYS OF PEACE

In the context of the closing sentence of the preceding chapter, I will now attempt to describe situations that when seen in from a removed perspective are clearly utter chaos, but in their contemporary setting can appear to be desirable normalcy. That chaos / normalcy I returned to was like this. Our house had survived, without any more scratches. There hadn't been any more bomb damage, and artillery fire hadn't reached it, for reasons I'll come to shortly. The lilacs were now in full bloom, and so were the forsythia. The grass had begun to green. The trees along the street were all green, and everything looked neat and tidy. Of course, the pine tree forest nearby was as unscathed as ever. Elsewhere, there was hardly any new damage. Things hadn't changed since I had been there two-and-a-half weeks before, which was historically an eternity. And those kind and gentle people, Oma and Opa Krause, were there, and so was Christel. Again there was that happiness about people having made it. Our roomer, Mr. Kaufmann, had also returned. And so all was well, or so it seemed.

I learned that a week or so previously, Russian troops had

arrived and occupied our area, and there had been some looting of its houses. The fast advance of the Russian troops had precluded extensive shelling of our area, but then they stopped advancing. Why? I described, in several chapters, my local environment but under different circumstances. There was this relatively deep, valley-like ditch for the railroad and commuter trains. It was that part of the railway on which, eight years before, Mussolini had arrived. And then there was the overpass of the Heerstraße leading straight into downtown, where Hitler would accompany his visitors into Berlin. Other times, he paraded himself on this boulevard, from downtown to the Olympic stadium.

All that glory was forgotten in 1945. At this time, the railroad ditch was quite a difficult gorge to cross, apparently even for tanks – you really had to cross that ditch via the Heerstraße bridge – and a tank barrier obstacle had been erected. I'd seen it early in April; it was a formidable obstacle.

Many tank barriers and so-called obstacles had been erected throughout the city, though, I didn't see many on my travels through the city. In any event, the Russians had a joke: How long does it take to overcome these tank barriers? Answer: 2 hours and 3 minutes. The two hours were spent laughing and three minutes to get through. Well, this joke didn't apply to the barrier across the Heerstraße Bridge; the Russians never broke through. Later, they just went around it some other way. Afterwards, a whole bunch of 14 – and 15-year-old Hitler youths – I was told well over a hundred–were found dead all around it: they had defended the barrier.

While all that happened on the strategic level, our area was at the Russians' disposal; they had their rape orgy. Luckily in our house, there was a kind of wall closet occupying the space above the stairs from the lower to the next floor. That wall closet could be accessed from one of the upstairs rooms. Opa Krause and, I think, the roomer who had been there already, had devised a system in which they placed a tall cupboard onto a rug. When the Russians approached the house, Christel would climb into the closet and then the cupboard would be slid in front of the wall closet door. How often they did this, I don't know, but Christel remained untouched. Where Oma Krause was, I don't know either. However, the situation was different for our neighbors, a couple in their fiftieth year. I mentioned them before; he was blind from a WWI injury. The Russians gang-raped his wife, forcing the blind man at gunpoint to hold her down while they raped her. By the time I came home she was still in shock.

In our garden, a man from an organization named after its founder and operator, Todt or just OT, was buried. Why was that man was buried there?

The Todt Organization was a successful operation of a different kind of conscript, slave labor; it built the so-called Atlantic Wall, a series of bunkers and gun embankments along the coast of Normandy. A few are still left; they were indeed formidable and one can still see them. These people built airfields, high-rise bunkers, and all kinds of, let's say, peripheral war installations. Nearby, there had been a camp for several hundred OT men, as they were commonly called. What were they supposed to do at the end of the war? That particular man had befriended Opa Krause, and apparently, he (Krause) helped him defect from the Organization. Unfortunately, he timed it wrong, and Russian soldiers spotted him in his uniform. He ran into our house, the Russians behind him, and they gunned him down on our staircase. I don't remember whether Christel was hidden in the hanging closet, right above these stairs, but I'm sure she was. He got buried in our garden, but later, a commission recovering war dead couldn't find his identity. Opa Krause kept his name and address in a little book he carried with him but one day, the he was arrested by the Russians and has never been heard from since; the identity of the OT man vanished with him and his address book.

The OT camp became important to our survival. When, why, and how it was abandoned, I don't know but it was, and there was lots of stuff left, particularly food. Our entire area descended upon that camp and carried away whatever could be carried. Even after I came home, there was still some stuff left in the camp. In any event, we had at home lots of flour, potatoes, dried vegetable, some butter. It carried us through the first weeks of the occupation. And as to water, I mentioned earlier the horse-watering, hand-operated pumps all over the city. One of these pumps was right in the middle of our housing development, and there were no lines; you just had to carry the pail about a thousand feet. The pump has now been put out of commission (which I think was very stupid. Who knows what people may need in the future?). The pump body is preserved as a kind of local landmark, which is a good idea.

But I have to tell my story more on a day by day basis.

I don't remember the exact sequence of the next three events, following my arrival home, but that doesn't really matter because they are not related in time to each other.

I returned home on May 5th and of utmost urgency was getting rid of my colony of lice. I should have kept the clothing with which I had safely gained my freedom as a kind of souvenir but getting rid of the lice was more urgent than collecting memorabilia. How do you get rid of lice without DDT or whatever? I dragged lots of pails of water from the pump home, filled the bathtub, threw away all the clothes I had worn out of the subway, and drowned whoever was dwelling on me. Luckily, some of my boyhood clothes were still left in my closet that even still fit me; they were, of course, free from pests.

The next important event was that the Russians decided that they wanted our houses for a bit, because they were opposite the larger ones where the Opel executive lived, also my good friend among the nobility (he wasn't home yet), and the Radio Berlin Symphony orchestra leader. Russian officers wanted to live in the larger homes, and their underlings across the street, in the smaller houses where I lived. And so Oma and Opa Krause, their granddaughter Christel, our roomer, and I had to move out; we took rooms in the house in the back of our garden. That was a big house occupied by one man only, Mr. Torno; his family was somewhere in the countryside. He had prevented his house from even being "visited" by Russians by constantly wiping the floor near the entrance with Lysol, and he did this *over* and *over* again. It stank to high heaven, but he did this only near the entrance so that whenever Russians came close, they smelled this and muttered "hospital" – hospital was associated with sickness, and so they left. That worked up to a point, but after we and several people moved in and slept on the floor, the smell dissipated, and the newly-influxed Russians began to look for girls. Mr. Torno didn't have the wall closet to hide Christel or anybody else in, so she and one of the Krauses left to go to Schöneberg, where I had found Lotte Ide a few days before. An elderly couple who were also staying at the Torno's house were incensed; the Russians had threatened to kill everybody in the house if Christel wasn't there in the evening, so this couple insisted that Christel should stay and be raped. Well, she didn't, of course; at night, Russians came and, at gun-point, forced me and others to look for the girl. Whatever happened, I don't know; at one point, they simply left and didn't shoot anybody. It still stank like Lysol, to some extent.

I've often wondered on what basis people made decisions at that time. How do you cope rationally with a totally irrational scenario? The answer is really quite simple: you deal with whatever practical problem you're confronted with. That sounds simplistic, but what I mean is: you don't try to change the course of history, you try to stay alive, you try to deal with your own problems at hand, but you don't (or at least, shouldn't) forget that your own problem might not be limited to that; it may involve others. Again, is that too simplistic? Perhaps, but it's merely a reminder that the situation we found ourselves in involves no sophistication of any kind; that was all stripped away and what's left is what you might call "basic, human behavior." And so Christel remained indeed untouched, but later her grandfather, Opa Krause was captured on the way back to Schöneberg, for no reason at all; just abducted by a Russian military patrol and put in a concentration camp where he died shortly thereafter. I have very fond memories of this wonderfully kind and gentle man who never harbored any idea of ever harming anybody, and he ended up as a victim of punishment many possibly did deserve, but not he.

The third noteworthy event occurred around V-E day and thereafter. I don't recall whether we'd already returned to our house; it doesn't matter. History records that, on May 7th, Germany surrendered; what exactly did that mean? In reality, one should not be deceived by the pomposity of such a nonsensical label. On that day, May 7th, a bunch of totally powerless German generals affixed their signature to a document attesting to the surrender of the German Army, in the name of something that had ceased to exist as an organized, sovereign, political entity – a state that no longer existed. I'm not arguing legalistic niceties, but a factual situation. The German people's right to self-determination had ceased to exist. In Reims, the German Admiral Friedeburg signed a document and on the next day, Fieldmarshal Keitel signed that or another document in Karlshorst, a Berlin suburb – events which may be of interest to abstract, legal theory scholars. As a reality, they were meaningless and understood as such, but I suppose, strictly speaking this may not be entirely correct; the documentation may have been needed to instigate the surrender of German troops.

Nobody I know of cared about this; it didn't matter, it had no effect on people's lives, then or later. Whatever was done, whatever happened, whatever came into existence simply defies placing into a legalistic frame. In my mind, the written surrender wasn't, in fact, a legal action; Germany simply ceased to exist, not by any oral or written declaration, but from a complete conquest and the dissolution of any existing political and governmental entities. It ceased to exist because, legally or morally, nobody, absolutely nobody, could have mustered any kind of legitimization, political or historical, to speak on behalf of the German people. Even stronger, Adolf Hitler had destroyed the moral claim of Germans to be a political entity. The question was, could Germany be restored as a political entity? At that time, it was far from certain, but more importantly, did people really care? Over fifty years later, we can be glad and happy that soon there was a restoration, that there were people who picked up the remnants and formed a new entity, and with patience, that entity reached some kind of completion, when in 1989, the infamous Berlin Wall came down. I see all that, not as a political continuation, but as a new creation that began some time after 1945.

I've entered the foregoing discourse as a kind of reality check against claims by historians. I tried to tie a connection between personal experience and history, and as to the latter, I believe that, not just for me, but for many people there was a lacuna, a void, that can never be bridged except through legalistic fiddle-faddle. While the demise of Germany as an entity was of global, monumental importance, for us, the surviving people, it was very different. We existed in a frame of complete amorphousness. On the day following V-E Day, the Russian troops were allowed to discharge any and all ammunition in their possession. Whether or not they had the express permission to shoot at anyone or anything, I don't know and, to be sure, had no desire to find out empirically. Rather, it was a good idea not to be seen in a window or walk out in the street. It was a rather noisy affair. To us it was more real and more cogent and relevant than the signatures in Rheims and Karlshorst; it negated the very existence of Germany as an entity.

Well, I'm sure that many people remember V-E Day differently. Jubilant parades around Piccadilly Circus, along Broadway, and even in Red Square were the order of the day, rightfully deserved by all those who participated in bringing down one of the most evil persons in the world; and in the course of it all, Germany was destroyed as a continuing, historical entity. It had to be completely re-created. But forgive me for asking this question: What had I done to deserve this? I was an innocent bystander, or was I? Isn't this a rather meaningless term?

After I moved back into our rather messed-up home, I tried to make some order. The Russians had built an outhouse outside in the garden, right where the OT man was buried. They'd looted the house but had found no interest in my youth clothes which barely fit me but had to do. The china, linens, and books had been of no interest to them; but, of my mother's clothes, some, but not much was left. There was some stuff that didn't belong to us, and so, the practice developed sporadically to put such items in front of the house. We, in turn, went along the street to see whether somebody else had put out stuff that might belong to us; indeed, I managed to recover some chairs and a rug, and took them home.

Believe it or not, something like a normal life gradually returned. To even put it in such terms is ridiculous; but consider: "Normal" simply meant that you had a roof over your head and repaired it as best as you could. I mentioned earlier that we'd stored the double windows, with panes still intact; when we removed the cardboard from the broken windows, lo and behold, there was light. There were no more air-raids, and the Russians were gone. Some food was in the basement, to which I added stuff looted from the OT camp. The sun was shining, the lilacs were still in bloom, the grass was now really green; what more could you want after five-and-a-half years of war? Basically, you stayed put. Occasionally, some acquaintance would arrive, and happy reunion scenes took place all over again.

One place we made sure to keep away from was the tank barrier I mentioned earlier because they were recruiting "innocent" passers-by to work on dismantling it. A day or so after that was completed, I was walking in the vicinity, when suddenly, a car

stopped next to me with some Russian officers motioning for me
to join them, which I did. I don't have to mention that I was very
scared, particularly as we drove toward the forest and then into it.
I was convinced they would shoot me. But they seemed to be very
friendly, and soon, they showed me a map of the area, quite updated
except that, at some location, there was written-in a square as a
marked site; it was clear that we were driving to that site. It also
became clear to me – much to my relief – that they wanted to know
if I knew what that was or could be. Fortunately, I did: it was the
site where the German army had planned to build the German
counterpart to Westpoint / Sandhurst / Saint Cyr. And I was able
to explain to them "university – soldat – officier," which I think they
understood. We walked around what was, in fact, an abandoned
building site, and I wasn't shot. They drove me back, and even offered
to drive me home; but I gestured that I would like to be dropped
where they had picked me up.

Another, and rather large, event was the announcement that
a bakery had opened somewhere. It was now the middle of May,
two weeks after the capitulation. We got fresh bread. Of course,
you had to stand in line for hours, but you had nothing else to do.
In terms of activity, standing in line for bread, and later for other
food, and getting water from the horse pumps was all there was to
do. Well, not quite. You were supposed to do clean-up work, but
after several years of learning how to get away with doing nothing,
it wasn't too difficult for me to take it easy. As I've said, spring 1945
was very beautiful. The lilacs were still blooming, so was the plum
tree in our garden, and there were lots of spring flowers. And so I
sat in the garden, doing nothing, not fearing any bombs. What more
could you want?

Of course the foregoing is, in a way, crazy, because it's very dis-
concerting to be surrounded by a totally non-functioning civilization.
No electricity; no running water; no telephone; no transportation;
no newspapers; no radio, but lots of rumors; no mail service; with the

exception of the one bread store, no other food source. You learned that you can make do with very little and still be content. The lack of transportation invited lots of walking to look for friends, or to visit with them just to see how they managed. Quite a number of times, I went to see the Ides. At some point, we even went to the movies and saw some Russian war movie; it was quite awful, but after all, it was a movie! I went there with Christel and a friend of hers, Anita. To go out, the girls made themselves as unattractive as possible by smearing some ashes on their faces; after all, the Russians were still on the prowl. Of course, they could have stayed home, but not week after week. So, peace seemed to have arrived, in some fashion.

Little did I know that something continued that had begun earlier and would continue for quite some time: ethnic Germans were driven away from many parts of Eastern Europe. Millions of people, and not just soldiers, were carted away into Russia. Jews often complain that other victims of WWII, in later times, call their fate a Holocaust, because the sole criterion for separating Jews from the rest of the population was that they were Jews, and no other reason. But exactly the same thing happened in Eastern Europe: being an ethnic German was sufficient reason to be carted away. Some day, this might be recognized. There's no difference in being put to death by hunger or cold or a gas chamber, with the sole reason being membership in a particular ethnic group. None of these facts was immediately known; but soon, I, and I'm sure, many others, learned about the death camps and gas chambers for the first time. Of course, I was shocked, to the point of disbelief at first. If there'd been even an inkling of something like that, I sure would have wanted to know more. As I have tried to explain, I was increasingly critical of the Nazi era and was, in fact, groping for confirmation for my aversion. Still, what was revealed then was too terrible to have anything to do with reality, an aspect which I will discuss shortly.

-23-

BACK TO SCHOOL (REALLY!)
– A BEGINNING OF SORTS

Nothing is more exuberant than the elation you feel after having escaped a catastrophe, and being well on your way out of that catastrophe's wake. This was how I felt when, in late May 1945, I inspected my old school and found it intact. Sure, there was some damage, but the school as such was still there. Some of the old buildings, even some of the simple, wooden structures, still stood, and there were even some added structures. Often, people find a focal point in a crucial time. For me, discovering that my school was basically still intact was a major point in my recovery, as far as understanding what all this was about. But the school was closed. Yes, we'd survived physically; yes, we found more and more of our friends and acquaintances had also survived; but now what? Was mere physical survival enough, or was there more to life? A normal life was little more than a dim memory. Did life really consist of a façade, behind which to scrape morsels from the gutter for survival and be happy with it?

This might sound stupid to many people, but in fact, our lives had consisted of a school as a kind of separate world in war-torn

Germany. Now, there was no school. So, life seemed to be nothing but a mere perpetuation of physical survival, and that appeared to be in the offing for a long time to come. Or was there more to it?[45] What did happen after the surrender, and after the immediate threat of violence from Russian soldiers ceased to be a clear and present danger?

During the month of May, I remember some violence concerning and as related to the Russian soldiers' conduct. But, as I've already said, I was sitting in the garden and, when not fetching water, enjoying the lilacs, many other spring flowers, the blooming of our plum tree and later of the peach tree. I must admit that I had reached a pleasant state of complacency and didn't really care about anything. I just didn't want to do anything; well, no, that isn't quite correct. I didn't want to *have* to do anything. You might say that I lived in a state of passive stupor, but no, that's not fair, either; I was just recovering emotionally, and was totally oblivious or outright ignorant about what normalcy in life is all about; excitement doesn't have to come at gunpoint. You can also accuse me of having a selfish attitude; fair enough, but what is selfishness? What does it mean, under the circumstances? I had just, without realizing it, emerged from a kind of society, now defunct, which considered selfishness of the population to be an absolute evil because it interfered with the selfishness of the powers in charge. I think that this respite after the war did me a lot of good, in teaching me that the selfishness underlying self-reliance and even capitalism is what makes the free world go around. I didn't know that then, and so, without ulterior motives, I enjoyed my loafing, my doing nothing, my unadulterated joy that I had survived this mess.

Toward the end of May, I came across Ms. Hüttman who had taught us history and German literature in Wittenberge; she had

---

45 I pose these questions, fully aware of the fact that this view may be examples of a post modernistic or relativizing view.

stayed in Berlin to the end. In fact, of all our Waldschule teachers, she was the only one left on location. She was a very determined person, lacking even the minutest amount of charm, but she wasn't intimidated by anybody, anywhere, anytime. She announced that she was going to rebuild the Waldschule. I don't believe that, in subsequent years, there was ever any event that had affected me emotionally in any comparable way and could parallel the mere prospect of re-opening of our school. I have no idea under what authority she acted. Some people have argued that, after the war, the Russian authorities fostered the reopening of schools. In such a general form, that assertion is certainly not true. In the Russian zone, there were high schools that remained closed for a year or longer.

I strongly believe that this time saw an emergence of true, pioneer spirit. Ms Hüttman certainly had it, and I conjectured that, in the Russian Major who was responsible for the area, she encountered a kindred spirit. Oh sure, he may have been a Communist by way of an implanted belief system, but obviously, he *did* authorize the opening of our school without central orders from "above." How do I know that? Very simply, no other school in our area, or as far as I knew even further away, reopened as early as ours. If there had been a general order on the part of the Soviet military authorities, there would have been, let's say, a greater degree of similarity in "official" action throughout Berlin. Well, there wasn't! So, then how was this possible? How could the school be opened without a general command on the part of the Russian authorities?

I won't bother you with the many, possible philosophical elements, but at that time I experienced directly the difference between West and East Germany, which later became apparent: the difference was the result of independent action by spirited people who, in spite of some governmental supervision or interference by the Western Allies, made things work. In the west, they succeeded, but in the east, they did not. One mustn't forget that, in the U.S., there was a significant amount of political influence by the New Dealers, the

American version of socialism. And Great Britain had just voted a Labor Government into power. So, there were very strong socialistic tendencies in the West. But, fortunately, democracies are pluralistic, and so enough independence emerged in the west, bolstered later by election results.

In the east, a system was immediately installed that relied on orders given from above. Whatever kind of -ism you may wish to call this does not matter; the difference between the West and the East, as it affected Germany (maybe all of Europe), at that time was the difference between the confused laborites' – New Deal socialism of the West – and the dogmatic and overtly oppressive socialism of the East. The latter stifles any initiative more than the former, and that was the root of the unequal road in East and West toward betterment after the war.

Now, what does that have to do with my own experience? Doesn't it sound like a presumptive, learned treatise-assertion? Maybe yes, maybe no. Please remember that I was in the process of learning things. The only free market experience, pragmatically as well as philosophically, was the black market. I distinctly remember that, at that time, we were "officially" confronted with barrages of different socialistic "ideas;" well, nay, we in the west were opportuned to look on one hand at a rigid, government controlled way of life, as proposed by the east, and that was, believe it or not, on our side contrasted by a rather diffuse fuzziness of laissez-faire. Now in the western part of Berlin, we had a peculiar situation. Local authorities hadn't yet been installed (and if they were, they weren't noticeable). The Russians were getting ready to relinquish the western part of the city to the western Allies, so there was some kind of emerging power vacuum within which an independent person could act. I believe that that is exactly what happened in our school. I am convinced that Ms. Hüttman reopened the school on her own authority, accompanied by a Russian Major who couldn't care less because in a month or so, he would leave the area anyhow. Our school reopened on June 6th, less than a month after the German surrender, about five weeks after the fall of Berlin. I know of no other school that opened so early. In fact, in some parts of the country, schools didn't open until fall and in some places, even later.

I will never forget the day when our school reopened. Three from my class: Hannelore Gammler, who'd been in a boarding school in Saxony but had returned to Berlin in the middle of April; then there was Wolfhart Krönert who, like me, had been fortunate enough to be in Berlin and had separated himself in time from the armed forces. He was a year-and-a-half older, and thus hadn't been with us in Wittenberge as LwH. Some of the students had been in our school before, but quite a number were from other schools which had not reopened. All the kids had stayed in Berlin, or returned just before the Russians sprung the trap. And there we were, a rather motley group of kids, most pretty scared. Many of the girls had been molested by Russian soldiers. The others from our LwH group and older guys from the school hadn't returned. At that time, I had no idea what had happened to them. The girls from our class, as well as younger kids, hadn't yet been returned from their evacuation quarters in Henkenhagen.

There were, of course, some teachers, but none of our old group; many of these new teachers were jobless people from other professions. For example, our physics/math teacher was a jobless engineer. Our English and French teacher had been, I believe, a translator for the German foreign office. So, school began. Not much at first, but that didn't matter – it was a beginning. In time, the scope and intensity increased. Later, kids from the Henkenhagen evacuation returned and, one by one, several LwHs returned, often after quite adventurous travels across the border between British and Russian zones, and then through the latter into Berlin. I don't remember whether any of these returns happened while the Russians were still in the western part of Berlin.

Traversing the Russian zone was very dangerous because the Russians often recaptured POWs from the west and carted them off to Siberia. Luckily, none of these returning kids was caught. As I write this, near the end of this millennium, I'm still in contact with several of them including, in particular, the two from my class who were with me at the school's reopening. It is interesting that, when we get together, we rarely talk about those times. We certainly remember that we coped, but don't want to reminisce about how.

With the renewal of our school, the summer of '45 came. The lilacs had stopped blooming, but many flowers still were; it was one of the warmest and most beautiful summers ever. The water supply began functioning again, a little trickle at first, in an outlet at a very low point in the basement. But when you put a pot there, it gradually filled, and then another one, slowly but sufficient; so that the time of having to carry water was over. Electricity was restored, available for a short time every day, but it was just another step in the beginning of normalization. I also don't remember when radio stations (armed forces broadcasts) began, but we had no radio anyway; it had been stolen.

A month or so after school started, the Russians left the western part of the city and the Western Allies arrived, each allotted a certain sector; we were in the British sector. Obviously we were very happy about this change of events, except that our street, Marienburger Allee, became again an area of interest for occupation forces because of the bigger houses, so we had to move again. This eviction, however, was done a in a bit more civilized manner as we were given more time to leave. This time I moved by myself to a small apartment building, to a top floor, single-room apartment above the apartment of the Seifert family I knew from elementary school. Detlev Seifert had been my schoolmate but had become a victim and casualty in the last days of the war. Mrs. Seifert and Detlev's younger brothers were elsewhere. Only Mr. Seifert was in that house, and through him, I got the apartment. All the people / roomers who had stayed on the top floor had left Berlin before the end of the war. The whole affair didn't really interrupt my life, and most importantly, with the arrival of the British troops, the population's food supply increased and became more or less regular. Food was rationed, of course, and the rations didn't make you fat, but the worst was over.

Shortly after I had moved out of the Marienburger Allee – I was still allowed in that street by the occupation forces – I was going back for some reason and saw my mother carrying a heavy backpack. She was quite exhausted and wondered what had happened. She could see that our house was still standing with hardly any damage – she didn't know that in advance – but there were all these British soldiers around: now what? My being there in the street, just at the moment of her arrival makes you wonder about coincidences. Obviously, we were overjoyed to see each other, and I took her to the place where I stayed. Her arrival indicated that, in July, some train traffic had been restored into Berlin.

Very soon after my mother returned, she was requested (well, call it "ordered" or "requisitioned") to serve as a cook in a non-com officer's mess in a street nearby. Technically, it's a degrading way of being treated, being ordered into a subservient position for the occupying forces. In reality, though, it was a godsend. She was a very diligent person, and her superior cook was a very nice chap. Not believing in leftovers, he allowed her to take home all food that was left from the day. The cook was typical Army and followed some book. I remember, when they made a roast, he discarded the meat juice and made gravy from packaged stuff. My mother brought the real, good stuff home, so we ate better than the British soldiers. Obviously, our sustenance vastly improved, and our little room became a favorite visiting place for many hungry acquaintances. It helped us and others to bridge the gap from our dwindling supply of stuff we had "taken" from the OT camp, up to the stabilization of the not-yet-functioning, regular food supply. Soon, we were allowed to move back into our house. The British soldiers stole some things like china, but that wasn't too important. Much more important was that they'd rebuilt the wall that had collapsed between the dining room and kitchen during the 1943 air raid. It would have been impossible, at that time, for us to get any material.

In general, "public life" was improving. Even a few restaurants were open, particularly on the main promenade of West Berlin, the Kurfürstendamm. Some movie houses opened with British and American movies. Old German movies were suspect, and new ones hadn't yet been made. Radio stations came into existence, and there were, of course, the Allied forces' radio stations. I really don't remember when we had a new radio, so that wasn't important. However, newspapers began to appear rather soon after the end of the war; they were published under Allied supervision. Whether or not the journalists and writers were the same who had, for the last 12 years, written the adulating Nazi garbage and just, let's say, had switched allegiances, I don't know. But since the entire Nazi era had lasted only twelve years, there were probably many journalists and writers from the years of the Republic who were not allowed to write again. In any event, it was quite clear that we read, for the first time, some reliable information (for people of my generation, that was literally true; it was for the first time in our lives because we had learned how to read after Hitler came to power). There were many accounts about what was and had been going on everywhere, without glorifying or justifying it.

Certain newspapers were published under American supervision, others under British supervision, still others under Russian control. In Berlin, all of them were available to us, including, in addition, papers just for Berlin, "organized" by sectors of occupation. All in all, it was interesting to compare them – our first encounter with "multiculturalism." We were offered an abundance in variety, which was completely new to me and my generation. I don't recall specific differences, which might also be an interesting object of study, but in retrospect, the battle for the political mind of the Germans had begun.

-24-

SUMMER 1945 – CONTINUING THE BEGINNING

Many interesting aspects began to develop, some of which I want to dwell on a bit. The first item concerns our school, and the new principal who had, mostly on her own authority and resolute attitude, reopened it. It's difficult to consider this event, and particularly the initial phases, adequately. Of course, everybody everywhere had to cope with the ruins: ruins of homes, offices, and workplaces generally, and many facets of everyday life. Often, there wasn't complete destruction, but damage comes in different degrees of severity. Fortunately, my home had survived more or less intact, and damage to the school was relatively minimal, certainly not insurmountably difficult. However, there was another kind of ruin to cope with: the destruction of the social fabric. And as a consequence, Ms. Hüttman soon found herself in the middle of conflicting forces. As long as there were Russians around, she had to cope with them on penalty of just being stopped in what she was doing. However, soon there was the beginning of a local German administration.

Right from the start, these local administrations were dominated by Communists and Social Democrats working hand in hand, and having in common a hatred of the "bourgeoisie." A high school was, to them, a symbol of class division and privilege. Today, this shameful coalition, particularly as far as the Social Democrats were concerned, is glossed over and brushed aside, and they hope, forgotten. What is remembered today, and with great fanfare at that, is the official combination of Social Democrats and Communists in the East, and the overt split between them in the West, but that was well *after* the initial fraternization phase. The split in the West was possibly motivated, on the part of the Social Democrats, by the prospect of cooperation with the New Dealers and Laborites.

Why do I mention this? Simply because Ms. Hüttman had to pacify the local Communist / Social Democrat clique. Next in line, during that phase, were the British authorities but I think they were the easiest to work with as they were well-versed in dealing with colonials (which is what we were at that time). Their main goal has always been not to make the natives restless. In that, they adequately succeeded. And finally, there were, of course, the worried parents who had seen their lives destroyed, or at least significantly impaired, who'd been worried sick about their kids and now hoped, finally, for something better. That, I conjectured simply from my experience, a little over 10 years later when I became a parent. People had little influence on the schools their kids went to. Intuitively, I believe, however, that people must have realized that, after the weeks and months of horror, they wanted to ensure that their kids were finally in a relatively safe place. The foregoing factors and political forces are nothing that I've conjured up after more than half a century. They're the result of collective impressions as I *do* remember them, reinforced, indeed, by newspaper accounts.

I distinctly remember the arrogance of public officials, by observation and comparison, and how little they cared, as far as schools were concerned.

It's not surprising that, in her maneuvering here, Ms. Hüttman was in a difficult position; no doubt, she displeased some people. As I mentioned, she wasn't exactly endowed with great charm, and that worked against her. One aspect was her interdiction that teachers – including the former principal – who had been a member of the Nazi Party, weren't allowed on school grounds; apparently she enforced this rule in a rather abrasive fashion. To this day, some former students hold that against her; to the point that, it sometimes appears her memory at the school was purged. Admittedly, it wasn't nice, but under the circumstances, it was simply necessary. After all, we'd never been a Nazi school, and reopening the school and keeping it open was obviously of paramount importance. She steadfastly re-organized the school and worked towards the highest grade for reaching the *Abitur* (graduation, following a formal final examination) as soon as possible.

As I mentioned, several former LwHs and evacuees returned during the summer. The highest rank among the returnees was a lieutenant. We also had a master sergeant. Some girls had also been in the air force as telephone and radar operators; apparently, that was, primarily, a source for amusement and not something to either gloat about or be ashamed of. Things stabilized, and so did the teaching staff, into a very congenial class atmosphere, aided by our own past experience in which it was rarely, if ever, "us" against "them." This was the return of the school's past atmosphere; the students and teachers from other schools adapted quickly. Even though there was no playing anymore with the teachers, the teachers very quickly realized that we were no longer little brats who wanted to get away with doing as little as possible. We gratefully picked up the pieces and put our lives together again.

The old saying, *"non scholae sed vitae discimus*[46]*"* was completely turned around. Life had already taught all of us, teachers and students

---

46 We learn for life, not for the school

alike, many lessons, including the fact that we, the students, had learned in a few years of experiencing war-end scenarios more than the teachers had learned before that time. They understood very well what we had been through, and we, to a limited extent, knew that life for them hadn't been easy either. They never considered what we had to say, whatever that was, as back-talk.

Likewise, what they had to say to us was never presented in a patronizing fashion. In terms of behavior, we were never unruly, but I don't think that that was a kind of "heritage" from the Nazi era; rather, we'd matured. Almost as an insignificant aside, they tolerated, for example, that we smoked (totally unheard of before), that we carried on black market dealings (which I'll say more about shortly). Maybe these early teachers' greatest achievement was that, after 12 years of dictatorial – authoritative – "rule", they realized that real authority and respect must be earned and can't be expected, particularly if there is no "authority" to force it down anybody's throat. They were well aware, and so were we, of the non-existence of any real authority. (An occupation force was a reality to be reckoned with, which has nothing to do with real authority based on a moral obligation.)

-25-

REALITIES

Now, I want to integrate into my account one aspect that became very important in postwar German life – actually, all over Europe – which I haven't found adequately dealt with. It concerns the so-called black market. Presently and for quite some time, and for many people probably, the very term "black market" has a connotation of illegality, crime, drugs, and in general asocial behavior, subversion of the existing order, anarchy etc. etc. Of course, all of these may be true at some time or another; it's a matter of perspective. The black market is simply a pattern of distribution of goods which are in demand, and which the existing order (if such exists at all) is unable to supply, or only to an insufficient extent. Now, let me relate something about certain realities concerning survival in Europe after WWII, and perhaps, many places before and after.

The black market was the means by which large amounts of goods in demand were channeled into the then general "economy." These goods wouldn't have been available otherwise; they had to bypass government regulations. Admittedly, these goods were sometimes taken (stolen?) from the general organized supply (if there was one). However, in many instances, they were channeled into the economy in a manner that simply eluded official channels. Through the PX and NAAFI[47] stores, and many other channels, goods actually destined for the Allied soldiers found their way into the economy of the occupied peoples all over Europe.

Let me be blunt about this: there were Germans, Frenchmen, Italians, etc. who were starving, wanting to smoke and, once in a while, have a cup of real coffee. And here were American GIs and Brits offering coffee, cigarettes, chocolate, tea, and also butter. Where did they get it from? We, the prospective buyers, weren't in the least interested how the Allied soldiers got their hands on these goodies, whether they were allowed to deal with us etc. etc. Decisive was the fact that that stuff was not available otherwise.

But then, there was the other traffic: the prospective customers for these goodies had nothing to offer in terms of currency. So, they sold Leica cameras, gold for inflationary prices – and anything else they had – to buy what they needed. I'm convinced that a very large number of people in Europe survived in large part because they bought black market food; for untold millions, a good cup of coffee, together with a cigarette, made you forget for a bit the otherwise pretty miserable existence. Often, there was outright barter, say, of x milligrams of gold for a pound of coffee or a carton of cigarettes or a pound of butter. We sold an old, not very good piano for 100 pounds of potatoes. This is not a black market, in the morally-criminal sense; but an uncontrolled, and thus, a free market. Some people later called this a sell-out of Germany, of giving away what little valuables were left that survived the bombing and looting, for perishables and consumables. This may sound convincing in the abstract, but you can't eat or drink gold, and if that's all you have to exchange for what you need to physically or emotionally survive, that may, ultimately, tide you over until you can recoup what you've lost. I understand Germans went on a gold and diamond buying

47 The stores for the American and British forces, respectively

spree just 10 years later.

Why have I dwelt on the foregoing discourse? The entire so-called economic miracle is based on survival, not just of people, but of the free enterprising spirit. Am I speculating? Not at all. I saw and experienced it in the years that followed and, in a way, I'm proud to say I participated in it, throughout my professional life. What I've said is a generalization, based on my own experience for many years. In fact, subsequent history confirms it over and over again. Also, in my own experience, schools and universities rapidly became centers of black-market activities. In our high school, we bartered / bickered / bargained / peddled cigarettes and coffee and who knows what else. Our black market did not develop into an enterprise on a grand scale, but just enough to put a few extras into our pocket and to make survival a bit easier. I'll add that I never converted my mother's spoils from her cooking for the British soldiers into a profitable enterprise, though I emphasize that I really don't consider this particularly laudable. In fact, you might call it stupidity, except that we shared the spoils from the victors with relatives and friends; that, indeed, was the right thing to do.

After newspapers began to appear, we learned about the horrors and atrocities Germans had inflicted on others. We didn't learn at that time about the atrocities that were inflicted upon Germans in a tit-for-tat fashion throughout 1944 and '45, and which continued in so-called POW camps (at that time, in reality, concentration – forced labor camps of the Allies). A lot has been written on the subject of German atrocities. I have, in previous chapters, reported on the very limited aspects of these atrocities I came to know. The scale of these atrocities was, of course, completely unknown to me or to anybody I knew, or who may have told me about them, knowing my adverse attitude toward the Nazi regime.

In the first post-war years, step by step, I – as well as others – began to realize the enormity of the crimes that had been committed. They were reported in the new newspapers. But why did I believe them then? In the past years, that is, during the Nazi era, I'd painstakingly accumulated information that made me increasingly believe in the truth of the surmised wrongness of what was going on. That sounds like a mouthful, but after so many years, it's very difficult to put into words the growing suspicion that there was something very wrong with Germany; often, you couldn't really define it. In a different way, I've stated this before. But now, after the war, the scenario became more obvious. The aspects and emotions of understanding hadn't really changed at all, but now there was an enormity involved which defied description and belief.

My initial reaction was similar to many people's: something like that couldn't possibly have happened. However, it didn't take me long to realize that, in spite of the unbelievable enormity, it was a kind of confirmation of what I'd suspected for a long time. Not, of course, the mass killings, but the notion that the Third Reich was a criminal enterprise. The enormity was simply the consistent multiplication of an action – killing a person for what he or she biologically is – and transforming that action into a machinery of efficiency and thoroughness. Germans are famous for such characteristics, and it didn't take me very long before I realized this deadly combination. I don't remember that this was discussed in school among the students; in a way, it simply seemed beyond comprehension. On reflection, now, half a century later, what could we have discussed in school? Obviously, we hadn't participated, and if anybody knew anybody who had, it couldn't have been expected that it would be mentioned.

There's still, to this day, an extensive (*ad nauseam*) discussion of German repentance, etc. etc. – compared with the persisting recalcitrance of the Japanese who ignore their past no matter what. I have to say that I both despise and admire the Japanese for this. I despise many of them for failing to take a decisive stand on a moral issue after so many years. But I admire them for having apparently taken consistently a collective stand against the concept of collective guilt, a position which to this day, has eluded the Germans and which has put them into a position of being the continuing whipping boy.

But going back to 1945, I must make a point here which social scientists, psychology-generalists may have ignored. As time goes by, ignoring the following aspect becomes easier.

These enormous Nazi crimes became known to a greater and greater extent during the first phase of the post-war era. I described the euphoria we went through every time we met somebody who had made it, too. But there's another side of the coin: the gnawing uncertainty, which, at the same time, a large number of people felt about the fate of many loved ones. Luckily, I was spared this emotional torture. I was united with my mother in July 1945, about a third of a year after we had last heard from each other. However, millions were not so fortunate. Later, a young woman with a little boy stayed in our house, and she never learned what had happened to her husband. Others knew that a loved one had survived but did not know when he would come back from a POW camp. And then, there was the mass exodus from eastern Europe and the eastern part of Germany – not East Germany, but Silesia, East Prussia and Pomerania, which by now was all made into a part of Poland. There were also the people the Russians put into concentration camps. And so, many people were occupied with worry about relatives or people they'd known. To ask them to occupy themselves extensively with abstract matters of justice, concerning people they didn't know personally (Jews, gypsies), was simply unrealistic.

In the fall of 1945, the so-called Nuremburg trials began. It invoked among my friends and myself fairly little interest. The outcome of this trial is still heralded as a victory for international justice. But then, and today, I felt it to be a mockery. To have a Soviet judge sitting on the bench robbed these proceedings of any legitimacy; it was *"vae victis,"*[48] pure and simple. I don't believe that it carried

---

48 Woe to the vanquished

much moral force at that time. That some severe punishment was in order is without question, but it should have been meted out from a genuine, international tribunal and not from one that included one of Stalin's henchmen. The Nuremberg trials and judgment will stay in the history books, but let it be known that this kind of international "justice" will be tainted forever; it had nothing to do with justice, it was nothing but an act of revenge. Several very honorable American and British jurists were attached to these proceedings; I'll never understand how they deigned these proceedings, how they could believe that they were engaged in the administration of justice while on the bench with this murderous, Soviet scum.

-26-

FINAL SCHOOL DAYS

In the fall of 1945 – I really don't remember details, nor how it actually materialized – I must have exhibited what today would be called post-traumatic stress syndrome / disorder. I believe others had it, too, in different ways. For me, it developed as an on-and-off, don't give a damn attitude. I very much enjoyed going to school again, for many months now, but for some reason – actually for no reason at all – I started to cut classes here and there. Fortunately, it didn't last long. Our class and school population had stabilized, and the teachers were now well established. A few of the old teachers had returned. Others were at odds with Ms. Hüttman's personality and went to different schools. Our rather ambitious principal wanted our class to stage a play, probably for school propaganda. For reasons I don't recall, or maybe never knew, the Faust drama by the British playwright Marlowe was chosen.

I wasn't enthusiastic about it and sought to get myself a good part with little to do and say. I'd chosen the part of one of the deadly sins, laziness. We read this play in class, and when it came to my part, the entire class burst out laughing. Hüttman, who also taught German literature, wasn't amused and decided I should play Mephistopheles, obviously the second-longest part of the play and, I had to admit right away, the most interesting one. In many ways, the Faust part was boring; playing "evil" is always more rewarding, and I soon loved it. The play was directed by a fellow classmate who was interested in the theater and wanted to become a stage director. In fact, he was, until not long ago, a director in Zurich. My initial, laziness-motivated skepticism faded rapidly. We all had a wonderful time putting on this play. It was a great success; it was even written up in the newspapers. We added several performances over and beyond those originally planned and made a pile of money for the school.

I must have been fairly good as an actor. I told my mother who was, of course, attending "opening night," that I was the very first person on stage to say anything. Later, she said that she believed I must have been mistaken. Well, I wasn't, I really must have sounded rotten and evil to an extent she hadn't known. Maybe I should have become an actor. People actually talked about this Faust performance for years. But, there is more to it than that: I believe it gave all of us a sense of accomplishment we hadn't known before; we could do something beyond just surviving; we participated in something called culture which was for us, for all practical purposes, just an empty word.

The winter of '45 to '46 was very hard, but our energetic principal Hüttman managed to get the school some coal. It wasn't particularly hot, but passable in the classrooms; I don't remember that we ever closed for lack of heating. In some post-war accounts, such closures have been asserted. I don't believe this is correct. Never mind, for better or worse, we stuck it out. Life returned gradually to what was, relatively speaking, normal. Of course, food was rationed and not available in great abundance. Produce was very rare; fruit, practically non-existent. The school black market flourished, to some extent, and we began to prepare for the Abitur. That had been, in the past, a serious matter for the students involved. This first post-war Abitur was a challenge for students and teachers. We all understood that it had to be a success –"all" meant students as well as teachers. Tacitly this was a kind of insurance policy: remember, *Non vitae sed scholae discimus*. It was clear that it had to be a success for everybody but without becoming a sham. However, there was a problem.

An Abitur was "really" a kind of graduation to bourgeois privilege. The local Social Democrats didn't help, and the still Communist-dominated school administration simply ignored the need for an *Abitur*. I was a member of a three- or four student delegation which had a conference with a Mr. Wildangel, the Superintendent for all Berlin schools. I don't recall whether he was one of the Moscow returnees, but it was the Communist policy to be nice to children (the wave of the future), so we had a good meeting. Whether this did any good I don't know, but at least we didn't make matters worse, because he did give permission for our final graduation examination which took place in July 1946, and later, in other schools as well.

The examination was conducted under the chairmanship of an elderly gentleman, a Mr. Naumann; he had been recalled from retirement and was very jovial indeed. I don't believe that he was a Social Democrat. He reminded me very much of my German teacher Ölze in Bunzlau, who had been a deputy for the Conservative party in the Federal Parliament.

Everybody passed, to nobody's surprise, and it was a glowing success for the principal, the teachers, the students, the school, and the city. Mr. Naumann gave a fine speech in which he recognized, in a very guarded way, that our education may have some gaps, but this was more than balanced by life experience. Strictly speaking, this wasn't entirely correct, because war doesn't teach you the foundation of civilization.

But ultimately he was right, because a very sizable portion of our class developed into professional people. Of those with whom I have some contact, none turned out to be a failure.

We held a kind of post-graduation prom, and then high school was over. I didn't realize at that time how much that *refugium* had meant to me, but the still existing, continuing, and resumed ties with quite a number of former classmates, to this day, speaks louder than words of praise. I didn't realize until later that, through this school, I had survived an unbelievable trauma, ranging from the Sudeten crisis in 1938 to a point in time in 1946, in which planning one's life for the future was no longer an absurdity.

-27-

WHAT FUTURE?

I am, possibly by nature, to some extent quite naïve, prone to living in a dream world, sometimes just disregarding adverse reality. Up to the time I was 18, particularly during the entire late Nazi era, the LwH time and the immediate post-war period did not cause me to worry about my future. I'm not talking about physical survival; I'm talking about life. Looking back, however, I think many of my classmates weren't that different, so maybe it wasn't just me, maybe it was a natural defense mechanism which we used to shield ourselves individually against adversities. Maybe the school had served as kind of communal shield. Be that as it may, even before school was over and before we had the Abitur behind us, the question arose or should have arisen, *now what?*

Today, it's quite normal that everyone in their late teens seriously contemplates the question of what to do with his or her life; here, the independence from parental supervision plays a very important part. Before I examine this point, I just want to state, in a position of quite incredible arrogance, the idea of not going to the University didn't enter my mind; I never considered not studying as an option. I'll come back to this later; first, I want to say that the question of being independent from parental control, in my case from my mother, simply didn't arise. I strongly believe that the situation was basically similar to that of all my classmates, even including those who didn't return to our school right after the war. We never got together to complain about the unreasonableness of our parents etc. etc. I mentioned earlier that the war years themselves almost negated the customary strain between a pre- and early- teen and his or her parents. There just wasn't the opportunity to get into trouble.

Well, no, that is incorrect; we could have formed street gangs, using the black-out for unsavory activities. Well, we didn't; it just didn't occur to us. Particularly, what exactly was it our elders deemed appropriate? Their world had just fallen apart, in a way much more than ours; their world had been destroyed and didn't serve as model; our world hadn't been formed yet, and we took from around us whatever we could.

Following the war, the joy of knowing that my mother (as to me) and I (as to her) had survived overshadowed everything. Looking back, after I came home – three days after Berlin's surrender – and many weeks before my mother came back, I had taken care of things to the extent that was possible, and so had many others. Without being told what to do, I'd indeed grown up and learned to act responsibly. Having survived the military's cunning atmosphere, I'd basically been salvaging as much as possible. When my mother came home, our house was occupied by British soldiers (which I couldn't do anything about), but I had a place for us to live. I'd salvaged some of her clothes, lots of our household stuff, and other necessities. I simply offered her an admittedly very simple, very rudimentary homecoming and way of life – of the same kind I had been living up to that time. In addition, I went to school (without being told to) together with friends of like spirit; we were going to school to catch up, not because some grown-up told us to. I had also made contact with my friends and friends of my parent's generation. Well, I did some black-market dealings to augment what I thought I needed, e.g. cigarettes. And so, in retrospect it was apparent that when my mother came back, she found a grown up, adult son, who as best as was possible under the circumstances, had taken care of things, not just for himself, but of family matters and had prevented looting by people other than occupation forces. In fact, it was she who had come home. I was home (sort of) to receive her and, in a way, to welcome her.

It was obvious that, at that point, she couldn't just take over as a parent, and she had enough insight and intelligence not even to try. She recognized (and I did, too, without verbalizing it) that there was now a partnership between mother and son as co-equals. I quite believe that, in many cases of my contemporaries, the situation was similar. Teenagers, time and again and the world over (and I expect going back to hunters and gatherers), had to prove themselves and were expected to vie for independence from the old folks' dictates. In our generation, it simply was different. We proved our worth already (after all, we were alive!), well before the normal time for this had come. Am I unduly generalizing beyond my own experience? Not at all, because I'm including what I learned from my contemporaries with whom I had contact. We'd proved that we could stand on our feet; we'd proved it to the world, simply by surviving. And not only had we proven it to our parents, most importantly, we'd proven it to ourselves. The book I've alluded to about the impact the war had on the Luftwaffenhelfer is very ambivalent about the relationship between parents and returning LwHs. Apparently, there are too many variants and special circumstances if the returnee had been a POW but his findings seem to be quite clear: that there were no problems when the parents understood that the returnee was no longer a child subject to their direction. I was fortunate that my mother indeed understood.

I mentioned a certain naïveté on my part about lack of concern for the future. But maybe that naïveté was simply an aspect of taking things one step at a time, a realization of the need to cope with the immediate future and not to make yourself sick over the time beyond. Maybe I (and others?) intuitively rejected the idea of long-term planning as unrealistic and to looked instead for opportunities as they opened up.

So, my mother and I entered into an implied partnership (aren't legal terms horrible?) or perhaps, more accurately, an unspoken understanding. We'd stuck it out together through the first part of the war, were separated toward the end, and re-united in summer of 1945; it was obvious that it was appropriate, or from both our points of view, practical (opportunistic?) to continue to stick it out together.

Now, please don't assume that I posit here my relationship with my mother as a Rousseau kind of social contract, or do I? Was a pragmatic appraisal of advantageous behavior at the root of our staying together for the next ten years? Most certainly not in an absolute way. No doubt, an emotional component was involved, but was that component stronger than or at least as strong as the pragmatic aspect? I indirectly stated the reason I pose this question: after high school, I simply wasn't concerned with making a living. That lack of concern was most certainly based on the fact that, indeed, I'd stayed alive without what you'd call a regular income. Intuitively, that means I was convinced that I was entitled to live at home as long as I wanted to. I didn't feel in the least any moral or pragmatic need to make a living. Did I take undue advantage of my mother at that time? Not at all, because we'd formed this implicit partnership of mutual dependency.

I raise this issue, however, in a contemporary framework, where it makes sense and is one of the critical social issues. But, at that time, such a social issue would have made no sense at all. Families simply shared resources in order to survive, to get on with their lives. Our house, which miraculously survived, was the place for me to stay. For example, to go and look for a place to stay among ruins or the scarce living quarters, often partially damaged, would have been exceedingly stupid; in fact, it would have been outright immoral. I would have been taking away living quarters from among the many who'd become homeless because of the war and occupation.

In the Communist-Social Democrat alliance aimed at stifling the bourgeoisie, they decreed that pensions not be paid. They were paid in West Germany, not in the East; all of Berlin was dominated by that alliance, and they followed the East in their disgusting approach, just to punish their old, bourgeois adversaries. So, my mother had no income. I must admit, with a sense of realistic pride, that it never occurred to me to sacrifice my future, to stop thinking about more formal education, and instead get a job to keep us alive. If somebody believes I should have at least thought about it, frankly I don't care. I feel no remorse about it. I simply felt strongly that I was entitled to study, simply because I wanted to, and there was no reason in my mind why that shouldn't be possible; after all, universities continued, so why shouldn't I benefit from it?

We managed by renting out rooms in our house. This doesn't sound like much, but you couldn't buy anything anyhow, and rationed food was very cheap. Of course, my mother could go to work, and I don't understand why she didn't, but it was a prospect that did not appeal to her – until we came across a good idea in good old (albeit, small scale) capitalistic fashion.

I don't recall how it started, but we began a business of making handbags. I had designed them generally and "engineered" them for practical construction. Basically, they were made of cardboard, which we covered with material people supplied. We had the cardboard, but I don't remember where we got it from. Since practically anything was useable for this, the material was no problem; people always have some scraps. Our dining room was converted during the day to a workshop for my mother and a number of elderly ladies who were in the same situation: the Communist-Social Democrat coalition had stopped their pensions. We didn't get rich, didn't bother with any license and most certainly didn't pay any taxes. I don't remember any dissatisfied customers. Since, as I said, you couldn't buy anything in the stores, we certainly had no problem in selling these handbags. In winter, we heated the dining room with a small furnace, and when I came home from studying we all sat around the dining room table; it was almost cozy. I could indeed embark on an academic education.

By the summer 1946 the universities everywhere had begun to dig out from under the rubble. In Berlin, we had basically two universities in addition to some schools of higher learning for engineering, fine arts, and music. There was the Technical University, basically a highest-level engineering school, with some additional natural science for broadening its scope, as well as mathematical departments. For pragmatic reasons, I concentrated on seeking admission to that school, though I must confess its being considerably closer to home was an additional feature I liked. But then, there was the time-honored, history-laden Humboldt University in the center of Berlin. Intuitively, I was drawn to it. What did I really want? How could I formulate and particularize my academic goals? What was my contemplated major? What job position, career goals was I pursuing, what specifics was I heading for? I put these questions in modern terms for reasons of contrast, because at that time they didn't mean anything at all; or I can say that none of the above was applicable. I had no such goal whatever. Then, what did I want in an institution of higher learning? Very simple: I wanted an intellectual blow-up; I wanted to wallow in ideas. Well, ultimately, I wanted to know, in terms of Goethe's *Faust*, the fabric that holds the world together. Well, not quite, even that was too pragmatic and practical. Soon after I started, I engulfed myself in the abstractions and the esthetics of pure mathematics. I enjoyed the beauty of some mathematical theorem's concise proof, having no practical value whatever. I simply enjoyed the merger of logic and esthetics. But I'm getting ahead of my story.

Sometime in 1946, I applied to both universities; some foul up occurred in the Technical University, but I was accepted in Humboldt. I was lucky because, as I hinted, I had no contingency plans whatever and my relative youth (actually the normal age for normal times) was a negative factor because of all the veterans. This was the second semester the University was opened after the war, but it was really the first time that it operated on a full-scale basis. We were 40 students admitted for Mathematics and 40 for Physics: Not very many. Still, I accepted my admission as something I was due. What naïve arrogance! But deep down, it was a time when I began to feel I had been on the wrong side of the past conflict for no fault of my own. For example, I didn't feel it unjust that Hitler Youth leaders and Army Officers weren't necessarily barred but put in low probability categories, as far as admission chances were concerned. So, I had no qualms that my admission status was higher than theirs; I guess it was just my way of expressing my teenage rebellion against the situation that had marred my childhood.

Generally speaking, many POWs began to return then. Returning veterans began filling universities all over the world, but the victor countries, of course, had it relative easy to adjust, expand etc. Studying in Germany meant making do with what was left and could be repaired with relative ease; one made do with the remnants. So, in the fall of 1946, I began to attend classes at the Humboldt University.

-28-

UNIVERSITY – THE NEXT SHELTER

In the early months after the war, there was no means to go to downtown Berlin except on foot; in the really early days, you didn't go anywhere except when you absolutely had to. I walked quite a number of times to Schöneberg to see the Ide family. The scope of one's sojourn was also limited by the curfew.

But in 1946, with the elevated train system running again, you could indeed reach downtown. I mentioned that in early '46 I was a member of a delegation to negotiate with the school authorities; obviously, we got there and not by walking. Later, I went downtown to apply for the admission to the university; also, there were interviews etc. These trips were like visiting another planet, but it was also the area where I'd spent the last days of the war before the fall of Berlin.

Most of the time after the war, I stayed in our suburb, with its trees (remember the lilac) and all the green that covered the damage; it was a world in which, physically, much was still intact. Not so downtown. I'd seen the city in flames, its crumbling ruins, artillery bombardment, a kind of three-dimensional catastrophe movie in which you were a participant. Now, after some time had elapsed, it was something else to see the result of all this, after the shooting and shelling had stopped. There was, on one hand, a much stronger realization of the destruction, of the ruins with the dead-looking, still-standing but empty façades. The rubble was off the street, but nothing had been rebuilt except in a way of makeshift, superficial repair. No new construction was even talked about. On the other hand, seeing the downtown area for the first time in 1946, then on a daily basis, brought a sense of wonderment that anything was left at all. There were rows upon rows upon rows of burnt-out houses[49], facades with vacantly staring holes that once had been windows, sometimes entire walls, sometimes just portions, or even heaps of rubble. And on the streets where some cars could drive, people were standing, walking, talking – seemingly oblivious to the ruins. Even so, some useful structures still existed. In May of 1945, I'd just experienced incessant barrages of artillery and hadn't been in the mood for sightseeing after emerging from the tunnel and trying to get away from the Russians. Now, I was genuinely amazed how much of downtown Berlin had survived.

The outer walls of the University were intact, and some classrooms on the lower two levels had needed relatively minor repairs. Next to it was the main, old States-Library (the equivalent of the Library of Congress). Many parts were still intact, and there were even books in it, but it was surrounded by rubble. So, in the fall of 1946, I changed my ambience from the pleasant, plant-covered, tree-lined and basically intact home – near-school scenario, with its simple but basically intact wooden structures, for a stark environment of a few, originally fairly-majestic, stone structures of the last century (which still exhibited some majesty). As I mentioned already, Prussian architecture was never particularly grand, but there was a certain grandeur left, a kind of cultural survival. Since then, part of it was destroyed by the East German authorities who were politically motivated. I sincerely hope that the present city

---

49 Documentaries have amply shown this scene – Berlin, Dresden etc.

planners, at the turn of the millennium, appreciate the importance of architectural continuity.

Almost every day, I took the train of the reconstructed, elevated train system for about a half-hour ride through dilapidated, and only rarely-repaired or re-constructed, ruins to the center of Berlin. I walked in streets lined by ruins and burnt out houses to the University to attend classes; what a way to begin your higher education.

Well, what indeed! In high school, intellectually and emotionally, you can expect only so much satisfaction (or not). But in this or that field, different for each student, you get a sense there must be something more and beyond what you got thus far, and I do not mean just more tedious details. You begin to yearn for that something more. I believe that this kind of yearning is the determining factor in one's quest for knowledge. For me, that was, of course, mathematics and theoretical physics, in an intertwined manner. I've mentioned that I wasn't much – if at all – concerned about pragmatic aspects of a job training to make a living. In fact, I sought that "something more" without knowing or actually wanting to know where it would lead to and what to expect. Maybe that was a part of the general experience we underwent: don't ask what "it" may lead to.

The first semester at the University was a mind- and eye-opener. After trudging by train and on foot through ruins and rubble, I listened to Professor Schmidt's lecture on differential / integral calculus. We had had calculus in high school in a technical, mechanical sense, and in my arrogance, I considered skipping classes – I knew it all. To some vindication, I must add that, very quickly, I abandoned such foolishness. Almost literally, I sat at the feet of this intellectual giant, who developed this seemingly technical-manipulative concept into a world of formal philosophical esthetics. He had no notes, no book; after entering the classroom, he asked somebody in the front row where approximately he had left off previously. And off he went, in a gap-less continuation of his lecture, presenting it in a prose which, if recorded, could have been immediately converted into book form without requiring further editing.

And then there was a professor whose name I've forgotten, very tall and also quite old with a white beard, the prototype of a university professor. He taught theoretical mechanics, a subject that can be made unbelievably dull, but he developed it as one of the basic concepts by which reality was divested from divine intervention. Need I tell you that I was blissfully in an intellectual heaven? What difference did the ruins make? And the need to make living was shifted ever further from my mind.

And then there was Professor Gerthsen, who taught basic physics. We didn't have any books, but I believe he had prepared lecture notes which later were made into a book (I still have it, and often have consulted it throughout the years as a basic text). Papa Gerthsen did not bother with epistemic questions about the knowability of the physical world; instead, he presented physics as a way of looking at happenings that can be analyzed and then mathematically described. What did he actually teach me or us? I can't put it into a definite frame, except that he enticed us to look deeper into phenomena covered by a descriptive Physics, being descriptive mathematically and verbally without bothering to make things unmanageable by introducing the instrumentalist / realist dispute. He taught us that descriptive physics suffices for many purposes, leaving open whether this suffices for a real, in-depth understanding. I confess that this was something I learned much later, and after long reflection, but Papa Gerthsen planted the root of interest.

But then there was, of course, another side of life. I think that the winter of 1946 to '47 was the absolute bottom, in terms of physical existence, at least in Berlin and possibly in other places as well. There was no coal for heating, and it was a very cold winter. The food supply had been stabilized for quite some time, on a low level, but the severity of the temperatures interfered with everything. In the morning, I'd wake up because my face touched a layer of ice that had formed from my breath on the bedsheet. Well, okay, I got up, traveled, and went to class in the university to recover from the rather rude awakening, by engulfing myself blissfully in a well-reasoned theorem. This may sound rather stupid, but it's what kept me going. Forgive me, and this might sound awfully like a platitude, but there is the saying: "Mind over matter."

Let me put it differently: I strongly believe that being about 19 or 20 years of age, my intellectual curiosity had its greatest impetus from the adversities which the world presented me. I was able to keep my studies completely separate from the dilapidated circumstances under which I satisfied my intellectual curiosity. Did that mean that I lived in a dream world, oblivious to reality? Quite possibly, because I'd found a new *refugium*, one very different from the one before; it wasn't a setting among trees and flowers, but centered around the reading room of the State Library. The library books were one thing, but another thing was the simple fact that it was heated. In addition, there was nothing for a student to do except studying and staying alive. I'm sorry to say that my social contacts were very limited. I often spent time with a former schoolmate, Horst Scheunemann; I mentioned him earlier; he was the one who, in his early childhood years, experienced the Hitler Youth as nothing but bunch of thugs. Beyond that, further companionship was difficult because most students were older, many much older – mostly returned veterans. And the girls were also much older; math and physics were male-dominated anyway. Otherwise, I wasn't oblivious to reality; I financed my studies with black market dealings and helped my mother in our handbag enterprise.

But over time, I began to realize – very slowly at first – that financing my studies through black market dealings and helping my mother make handbags may indeed be good for keeping me in the University, but believe it or not, after a few semesters, I began thinking about how I could make a living through proving beautiful mathematical theorems. In other words, I had blissfully wallowed in formal aesthetics, and having done that for quite a while, I began to realize that, for me, that wasn't a goal in itself. I needed some reality, so I began to shift to physics, and soon, as I will explain, to atmospheric physics. I don't remember why I didn't stick with straightforward physics, a field that as such continues to enthrall me to this day. I guess I missed the personal touch of learning.

I'll explain. That element was prevalent throughout my high school years (I come back to that, time and again). The first university years were dominated by towering figures of intellectual grandeur; no personal touch there, and none expected – more often a kind of adulation, even adoration, quite fitting the abstract notions that were involved; bliss in a world of concepts.

Then in 1947 I met – I don't remember how it came about – the chairman of the meteorological department, Professor Ertel, who specialized in theoretical meteorology, that is, physics applied to the atmosphere. In many fields and sections of physics, there are neat solutions to simplified problems. But the physics applied to the atmosphere presents a very complex, fluid, thermo-dynamic problem. We hit it off personally, right from the beginning. He was a towering giant in his field; in his person he was short, over-weight, and very congenial. How he came to be overweight in that time escaped me, but he always had lots of cigarettes and was very generous with them. The department consisted of himself, one or two "assistants" (like assistant professors or TA's or something in-between), and about half a dozen students. None of them was interested in theory, but in the witchcraft-like art of weather fore-casting. And so, very soon, I became a student of his; I had indeed found another *refugium*, more personal than ever before. I spent more and more time in the institute which was in a West Berlin suburb, a small building right in the middle of the University School of Horticulture. I learned a great deal, just by discussions with Professor Ertel, and I believe he enjoyed our conversations. Most importantly, he made, time and again, numerous suggestions on what I should be reading.

Looking back, I made the right choice shifting to this department, even though I never practiced as a meteorologist. I didn't know it then, but if you study at a real university, not a glorified trade or craft school, it doesn't matter what you study. The substance are details; what you learn is how to think, methodologically, scientifically, maybe just in an orderly, that is, well-reasoned fashion – which has nothing to do with the horrible German obsession with "order." I didn't realize it then, but for example, if you're good at managing something, most likely you can manage anything. If you learn to deal with some aspect of something on a scientific basis, you can use the methods you've learned and apply them anywhere. You learn to solve problems in an intellectually adequate and acceptable fashion; you learn the nature of an explanation and specifically how to arrive at a scientifically acceptable explanation. Ultimately, it makes no difference what the subject matter of these problems is. When I graduated several years down the line, I was a certified meteorologist – a Diplom Geophysicist. For the purpose of an immediate job search, that may have meant something. In reality, I had behind me several years of very intense, personal contact with a brilliant theoretician in Physics, a man, who in his particular field, was quite unique in applying abstract concepts to that field. That is what he taught me, and as it turned out, it didn't matter what that field was.

I'll come back to Prof. Ertel time and again, and I will dwell on this quite a bit, but let me preview some aspects here. In a way, we were both living in a dream world separated from reality. He found his way to what he perceived to be a reality and that brought him, ultimately, into tragic conflict with authority. Remember, at that time, reality meant how you coped with the aftermath of the war; it has absolutely nothing to do with what today you understand reality to mean. Is this some philosophical gobbledegook? No, it is simply this: How Professor Ertel coped with that aftermath brought him into conflict with the authorities, and in effect, terminated a career which could have been brilliant and glorious. Possibly, I was fortunate (or sufficiently astute) enough to always pull myself back into reality and not let a dream world push me onto a path where coping with reality becomes impossible.

-29-

BERLIN IN THE LATE 40'S – THE BEGINNING OF TURMOIL

Now, I'll now turn to other aspects of my remembrance, only marginally to do with my studies, but they are the background against which important aspects for my higher education developed. First of all, the Humboldt University wasn't, at least where I was, a place of great black market activity, and my private "source" turned into a cocaine dealership; I didn't want anything to do with that, so in the summer recesses, I took some jobs. I'm not certain on the timing, but one summer, I took up with the construction department of the newspaper "Berliner Zeitung," which was in the East. The department was quite important because its function was to provide and to maintain facilities for the newspaper staff in downtown Berlin. I did some, let's say, rudimentary architectural work which was quite interesting in itself, but that's not the reason I relate this here.

The department was headed by a man with the unusual name Levis-Litzman. He was one of the Moscow returnees; he'd belonged to the so-called National Committee Free Germany[50]. I believe this group was founded by Fieldmarshall Paulus and a General v. Seidlitz. Paulus had been the commanding officer of the army that capitulated at Stalingrad. A timely retreat and consolidation of forces would have prevented that disaster. So, not surprisingly, he became very disenchanted with the Nazis and was joined by other officers in captivity, including Levis-Litzman, who'd been a pilot and was shot down over Russia.

The very existence of this group, which I'd heard of already during the war, posed a problem for me: namely, where is the dividing line between resistance against your own government, whose conduct is by civilized standards, criminal – and treason against your own people? I don't profess to know the answer, but I also must say that, to the extent I knew anything about the Soviet system, to me, these people were opportunists who tried to escape the hardship of being a POW in the Soviet Union. Well, so what, or where is the dividing line? In any event, I found it very interesting to meet a member of that famous/infamous but small group. I was impressed by his mild, friendly manner and nature – but then, a few years earlier, I had met an SS officer of the infamous Sonder-komandos, and he too was mild-mannered and friendly. Not then but later, it became clear that, for Levis-Litzman, this was just a "holding" position. A few years later, he became the commanding officer of the East German Airforce. Anyway, in my mind, he was an unscrupulous opportunist with no moral convictions, or else an individual with such strong convictions that he would do anything to further them, and be able to hide it behind the façade of a mild-mannered personality.

For my next job, I must reminisce a bit about the political scene. As summer of 1948 broke, the Western zones (not yet the Federal Republic of Germany) had a currency reform. There existed

---

50 National Komitee Freies Deutschland

a so-called Bi-zonal Advisory Board. I don't remember the exact timing; it doesn't matter. The German chief economic advisor, Prof. Erhart, waited for a weekend when all of his Allied "superiors" were out of town or whatever, and in one stroke, he abandoned, cancelled, whatever, *all* restrictive, economic regulations; no more clothes coupons, restrictions on use of raw material, etc. I believe that some food rationing continued, because there was still real scarcity (e.g. on account of war time depletion of stock). The main point was that industry was no longer regulated.

That Monday morning, the U.S. New Dealers and British Laborites called Erhart "on the carpet" and vehemently denounced his actions. They reminded him that, under the charter of this German Advisory Board, any significant changes in economic policy had to be approved by the military governments. Prof. Erhart acknowledged that and made his famous statement: "I didn't change any regulations, I just abolished them." By that time, it was too late to do anything about it; a floodgate had been opened, through which, not metaphorically but literally, goods were pouring. Nobody paid any attention anymore to any control of the supply and demand; the market had taken over: in fact, the black market had won.

On the Berlin political scene, the currency reform was the more overt action. It signaled to the world the de facto, economic split between east and west (just as 42 years later, the real unification of Germany occurred when the DDR in the East adopted the DM as its currency and thus ceased to have any say in monetary policy). The question was: how about West Berlin? The East answered with a currency reform of its own, which all but sealed its currency to one of inferior value. I don't remember who made the decision, but West Berlin became a part of the West Currency area.

The East "allowed" us to exchange a certain amount of the old Reichsmark into "East Mark," which we did to bring some order into the financial system; you couldn't just wheel in tons of Old

Reichsmark and convert it into New money. Be that as it may, West Berlin was now financially isolated from its Eastern Hinterland; we became an economic enclave. The eastern authorities – to wit, the Soviets – answered with the infamous blockade of West Berlin. Much has been written about it, and I want to limit this to my personal experience. However, I want to add here that my subsequent knowledge about the Potsdam conference assured me that U.S. president Harry S. Truman was indeed "guilty" of starting the Cold War by stopping cold Stalin's advance in Europe. This, of course, was consistent with his decision to counter the blockade by the airlift. He confronted Stalin with a position on what would be acceptable and what not; Stalin, obviously, wanted to test Truman on this, and Truman passed the test with flying colors. The airlift saved me and all the other West Berliners from who knows what. A balance was struck: The Soviets stopped the supply of food and other items to the German West Berlin population, but they didn't interfere with the movement of Allied troops and their supplies. Such an interference would have been an act of war. Stalin didn't dare to test Truman on this. So, the "raisin bombers" flew mission after mission into Berlin. It gave the Allied military a very convenient and realistic training ground for their airforce, accuracy and timing in matters of flight control, landing sequences etc. etc. Did it help them, a few years later, in Korea? I don't know, but I hope that the Allied bomber pilots' training in the Berlin airlift had some additional benefits concerning the survival of the free world.

Many more things happened in 1948 on a more general level; I'll come back to the more personal aspects of how we, the people, reacted to all this stuff. At some point, we had the first, real election; a municipal one at that time, but so what? I was eligible, that is, old enough to vote. The western Social Democrats found it more expedient to look for the New Dealers and the Laborites as their Allies, and to woo the western population by at least not embracing Marxism. At that time, they weren't quite ready to denounce it; that came later, when they realized their hopeless situation in the face of bourgeois giants like Conrad Adenauer, Theodore Heuss, Fritz Schäffer, Ludwig Erhart, and Kurt Kiesinger. At that time, the Social Democrats believed it was sufficient to be anti-Communist, and that proved to be the right card to play. Up to that election, the municipal authorities were strictly Communist-dominated. Unlike Vienna, downtown Berlin wasn't jointly administered by all the four powers calling the shots. So, the municipal administrative facilities were in East Berlin. We also had, throughout Berlin, elections for mayor and a city council; these were the first real elections, as far as I was concerned.

Still, looking back at them, I have some major reservations. Well, not that there were elections at all; this was something of major importance. No, my reservations cover something different. The Social Democrats fielded as "their" main candidate an individual who became quite famous, Ernst Reuther. I didn't know it at that time, but my own affiliation was differently oriented, which, at the moment, doesn't matter. It was obvious that this man – today we would call him the front-runner – would be elected with an over-whelming majority. However, he had been a Soviet henchman in the Ukraine, actively participating in the submission of the Ukraine under Soviet rule in the thirties, one of the bloodiest undertakings of this century which means a lot. After having done the bidding for his Soviet mentors, he left them. Quite possibly, there was an ounce of decency left in him, a mitigating circumstance perhaps, but far from becoming a qualifier as a champion of freedom. He left the Soviet Union, went into exile in Turkey, then came back to Germany. To this day, this man is, to me, a blatantly immoral, even criminal, opportunistic individual. But maybe this is a good opportunity to look at history in a cold, hard, realistic fashion.

Maybe at this and any other decisive juncture of History, such people are needed. Of course, I still wonder: didn't we have anybody available in the West of a more decent character to lead Berlin?

Possibly so, but maybe in critical situations, people of questionable nature are needed. Maybe another individual would have exhibited a more conciliatory nature (well, hold it right there; what is in the offing here is a person amenable to appeasement, and wasn't that one of the underlying causes of WWII?). Ernst Reuther, the former Bolshevik henchman, was, in the eyes of the Soviets, an unacceptable renegade. Oh, sure, he was the ideal anti-Nazi in almost everybody's eyes, but his being a renegade made him unacceptable to the Soviets; his early separation from them made him easily acceptable to the West. In fact, in that situation, his very unacceptability to the Soviets, while amassing a huge majority of votes, made him the ideal candidate to ensure the administration of Berlin's separation from the Soviet sphere of influence. Well, not quite; the Soviets, having won (at least in their own mind) the war, weren't going to give away the spoils of victory. Here we have a different way of looking at history. The former Ukrainian henchman of the Soviets became the champion of freedom in Berlin, right at the very moment the former Missouri gangster prodigy in the White House stopped Stalin in Berlin. Of course, the foregoing is a somewhat cynical assessment based on subsequent reflections; so, what does that have to do with my remembrances? I knew at that time some of Ernst Reuther's background, and I was confused about the background of Harry Truman and his association with the gangster Pendergast. For some reason, I didn't trust either of them and in retrospect, there were sufficient reasons. On the other hand, there's a direct recollection of what Ernst and Harry did, no question about it, and the question I raise is simply this: How come them? Do we really have to depend on crooks to fight other crooks?

-30-

BLOCKADE AND COMMUNIST TAKEOVER

After having "disposed" of general aspects of history, let me now turn to the details us folks "on the ground" were experiencing. Clearly, you won't find that in the history books; it would be too embarrassing for many. Here, I finally come to my second summer job as a student. In 1948, I worked as a statistician for the Berlin municipal administration. Today, you would call it computer programming, except there were no computers yet. There were, however, machines for tabulating statistical data and they, too, had to be programmed and I worked with them; quite interesting stuff at that time. Where these machines came from I don't know, but that isn't important. What was important was, without my knowing it, for the first time, I was exposed to the real world of data processing and liking it. Little did I know that, for the most part of my professional life I would be working in this field. But, at that time, my job duties and experience weren't that important. Much more important was the location of my job – it was downtown Berlin, just a few blocks away from the Red Town-hall of Berlin, which had miraculously survived. That town hall housed the newly-elected Berlin administration; there were hardly any Communists, but a majority of Social Democrats, and Christian Unionists, the bourgeois coalition of anti-Nazi anti-socialist movement. One day in the summer of 1948, I saw a well-organized group of "spontaneous demonstrators" walk through the city streets towards the town hall. These demonstrators were under the protection of the Soviet police, as I could clearly see from the window. The police were supposed to protect the city officials from an unruly mob; instead, they participated in the mob disposing of the duly elected city government.

So, I witnessed an occasion quite similar to the mob scenes in Berlin in 1919, in St. Petersburg in 1917, in Paris in 1789 and in Prague at about the same time. Maybe not that dramatic, but symbolically on the same footing. In a way, and even more important, what was being disposed of was a legitimately-elected city government, taking office after more than 12 years of Nazi dictatorship. Just a few weeks after its election, that government was disposed of by the Soviets, one of the victorious parties who had no better means to demonstrate that they were any better than those which a few years earlier had succumbed to them. I'll never understand how Germans could participate in that event. Here was a local government, the first that was freely elected after more than a dozen years in Germany; how could these people participate in such an act? Almost half a century later, pseudo historian Goldhagen blamed the German people as a whole as being imbued with the inclination to impose terror upon Jews. I was flabbergasted to see this spectacle. Were we Germans really that bad, just replacing one dictatorship with another, without any moral reservations? I've learned a lot since then, particularly that the same kind of danger lurks everywhere, in all countries; nobody is immune from the effect of mob mentality.

The deposed city government re-assembled in West Berlin, in the Rathaus-town hall of Schöneberg, which I mentioned earlier. Now what? Berlin was split into halves, and the Western sectors had their own administration under the newly elected city council and mayor. The Western sectors had their own currency anyhow, and the life-supporting goods were flown in. But let me say this: after almost fifty years, it's still very difficult to describe the situation. If I'd done so at that time, it probably would have been easier, except that I wouldn't have been fully aware of the craziness of the situation, and what I would have described then could readily have been discarded as complete gibberish. What I'm attempting to describe are, let's say, aspects of chaos. I want to be very precise on this. War, of course, is chaos, and when a war ends, the chaos persists to some extent, at least for quite some time. But that's a chaos induced by wanton, physical destruction, a chaos resulting from bombs, grenades, from the random action of people acting in a vacuum of lawlessness or even outright permissiveness, such as I have described. Now, I want to describe certain aspects of the chaos and how people coped with it.

History books describe the inauguration of the West Berlin city government as a triumph of the growing democratic order (the German obsession with order always shows through), which, of course, was true. Then, there was the orderly supply of food through the airlift etc., etc. But now, don't let that fool you. Earlier, it had already been the practice in Berlin that city folks traveled by train (by whatever train service was available after the Russians had removed the rails from one track of many two-track systems) into the countryside to procure additional food. The method was known as "hamstering." West Berlin was economically sealed from the Eastern Berlin sector as well as from East Germany (soon to become the German Democrat Republic, or DDR), but people from West Berlin could still travel there, in fact until 13 years later, when the infamous Wall went up. So, during the Blockade, people from West Berlin traveled freely into the Eastern zone to "hamster" food.

This was done two ways. In one, you brought along western goods. Where did they come from? Well, even during the blockade, western goods became "somehow" available in West Berlin so, you could barter. In addition, we in the West had DM West, which very soon established itself at around 4 to 5 times the value of the East mark. During the blockade years, the West German DM began to become the desirable currency in the east, a practice that still continues. With DM West you could buy food from the farmers in the East. Our handbag business had somehow come to a halt, and my mother's pension hadn't yet but would soon resume. But in the meantime, my mother went hamstering once a week or so. Now, I will turn to a rather interesting scenario.

In the East, there was kind of paramilitary police called the "People's Police." They set up checkpoints on railway stations to "inspect" people coming back from the East German hinterland, and took food *away* from the people, an act of outright governmentally-instituted theft. Was that just another example of the German obsession with order, or something else? Obviously, it posed a very difficult problem. They could have blocked the access to East Germany from West Berlin completely. But they didn't. Well, why not? The Communists in the East had just started to install their incompetent economic system and had, in a way, already capitulated. This stealing from the people was just another way of sluicing food, for which they didn't even have to pay, into their organized supply system. But letting a certain amount of food go through would encourage people to try to break the blockade. The Communists would take their share and let some go through. It's just as now, half a century later, the mafia runs Russia. In the late '40s in East Germany, the "authorities" weren't willing to make such concessions, so they had to re-channel the free market goods into the system of regulation. Well, the German obsession for order came in handy!

There are always flaws in any system, so there were ways around all this. I'll explain. First of all, even the strictest bureaucrats, or at least some of them and including even Stalinists, may have, at times, some human features left. It wouldn't look too good to take, say, from an elderly lady a few pounds of potatoes, a little bit of flour, some vegetable, so a certain amount of goods was allowed. What wasn't allowed was butter, eggs, meat. So the name of the game was to hide the good stuff in the potatoes etc, then get it through the check-point. Now, after this lengthy introduction (after all, I have to introduce the reader to all this insanity) I'll report how my mother did it.

My mother usually went – and I do not remember the reason for the original choice – to an area to the east of Berlin called "Oder-bruch." It's one of the areas which had been swampy but were drained by Fredrick the Great and rendered agriculturally useful. There were still farmers in the region; they hadn't been expropriated yet by the Communists but were a few years later. My mother found a particular village highly conducive to doing business. She bartered cloth material for whatever she could get. She claimed (may God pardon her the lie), that she got the material directly from British air-lift pilots. I think she also brought cigarettes, tea, and coffee, that was already, to some extent, available. For that, she got good stuff: butter, eggs (very tricky to transport) sometimes cheese (also tricky because of the smell), and homemade sausage. All that was hidden among potatoes usually, which, of course, were useful, too. Now, to get that past the checkpoints set up by the "People's Police," she used two methods.

The first one was based on a keen sense of observation. Each checkpoint had several lines, and intuitively she believed that not all of these border guards would be bastards. So, as she approached one checkpoint – I guess it was on her first hamster excursion – she took the chance with a man who she observed a bit and who looked to be a decent man. She showed him her backpack and boldly announced that she had only potatoes. She looked at him, he at her; would he believe her? Well, of course not, but would he do anything about it? No, he didn't; he let her go. From then on, somehow, she found out what his schedule was and timed her trips accordingly, to be "inspected" by him. This scheme worked almost throughout the blockade.

As an interesting aside, he actually came to visit with us in West Berlin, but not in a tit-for-tat fashion. He guardedly hinted that he may be interested in defecting, and we guardedly hinted that, of course, he would be welcome at any time, and we would do what we could to help him. I hope the reader will appreciate how ridiculous the situation was. We were being blockaded, and my mother was, in fact, a kind of blockade runner, and here came one of the blockaders, venturing into "enemy territory," hoping for assistance to escape from what on the surface was a superior position. But then one day, he was gone, and my mother never saw him again. Did he betray himself? I sure hope not.

But there was a second method of smuggling. During her trips, my mother met a guy who was certified insane. There were no insane asylums, and some people are only "marginally" insane (whatever that might mean). Now, get this: the German obsession with order led them to decree: If you were certified insane as evidenced by an appropriate document (of course!), you were allowed with impunity to transcend, or better, deviate from the existing order; that is to say, if you had such a certification, you could embark on disorderly conduct, behaving unruly and disrespectfully, barring physical violence. This guy was certified insane, and the authorities would just let him go and not excite him. This meant that, at a checkpoint, he just had to flash his "insanity certification" and was speedily waved through. He told my mother all this during one of the trips; my mother recognized that sticking with this guy would be advantageous. And so whenever that friendly guard wasn't on duty and later, after he had gone, my mother sort of hinted that she was with the "insane" guy and followed him closely through the checkpoint without having to show or say anything. I don't believe that anything was ever taken away from her; my mother was indeed a small-scale but successful blockade runner.

Now I turn to another aspect of the crazy lifestyle we experienced on account of the blockade and the currency reforms. I report more deeply into money matters and from a more organized perspective. The orderly German mind perceived that there was a problem. Many people living in the Western Sector worked in the east and were paid in East-mark, which meant their earnings would drop to less than 23% of a reasonable wage or salary. Conversely, people living in the East but working in the West made more than four times as much, if they changed their earnings at market value into East-marks. Altogether, there would a spread of 16 to 20 times between the real earnings of a secretary, a teacher, whatever, working in the East or in the West. The obvious remedy would have been that those living in the West but working in the East had to move to the East or find work in the West. But the bureaucratic mind (shrouded by a disguise of fairness), devised the following system. People living in the East and working in the West got, I think, only 20 or 25% in DM West; the rest, that is the bulk of their earnings were paid in East-mark on a one-to-one basis. The employer, of course, had to pay the full amount in DM West, but 75 – 80% to the government! How utterly disgusting, that these people had the West Berlin Government steal well over half of their earnings from them; surprisingly, the city government was still dominated by Social Democrats[51].

Look at it this way: in the East the government took away from the hamstering people what they had duly bartered, and the West government stole money from the easterners who worked in the West for the free enterprise system. Now, let's look at the other side of the coin. The governmental theft as outlined was "justified" thus: People living in the West but working in the East had the right to turn their low-valued East-mark earnings into West-mark on a one-to-one basis. Not all of it, just a certain amount, I think about 75 or 80%. Well, I shouldn't complain because my student job with the

---

51 To my way of thinking, Marxists are nothing but thieves, and at that time the Social Democrats still fit that bill.

municipal authorities paid me in East-mark, and I was allowed after some doing, to convert some of it 1 : 1 into West-mark. I fully realize that this was, strictly speaking, not right, but you took advantage of any loophole and I didn't make much. I then took about DM 40 West and at a rate of 1 : 5 converted into 200 East-mark and paid my tuition for the next semester. This now leads to another, and very interesting, extension of this crazy situation.

A friend of mine from the university (we still meet more or less regularly; he is, by now, a venerable retired professor) came from Pirna in Saxony, East Germany. We met at the Meteorological Institute. He really had nothing, but he had decided to live in the West, which was justified because the Meteorological Institute was in the western part of the city at that time. I don't remember the exact amount, but I think he was allowed to change 200 DM *East* into 200 DM *West*. I think he didn't have the 200 DM East, or not all of it. So, he had to borrow it, and after the 1 : 1 conversion by the West Berlin authorities, he took a portion of the West-mark and re-converted it into 200 DM East at the market rate of 1 : 4 or 1 : 5. Then he took another portion of his West-marks and converted it into 200 DM East at market rate, so that next month he had the 200 DM East to convert at 1 : 1 into DM West and so on and so on. Does this make any sense? Of course not, but I hope the reader understands that there is some insane logic to all of this: given the situation, you can always beat the system. I must add that this crazy scheme was strictly legal. But there's another side to this. Many functionaries of the East German state lived in the West, took advantage of the system, and had officially changed part of their east German salary converted 1 : 1 into DM West and then traveled (often by chauffeur-driven limousines) into East Berlin, working to the best of their ability to destroy the capitalistic system from which they greedily and without compunction benefited.

-31-

COMMUNIST TAKE-OVER, AT THE UNIVERSITY

I now return my story to the University and my studies in general. I don't recall exactly when we had student body elections – the first and the last ones; a number of candidates offered to serve as student representatives, and in open meetings, they gave campaign speeches. By popular demand, they were forced to state party affiliations, if any.

As a consequence, all Communist candidates were soundly defeated. I don't remember whether this student representation ever had any influence on anything[52]. I remember that the student representation in later years was chosen quite differently, either appointed, or where only "acceptable" candidates were allowed to run; obviously, the East German administration couldn't tolerate this kind of a freely elected representation.

On a more personal level, the following events stand out. At some point in 1948, the so-called Freie Universität, Free University was founded, with its locations in West Berlin. It became clear that

---

52 Probably not; the communists were too well versed in stifling any and all opposition.

the Humboldt University would soon be Communist-dominated. The founding of the FU evoked strong interest in me, but what bothered me, right from the start, was that, in Mathematics and Physics, the professors who opted for the FU were strictly second rate; the top people stayed with the Humboldt University. Why they did so I'll never know, but it greatly confused me. More important to me was Prof. Ertel's decision to stay with Humboldt. In this case, it actually meant moving the Institute from the West Berlin / Dahlem location to some location in the East. Even though we were quite close and he was by no means a Communist in an ideological sense, I never understood his tacit, anti-American position. He'd been in Chicago in his thirties, and something must have happened which he never "forgave." If he'd stayed in the West, with or without the facilities of that Institute, he would have immediately become a dominating figure in the new FU. Never mind that meteorology was a kind of obscure field; he would have been, by far, the most prominent individual in physical sciences. Instead, he moved the Institute to the East and became a noticed member of the so-called Academy of Sciences – modeled after a similarly named Soviet Institution. He decided, however, to have apparently a sham residence in the West to convert most of his East salary 1 : 1 into DM West. He was caught in 1961, shortly before the Wall was built, spent several years in jail, and died shortly thereafter. What a miserable way of ending a career that could have been culminated in a towering position of honor.

But at the time, I was caught in the middle. I'd hoped he would stay in the West but, mindful not to close out options and further mindful that in the beginning of the FU there was no meteorological institute, I moved with Prof. Ertel to the new facilities in a rather posh area in the East, a villa right on the Müggelsee, the largest lake in the Berlin area. There was a garden, a beachfront, and otherwise ample space for a library lecture space and study places for students, offices for Professor Ertel and for his major assistant. Even though it was now an hour train ride for me each way, and almost half an hour walk from the closest train station to the lake front, I was again in a wonderful environment for studying. So I stayed. Fortunately I didn't have to compromise myself with Eastern authorities. All of my fellow students stayed – which may account for the fact that a meteorological Institute for the FU was missing for some time. Soon, foreign lecturers would visit us in the Müggelsee quarters; other former students of Ertel appeared and took jobs as research assistants. Apparently, they came in the wake of the then-unfolding anti-Americanism among some intellectuals.

Still, at some time in 1949, I applied for admission to the FU, just as an option. There was some rather perfunctory kind of admission procedure, and there was no problem to being admitted except that I was now more fully aware of the second-rate aspects of the natural science school (there is no real equivalent translation for the German term "Fakultät"– it is something in-between a "school" and a "department"). The FU was expected to have a Meteorological Institute in the future, but that was apparently a strictly, pragmatically-oriented endeavor, little more than a trade school for weather forecasters. There just was no comparison to Ertel's theoretically-oriented department of atmospheric science. This was the pre-computer age, and the later star of the Western Institute, Prof. Sherhag, had not arrived on the scene. So, I was admitted, but I respectfully declined. I was fully aware of the growing East-West split, about the rapidly declining chance for a united Germany at that time. And yet, I was still naïve (about 21 years old) and didn't fully realize that my opting to stay with Ertel and with the intellectual challenge he offered would lead to a dead-end in terms of job prospects, unless I worked in the East and continued to live in the West. Ultimately, I believe I made the right choice to continue my education and involvement in theory and concepts to a demonstrable finish – a master's thesis, at least. Thereafter, I made a break (i.e. after I had completed the task I had set out in 1946 to get a University education in as best a way

I could get). So, in 1949, I continued my almost daily or at least rather frequent sojourn to the Müggelsee *refugium*, a period of study and discussions with Ertel at an increasingly more interesting level.

A decisive event in the spring of 1949 was, of course, the lifting of the blockade. As seen from West Berlin, it was an event which if you saw it in a movie, you would dismiss it and say: "Oh sure; but that's just a movie." But the reality was remarkable. That the blockade was about to be lifted was known for at least several days, even weeks. As it was announced, on the morning the blockade was off, a large fleet of trucks embarked upon Berlin, and freight trains began to roll in; by nightfall, the stores were full. Where emptiness had reigned for about a decade, goods were piled upon goods.

Of course, capitalism is what it is, an economic system, and not a philanthropic enterprise; we soon found out that lots of the stuff dumped on the Berlin market consisted of items the West Germans were already sick of or that didn't meet their standards (you can get fussy very quickly). I guess just as the Marshall Plan, good as it was, was a convenient way to dump "surplus" goods on the European market, it really didn't matter: who cares, there is nothing wrong with making money and getting rid of stuff if people actually need it[53].

The differentiation between East and West became visible literally over night, with the end of the blockade. The stores in the Western sectors were full, with rationing soon abolished. I still have my last rationing card, only partially used. Most noticeable was the influx of clothes, sorely needed after all these years, and even more important, shoes.

The East remained drab, though I remember that the Eastern authorities tried to get stuff into East Berlin to mitigate a little the discrepancy; but that, too, was fruitless. They did, however,

---

53 This is not the place to belabor the point, but as far as Germany is concerned, the Marshall Plan was primarily psychological; it appeared that its monetary significance was close to being insignificant.

decontrol staples like potatoes and bread and vegetables – we in the West soon had chocolate, bananas and oranges; the East had to make do with carrots and turnips. For me, however, this was an added, readily-fulfilled duty.

With cheap East-marks, I bought whatever stuff I could get on my way from the Müggelsee Institute to the railway station. Controls were abolished at that time, and I had no problem getting the stuff into West Berlin. But then the East instituted something which, in one form or another, pervaded the Eastern bloc countries. One aspect was the special stores for the Communist bigwigs, in which only they could shop (in the class-less society!). Later, that was supplemented or replaced with valuta stores in which, get this, you could use only foreign currency (e.g. Dollars or DM) to buy things. The rest of the population wasn't allowed to possess that foreign currency. Also, and well before this, the East instituted a kind of legalized black market; there were stores and primarily restaurants called HO, in which you could buy, at much higher prices, "real" coffee and eat "Butter-creme-tarts." I don't believe you could buy western goods such as clothes, except in the Dollar Stores. The price was that in DM East what you would pay in the West, considering the free market exchange ratio 1 : 4 or 5. If (I forgot exactly) a cup of coffee was 50 Pfennig West, then in the HO restaurant you would have to pay 2.50 to 3 East-marks, I think; however, it was even a bit more expensive. What a fine system of socialism!

-32-

THE SPLIT WIDENS – NOW WHAT?

A t home, the situation had improved since my mother again got her pension; the rooms were still rented out and, believe it or not, for a year or two,Waldschul-Chef Krause, then widowed, lived in our house. However, my mother, who had a strong-willed personality, clashed with the autocratic Krause, so he left. Financially, we were safe, and the currency differential helped a great deal. Why my mother didn't take at least a part time job I don't know, and it wasn't for me to ask; maybe the two of us were a match in arrogance.

This is a good place for some kind of cultural interlude. Very soon, Berlin became a cultural battleground, heavily subsidized – until the Wall came down which prompted all kinds of closures. I don't remember when it started – most likely not before 1948 – but I began to frequent the theater, not too often, but for select and memorable performances. *Faust* with Gründgens; *Macbeth* with Walter Frank, *Natan the Wise* with Ernst Deutsch, *The Flies, Mary Queen of Scots*, by Sartre come to mind. These very peaceful enjoyments were augmented by shows with Theodore Bickel and Marcel Marceau.

Then, there were art exhibits that had previously been forbidden as degenerate, and clearly, the lack of an adequate education on that particular era showed up. It was years later (many more years of maturing?) that I began to enjoy intelligently Kandinski, Chagall, Picasso, Matisse. I then enjoyed particularly Schmitt-Rottluf and remember that, years ago, I had been at a special exhibition in the National Gallery and how singularly boring that stuff was that had been deemed appropriate for Germans. I regret particularly that I lost out on music, not due to the war but to the incompetence of teaching. My mother was totally disinterested, no stimulus there, and in school, the completely incompetent music teacher taught us nothing. Added to that was the often-boring radio program that reduced classical music to little more than background sound; still added to that was third-rate, boring dance music with a few exceptions like songs by Zarah Leander and Ilse Werner. That changed, of course, after the war, but my interest in "serious" music was kindled much later, really not until I lived in Los Angeles, listening to live music, as well as having a good sound system.

In 1950, I began to work on my master's thesis; still there were the trips to the Müggelsee institute; it was easier to work there than at home, as it was crowded. In the Institute, there was the normal contact with others, debates (never political ones), and seminars. My personal contacts with Prof. Ertel were ever so engaging. I had the feeling that, indeed, he was grooming me to become his successor. I was ambivalent, fearing the day I had to make a choice between politics and what was obviously a very promising career. On the local level, I had no competition; my fellow students had other interests. The main assistant to Prof. Ertel was interested in Paleo-climatology; why he was the assistant, I don't know, maybe to balance a bit between the esoteric subject of theory and the even more esoteric subject of what the weather and the climate was in the past. I was heading, academically, in the right direction; I wouldn't become assistant right away, but as soon as the other man had his professorship, which he did a few years down the road, the path would be clear. I simplify things a bit but with the exception of a Dr. Schmitz, I had no competition. But Schmitz was older and would wait until Ertel retired (at least that was my impression). A potential, "theoretical lacuna" was staring at me, and I was heading to filling it. I put it intentionally into these stark terms, where the road seems all but a foregone conclusion. Of course, there's always another side of the coin.

Already in 1949 but more so in 1950, the political polarization became ever more noticeable. What exactly does that mean? To anybody who was willing and able to look at the unfolding socio-political scenario, it became increasingly obvious that if you contemplated making a career in the East, in the soon-to-be founded DDR, you had to kowtow to the system. Again, what does that mean? Did you have to compromise your personal integrity? Why should you? I'll explain how I gradually became aware of this.

Professor Ertel was already a member of the DDR-to-be establishment, as a member of the Academy, as I mentioned. Did they fully accept him? I doubt it; they accepted only their political cadres, indoctrinated Communists. The rest were useful tools. Undoubtedly, he knew that he was an internationally respected scientist, and they used him in this regard. Now, one day, he explained to me how science worked in the Soviet realm. If you were a scientist in the Soviet Union (and by implication, the same would soon be true in the DDR), you submitted a plan for research projects which you would undertake. However, this plan included lots of stuff you had already completed, that is, where you already knew the result. Additionally, not included was stuff you reasonably could expect to complete, as well as further projects. After you submitted that plan, you worked on something else, namely the stuff you hadn't submitted but expected to complete and then on the next project. Now after a year, you reported on your accomplishments, through submitted publications or otherwise. Of course, you'd fulfilled the plan because you'd completed it before, but lo and behold, there was some of the additional stuff you had accomplished; so, you had over-fulfilled your plan. The next year, the whole scheme (or shall I say, charade) was repeated. Do this for a while, and you sure will get the Stalin prize, Lenin Order of Merit, or whatever. Do I sound ridiculous?

Indeed I do, as it's a ridiculous system from an outsider's point of view. Admittedly, it was a clever scheme on part of the intelligentsia to beat the system. While living with it, you live with a maximal scope of expectations and rewards. It became very clear to me that, if I embarked on an academic career in the East, that is exactly the kind of atmosphere I would have to live with. Admittedly, the full scope of such a degrading way of life hadn't completely sunk in. Disgusting as it is, it wouldn't, however involve intellectual compromise. What do I mean by that?

To Professor Ertel and me and others it was also clear that there was no such thing as bourgeois, Western, anti-worker meteorology. It rains or shines on kings, capitalists, and workers alike, and neither class has a preferred handle on how to predict rain. In this ridiculous fashion, I want to introduce the fact that, by and large, the Communists kept out of the field of natural science. In other words, you could practice pragmatic meteorology, as well as theoretical meteorology, physics, mathematics, geology, without running afoul of Marxist doctrine. Or could you? The Communists didn't repeat directly the Nazi mistake introducing the notion of Jewish physics and mathematics. Isolated instances of outright aberration did occur, notably the Lysenko Biology with its catastrophic results for Soviet agriculture. But would that always be the case? In 1950, it so seemed, and it was difficult to assess the scope of Communist nonsense on a "practical" level. And I was suspicious.

On a more subtle basis and sometimes not so subtle, new students began to appear, quite different in character. Obviously, political correctness had become, well, maybe not yet a requirement

but an admission-promoting feature. They, of course, were spout-
ing their Marxist Communist garbage, the political party line etc.
Whereas before politics was taboo, except with friends, it made me
aware that I was heading towards a system in which, to a considerable extent, I would not only be surrounded by opportunists, but by
people who were believing the lies and mouthing the party line. Also,
I suspected that these people would compromise their intellectual
integrity whenever the party line required it. At that time I didn't
fully understand the ramifications. At that age – I was 22 – you see
things much more in black and white. But the handwriting was on
the wall. With increasing allusions to Marxism / Leninism as an
attempt to subvert natural sciences, there was clearly an attempt to
introduce the notion that you had to be a Marxist-trained individual to practice science for the benefit of the masses. Falsification of
scientific results wouldn't be too far away (I'll come back to that in
an interlude shortly).

So, towards the end of 1950, I was faced with this decision: can
I, with impunity, tie my professional life to the Humboldt University
as a place from which to launch an academic career? I wasn't aware
of any particular intellectual compromise I would have to face and
no matter that nonsense was sprouted concerning Marxist ideology, I was firmly convinced that practicing theoretical meteorology
would remain free from such intrusions. Much more basic, I began
to realize that the Communist system was just another system of
stifling control. I suspected at least that, in the offing, there would
be an attempt to introduce in some form the notion of a "bourgeois
science," never mind that in meteorology, this would be overtly
nonsense. However I began to realize (then! not 50 years later) that
no matter what your response in a specific field, you would practice
science in an environment in which you have to pay lip service to
whatever the power structure deemed to be politically correct. You
may be surrounded by people who kowtow to whatever epistemic
nonsense the powers that be dictate, and your intellectual life would

be little more than a continuing attempt to get around that. The latter analysis is, of course, the result of later reflection, but I claim that, at that time, at least intuitively, I recognized this to be the problem, particularly after beginning to see what kind of new students entered the academic system; in addition, there would have been the scenario of being constantly surrounded by the opportunists, henchmen, goons, and even true believers of that system – and after some long and hard reflection, I decided to finish my studies as fast as possible and stay out of that realm.

Now please forgive me, but years later I found that, in the contemporary intellectual scene in the free world, a frightening parallel emerged. The Frankfurt school and others of the so-called post-modernism seem to succeed where the Communists didn't. I had been wrong, I could have practiced theoretical meteorology without Marxist interference, but to gain a professorship without at least overtly paying lip service to that ideology wouldn't have been possible, or at least unlikely. But I could have always counted on the truth of mathematics and the pragmatic empirical approach of true scientists. Today, however, with post-modernism raising its ugly head, political-correctness simply wants to do away with any form of objectivity, replace it with social relevancy (beneficial to the masses) and replace scientific truth (or probability), even objectivity, with socially negotiated ideas, notions etc, etc. Frightening!

-33-

NOW WHAT; A CAREER CHOICE?

Towards the end of 1950, I was completing my dissertation and was heading towards a degree in Meteorology; actually, it was a degree in geophysics with emphasis on atmospheric physics. Whatever the label, I clearly seemed to have the option of becoming a meteorologist in one of two ways. I could have sought out a graduate position at the Freie University, which didn't have any graduates at that time. The alternative was to become a weather forecaster. Let me begin with the latter; here, I faced two problems. One was clearly my arrogance: I was a theoretician and not a weather forecasting craftsman like a frog. That arrogance was, in part, no doubt my nature, but it was also acquired from Prof. Ertel. He once published a paper delineating that an accurate weather forecast not covering the entire surface of the earth is impossible in principle, something that didn't endear him to his colleagues. But I knew that his position was theoretically sound. Weather forecasting, via computer programs yet to be written, was generally a thing of the future. But from a practical point of view, I faced a different situation.

Unknown to me, in earlier times, in the early forties when Germany was conquering step by step most of Europe, airfields were

240

built everywhere. Considering the general flimsiness of airplanes (by present-day standards) weather forecasting for flight routes was vital. It didn't matter much what the weather was tomorrow, rain or shine. Rather, it mattered a great deal what weather conditions planes would encounter within a few hours, and when they would (hopefully) return. Forecasts on that level were quite good already. With this at stake, Germany had found itself suddenly woefully short of meteorologists to staff the airfields (and probably flight controllers, maintenance people etc. etc). So meteorologists were trained in large numbers during the war using crash programs of fairly mediocre scientific basis.

Look at this pragmatically: what a way out for a young, scientifically-motivated man – I understand that science teachers were sought after – facing otherwise the drudgery and danger of military service in Russia, the Balkans, and elsewhere. So, a disproportional number of meteorologists were trained during the war. In the mid-forties, there was a reversal of German military fortune, and with it went the airfields. At war's end, of course, no airfields. The Allies availed themselves of these locals (they had to staff their airfields all over the world), but meteorology was certainly not the field of the future. Realizing that, I didn't even try to compete with this army of people who, even though not necessarily the best trained, did have a lot of experience; there was a lot of "witchcraft" and guessing involved anyway. My theory-oriented arrogance made the decision even easier.

And now the alternative. In the meantime, at the beginning of 1951, the FU had to some extent taken off. In retrospect, I made a rather short-sighted decision; there were no graduate students at the FU, and I could have written my own ticket. I had the basis for computer programming (though that didn't exist at the time) called numerical analysis, and I had studied certain solutions to problems which, in retrospect, were nothing short of an algorithmic analysis of the equation underlying air flow dynamics. Had I known about

computers at that time I'm sure my decision would have been different; it was just a few years too early. On the other hand, I still
wasn't so secure in my field that I could have dared to undertake
a doctoral program in an Institute almost completely devoid of a
genuine theoretical posture.

So with my graduation in 1951, my academic career came to a
halt, when in fact it hadn't really begun yet. Now what? Looking for
a job still didn't occur to me. Instead, I made some contact with the
Technical University, concerning fluid dynamics, and lo and behold,
I made contact with a Professor Mohr. We worked on a project on
the side for a year or so; he offered me a position as assistant, for DM
125, which didn't entice me very much. Through an acquaintance, I
learned about a position in a patent department of the AEG corpo-
ration, the second largest company in the electrical field. What in
the world was that? I had a vague notion of what a patent was, but
it had something to do with engineering and obviously well beneath
me. But why not take a look?

I approached the matter as a biologist may look at new species
of insects. I had an interview with the chief of patent department
(whatever that was), a very cordial, tall, and rather voluminous man,
and he offered me a position for DM 325 that would begin with
research. Well, that didn't sound too bad. I was impressed that he
made this offer just on the strength of my University Diploma, and
he was not in the least bothered by my specific background, having
studied atmospheric physics. I accepted – what did I have to lose?
I could always quit and frankly, since I had no knowledge of engineering (and some disdain at that) I expected to be fired within a
few days, and I figured they would have to pay me anyhow sufficient
to buy a shirt or two.

So on April 1st (as I remember it), I started that job in an environment very different from the academia I was accustomed to. As
I was told, I was supposed to do research, that is do some searches.

I realized that if I found out what I was supposed to be looking for, I would be alright. I put it into simplistic sounding terms because I didn't really know what searching in the patent field meant.

Three things became very clear to me. The stuff of interest was only a fraction as difficult as what I had been accustomed to while studying (and they would me pay for that!); my physics background, particularly good old Papa Gerthsen's lectures and notes from the first two semesters, provided ample background for the requisite understanding; and "patent people" knew that the patent field was rather obscure, so they expected, as a normal course of events, that they had to train people on the job.

I wasn't fired. They had just looked for someone with a solid, scientific background, never mind the field particulars. It was then that I first got the inkling that the substantive details of what you'd studied didn't matter much; what mattered was how you look at a problem and how you approach its solution. Since I'm a fast learner (I was at that time; almost 50 years later, it's sometimes a little slower), I found very quickly what I was supposed to or was expected to, if it in fact, existed. What we were looking for was novelty of inventions somebody had made in the company. But what intrigued me from the start was that the search was not limited to some nitty-gritty detail, but some concept, some idea in the technical realm. Gradually, I became aware that this was really right up my alley. So, without really understanding it, I was from the start familiarized with what patenting an invention was all about.

In order to make some sense of all this, it's necessary to give some kind of exposé about a company's patent department – what is it exactly? Initially, I didn't know, but found out very quickly. Whenever an individual in an industrial company has an unusual idea, fooled around with some instrumentation or meticulously worked some set up, or just tinkering and observed something unexpected, an invention may have been made. That invention may be entitled to legal protection, in the sense that others may not be allowed to use the idea and this or even other uses. A company's patent department's main function and purpose is to make sure that the ideas and uses developed by its employees with the company's money are being adequately protected for the company's benefit[54]. The controlling concept is, if you hadn't used the employer's facilities you wouldn't have been able to make the invention in the first place. And so my first job was to check whether ideas / uses, submitted often extremely sketchily, were really new; if not, there was no invention. If the subject matter is found on the basis of such a search / research to be novel, protection was sought for it. The career prospect that opened up for me was to do exactly that: to secure patent protection for such an idea. It dawned on me rather quickly that the protection sought was not that some lever is connected to some rivet etc. or some electric circuit element connected to a specific other, but protection sought was for the underlying concepts independent from the way it was used. That's a mouthful: it simply meant that I with my esoteric background in dealing with concepts was in at least as good a position, possibly even in a way better, equipped than engineers who had studied a multitude of nitty gritty details. And so I became a patent engineer.

After this rather abstract introduction, I'll be a bit more realistic and down to earth, except why should that interest you; and here, I will, at first again, be a bit general. I was, for a variety of reasons, at the right place at the right time. Unbeknownst to me and everybody else, the German economic miracle had just begun and I was in on it practically from the beginning. I won't bother you with economic abstractions but will describe the realities I faced and dealt with, and that fit into a general picture. Remember: in the beginning I said that I'll give an account, not as one of the policymakers and big wheels,

---

54 This is not the place to cover all of the ramifications and whether companies unduly exploit their inventors; Germany is the only country, as far as I know, in which employees are legally entitled to some compensation over and beyond their regular salary.

but as one of the people. So, simply, I will present a picture of how I and others on the bottom participated in this miracle.

When I said I was in on it at the right time, I mean this. The German Patent Office had been shut down with the end of the war but re-opened in 1949. Corporations had had to let their patent people go but had started reassembling them the next year, i.e. around 1950. AEG had done exactly that, rehiring all or most of their former patent engineers, and the department was in full operation (I'll explain why shortly). There was work aplenty, and it was time for them to look for new, younger people. In Berlin, I was their first hire from among the newly graduated; bear in mind that in general, hardly anyone graduated before 1950 – '51 because few, if any, had studied anything during the war. Soon, others graduated and joined the company, among them my then-to-become, long term friend Günter Keller. We hit it off right from the start and remained close until he died in a horrible car crash in 1975 (two cars – six people – no survivors). He was a few years older and was even more pragmatic than I was. When the time had come for him to be drafted, he looked around to volunteer for a service branch which ensured that he would always sleep in a white sheet-covered bed. So, he chose coastal artillery. They never shot where he was, and in 1945, there was a formal surrender to the British, almost with pomp and circumstances; he was home in Berlin fairly soon. He graduated from the TU as a physicist just a few months after I had. Soon, we were joined by a somewhat older fellow who had been in Stalingrad, was wounded and flown out in one of the last planes that left the besieged city; he, too, had just graduated as an electrical engineer. A little later, we were joined by a former naval officer who had also made it through the war but never talked about it. He had studied a bit before the war and had now finished as a mechanical engineer. Later came others, but we were, so to speak, the guard of the first hour. We shared the same office room together with two secretaries. Office space was still very sparse, though the facilities were very pleasant. AEG had taken over a former air-force building which had miraculously survived (I wonder why). We all embarked on a career as patent engineers. My original snobbism against engineering wore off, undoubtedly helped by an increasing paycheck. As I said, the DM 325 at first was soon raised to DM 385. Today, you have to pay that amount for one night in a hotel room, but at that time, you could get a room (without private facilities but running water) for DM 8 and I paid less than 10 Pfennig (1/10 of a mark) for the train ride to the Office (today DM 3.85). So the salary wasn't shabby at all.

As I've hinted already, the main reason for my being very satisfied with my job / profession – to the extent that I stayed with it for the rest of my professional life – was the subject matter which, as soon as I began to prepare descriptions of inventions deemed promising for protection in the right perspective, was always interesting. The challenge had very little to do with engineering, but more with the ability to extract from the nitty gritty workings of the "real" engineering, general aspects and underlying principles, to recognize the concepts, even if the "doers" themselves hadn't. It was like extracting from some physical concoction a kind of technical law, just as scientist extract from a concoction nature's laws of physics. Well-versed engineers, including engineering professors who worked for the company, had very much an idea of what they had been coming up with in the abstract. But that just added to the variety of what I was doing. I had very good rapport with "my" inventors, even though I can be very stubborn and opinionated; they understood what I was doing, and I believe I had an easier time at it than the straight-forward engineers. All this is not yet very exciting, but hold on.

The department had a number of senior patent engineers, namely, those who'd been re-hired following the restoration of the patent system in 1949. Soon, every one of them had one of us newcomers as an assistant or apprentice or what you may wish to call it. My mentor was a Dr. Barz; before he'd been rehired, he'd been

running a power station in the Russian-occupied zone, a job so stressful that he had suffered a stroke while still in his forties. But that
hadn't affected his mind and particularly, not his speech. He limped a
little, and one hand was a bit impaired. He was one of the most intelligent men I have come across; we got along splendidly. Each of the
senior engineers covered a certain technical field, and his was what
began to be known as industrial electronics. The transistor hadn't
yet made its debut (though Bardeen-Brattain-Shockley had already
invented something obscure). Industrial electronics was still clumsy
and cumbersome and looked at with suspicion by any "hard-boiled"
engineers used to dealing with relays and switches and stuff like that,
and not some funny electrons flowing somewhere invisibly. Now, I
come finally to my claim that I was "really" in on the beginning of
the German economic miracle; I've already described the personal
set up; now comes the real stuff.

The first aspect was this. I came in contact and worked with
engineers, many of whom had worked in the armament industry
and very diligently escaped being drafted as Nazi cannon fodder. In
one form or another, they had many ideas, some useful for the war
effort, some too premature. Now, they were, so to speak, let loose
to realize their ideas for peaceful purposes. As I learned, technical development consists only to a very minor extent of grandiose
schemes. For the most part, it consists of umpteen zillion little steps
of improvements. It may sound a bit pompous, but the cream of
German engineering embarked upon rebuilding their destroyed
homeland as best as they could, without governmental interference
but with a lot of hard work, and *that* was the "miracle." I can't tell
you how exciting that was, dealing day in and day out with clever,
dedicated people expounding principles that were soon underlying
new technologies and electronics. Even more exciting for me, Dr.
Barz began letting me deal with all the real, new stuff. My friend
Günter Keller was Dr. Steinbach's assistant, whose field was other
aspects of industrial control. Soon, Günter Keller and I were the

main experts in principles of control and feedback engineering (seems far down from atmospheric physics; well, not really, as it all is covered by differential equations).

Now I come to another aspect of the German economic miracle: where did the work come from that the people (and I) were doing? Of course, I can only speak for a field I became thoroughly familiar with. It has to do with steel production and steel-working. Most steel making and working facilities (e.g. rolling mills) had either been destroyed, or the Allies had "de-mounted" them (another word for stealing, looting and plundering) and carted them away and reassembled them elsewhere. So, almost the entire steel production and working industry had to be rebuilt including rolling steel into sheets and plates from which, among other things, to build automobiles. This steel rolling required very accurate control, or you waste steel and produce scrap. For this, for the first time, electronics was introduced, resulting on one hand in a lot of inventions I had to deal with, while on the other hand, these inventions revolutionized steel rolling. The process became much accurate than before; in other words, there was scrap-free production of very accurate steel plates and sheet with very accurate and uniform thickness. This, in turn, made steel plate and sheet production very economical, which in turn was reflected in a very economic production of Volkswagens, Mercedes and other cars. The competing industries elsewhere in the world thought they could make do with their outdated production facilities including the stuff dismounted and carted away from Germany. They had dug themselves into holes of their own making. This is just one aspect – chemistry and engine engineering are others – where novelty was forced upon the rebuilding German industry.

In my new career, I discovered that, as with most people, if I was interested in something, I was generally good at it, and when I was good at something, it interested me; that describes exactly my relationship to industrial electronics and feedback systems. But over and above that, I became interested in the legal aspect of the patent system and its ramifications. I also became interested in a basic discrepancy which Dr. Barz described to me: engineers think in continuing (steadily varying) concepts, while lawyers think in discrete, isolated concepts. Patent systems try to reconcile this discrepancy. So, as far as the giant AEG was concerned, I found myself in a unique position within their structure; unwittingly, I began to amass the most interesting technical aspects and opportunity to develop new concepts. Of course, I had no idea about this state of affairs. I observed that, with the exception of Günter Keller, my other colleagues, particularly those who had come in after the war and most of whom I haven't mentioned because they worked in other offices in West Germany, weren't working in technical fields of comparable promising excitement as where it developed.

I was amazed that most of my AEG colleagues weren't very or even only marginally interested in the excitement of technological advances. It puzzled me for a long time, and the only explanation I have is that there's a difference in working with technical improvements as just that, or seeing them as changes in underlying concepts. Well, what were they interested in? Possibly they were more "street smart" than I am, and I more idealistically naïve. I think they were, to a man, interested in social positions. All of those I knew who started their career in 1951 or later either died prematurely, moved out of the technical field, or became head of a patent department elsewhere; all except me. I was never interested in that kind of position. I was interested in managing concepts, not people. Not surprisingly, I was also the only one who went abroad with the main goal in mind of broadening my horizon of knowledge.

-34-

AGAIN, VACATION BUT WITH A DIFFERENCE

As long as you're in school or the University, the concept of vacation has a meaning of its own. It is a break between one period of learning and the beginning of the next one. It isn't in the least a matter of merit, nothing you have earned, just a period of time in which you do something else or nothing. While I was in the Waldschule (have you observed that, time and again, I come back to it) these breaks in the school year were often confusing. Not early on, when they were associated with trips to Bunzlau, my mother's home town, the Silesian mountains, a trip to the Alps, to the sea, some glamorous experiences and memories of staying in fancy inns, even hotels or grand hotels. But as the war progressed, these periods of no-school were confusing. Some funny work in 1942, then the *de facto* evacuation from Berlin to Bunzlau in '43 (could one go home again, did the bombing stop?) then furlough in 1944, a very precious time away from the military, a little bit of normalcy. Then nothing of the sort after the end of the war: we had school from June '45 to the Abitur. Then came the to-do with getting into the University, some job assignment to clear away rubble. I've talked about some jobs in between semesters, the construction department, a job as statistician with the municipal administration; in 1949, a job with Ertel doing some calculations and then, of course, the final stretch was just working on my master's thesis. And so leading up to 1952, I'd earned my first vacation, meaning I didn't have to go to the office and still got paid – unbelievable.

Now, going on vacation or otherwise travelling out of and back into Berlin presented a problem for many years – you had to travel through the east, i.e. the Russian-occupied zone. There was the so called "Interzonenzug"[55], with checking when you left Berlin and again when you left the Russian zone (now called DDR) and the same stuff on the way back[56]. I wasn't going to do that. The alternative was flying out of Tempelhof Airport, which I decided to do. It was somewhat more expensive, a lot more than a third-class ticket. Actually, by that time, nobody in my job (i.e. the patent department) had for any reason used the plane, into and out of Berlin.

Being the snob I was, the price didn't deter me. So in July 1952, I embarked on my first real vacation. At that time, flying was generally still something quite special. No mass tourism, no X-raying of baggage, no hurrying and crowding of any kind. My mother brought me to the airport by taxi, and there we had a leisurely meal in a pleasant, quiet, half-empty restaurant; no mass-feeding of a bunch of irate passengers whose flight was delayed. Then I boarded for my first plane ride. It was a DC-3, the plane that had made aviation history before the war and really began air travel. You entered from the rear through a flap-down door serving as a ladder and walked upstairs in the rather narrow plane to your seat. Then came the take off. Seeing Berlin for the first time from the air, the Grunewald, the Havel River, into the clouds and the sky, and most importantly,

---

55 Inter – zone – train

56 If you had a car, you could drive; I don't remember when that began, but the checking and control was the same, later actually worse.

into a very satisfying mood, was remarkable. I wasn't there because somebody sponsored me, or somebody ordered me and paid for it. I had paid for it, and I flew out of Tempelhof, the very place where I had been a few years earlier as a prospective Soviet POW. When we winged out of Berlin, a safe distance from the Russian zone, I finally experienced something you may call the pleasure of life, very, very different from the life I had been forced to live for so long.

I flew to Hanover and caught an express train (D-Zug) to Munich. The train ride from Hanover was another post-war first; the ride I had taken into the east zone in 1946 had little in common with this one, even though it was third class. But there were many vacationers like I was. No more hamstering, no refugees, just people out to have a good time – what a concept! After 50 years, it's hard to comprehend what a big deal all this really was.

We arrived in Munich early the next morning, then I took a train into the Alps, pretty much the same route I had taken 11 years prior, and I remembered it because nothing had changed there.

I stayed for only a few days at that location, enjoyed a ride into and visit to Innsbruck, a ride up a high mountain, the wonderful Maria Theresa street (not yet mobbed with tourists). Tourism was very much in its infancy since the end of the war, and the service was good accordingly. It was also reasonable: DM 7 to 9 for a room and three meals[57]. And then I went deeper into the Alps. After an unforgettable ride through the Inn valley and a bus ride, I arrived at a little village, Gaschurn, unbelievably picturesque. A real vacation. Let me relate two quite different experiences.

I stayed in the inn on my own. Group travel, usually by bus, was becoming popular, mostly for price reasons; such a way of organized travel I hadn't considered at all. However, in the inn, there was a group of people my age, not organized officially. I don't remember

---

57   At that time the equivalent of about $2.

how they got together, but I joined them; they were from the Stutt-
gart area which I found interesting, I was from Berlin which they
found interesting, and there was a girl I found interesting and, I
believe, vice versa. We took nice excursions together; all that seemingly not a big deal, but then, this was also their first real vacation
and so, yes, it was a big deal.

The other interesting event was a joint day excursion to Zurich,
Switzerland. We were fairly close to the border along Lake Zurich
and some very picturesque mountain range. And there, in Zurich, I
experienced a large city, a metropolitan center but without ruins. At
home, in the suburbs of Berlin and in Bunzlau during the war, there
were few or no ruins, But that is very different from a metropolis.
Now in Zurich, I saw, for the first time in well over 10 years, an
intact city; I walked through streets flanked by majestic, rich-looking
buildings and not burnt-out façades or rubble. What a difference
from the walk to and from the Humboldt University. Right now,
after so many years, I still feel the emotion seeing something intact
and seeming to offer a very hopeful future, of a life that was not
downtrodden by having to make do with what there happened to
be, of a life that had some kind of continuity. The beginning of my
trip by airplane was a fitting companion to this experience. Walking
through Zurich, I promised myself that I would return, and in a
general, as well as specific way, I kept that promise.

In fact, I kept that promise the very next year. I became aware
at that time (i.e. about a year-and-a- half at my job) that planning
for the future was no longer an exercise in illusion, an unrealistic
dream. So, no sooner had I returned from Austria that I began to
plan my 1953 vacation into Switzerland because I believed that there
were several of the most beautiful sights in the world. I also began to
realize I could afford it. Of course, the saying still holds that the Swiss
built nice mountains around their expensive hotels. So, I planned
this trip with a degree of particularity, bordering on the ridiculous
and never again achieved, but it paid off.

Please understand the setting. I made between DM 400 and 500 per month. Inflation hadn't begun yet, but even for a modest hotel / inn in Switzerland, I had to pay DM 20 for a room and 3 meals. I bought an excursion rail pass and then there was the flight, this time from Berlin to Frankfurt, and then the trip by train to Zurich, still third class (or was it called 2nd then? Anyway, not for long). I will soon describe the tour, because even by today's standard it was fairly remarkable, but I must share a kind of family matter.

I had an uncle, well, not really an uncle, he was the son of a sister of my paternal grandfather. That grand aunt, who'd married a professor of Sanskrit, had moved to Zurich and there his son, this uncle / second cousin, held a chair in ancient Indo-European languages. When I started to study, I had written him asking him for advice and possibly some assistance, secretly hoping that maybe I could study a year or so in Zurich. His answer was a very arrogant rejection, sort of hinting that Germany was intellectually finished anyhow, after the excursion into Jewish Physics and Mathematics. Pride on my part prevented me from replying but I promised myself that I would contact him again after I received my diploma. This I did in 1951, slyly asking him to be so kind to keep a copy of my diploma; after all, the Cold War was in the works, the Russians were around the corner etc. I didn't have to say it in my letter, the diploma said it for me, that I had passed summa cum laude. He promptly wrote back a very nice letter: of course, he would safeguard the diploma and invited me to visit them whenever in Zurich. And so in 1953, my first stop in Zurich was a visit to my uncle and his wife. He turned out to be a genuinely nice person. He showed me Zurich, and we had long talks, very different a person from what one could have surmised from our first contact. We kept up the communication for quite a while.

Following the visit with my uncle, I now continued on my vacation (i.e. the "real" trip began). Considering the times, it was just my second vacation, and hardly anybody in my office or even generally traveled at that time. Foreign countries were too expensive, people had different interests. And other things were more important – after all, many people had to buy everything new and had to pay "participating money" for getting into an apartment – a legal rip-off of the first order. Travelling still had an aura of exclusivity, and I planned to make the most of it, leaving nothing to chance and to maximize my pleasure as a returning visitor. I dwell on this a bit, because today you find comparable tours offered in package form, but I didn't have any "model" trips to go on (nobody I knew had done anything similar). I planned this to a point that seems ridiculous. I even planned in advance on which side of the train I would sit to maximize the view prospects.

Leaving Zurich, I went to Lucerne, took a boat ride, "did" the city, and spent the night in a hotel whose ancientness I marveled at, because it was combined with modern plumbing. Then, off to Interlaken, enjoying on the way one of the most fantastic vistas, the Eiger / Mönch / Jungfrau massif. My enjoyment was cut a bit short though because I'd planned to board a boat on Lake Spiez, believing that, as the map showed, I would be facing these three mountains while sliding through the waves. My map, however, had failed to show that a low-range mountain would block the view. Ah well, it was still wonderful.

Then on to Brig, a rather stark town positioned in the Rhone Valley with two features: it was the point from which to go to Zermatt and also it was on one end of the Simplon tunnel. I believe the Matterhorn towering over Zermatt to be the most awesome mountain view there is, dwarfed only by a ride up to the Gornergrat by cog-wheel train. A full day indeed. Then back to Brig and from there, the next day through the tunnel to Locarno on the Lago Maggiore for my first view of the Italian side of the Alps, Locarno, history-laden and beautiful. From there, with a narrow-gauge train, almost like a street-car, to some town to catch a train for the short ride to Lugano.

Lugano was my main destination: well kept, charming, with a wonderful lake promenade and flowers everywhere. There were two nice vista mountains flanking the town, charming Italian / Mediterranean streets at all angles, marketplaces, the main plaza in the center of the town covered in the evening end to end with tables. The main hotels were apparently not crowded; they, actually seemed quite empty. The cheap ones around the noisy plaza were brimming with people; I stayed in one of them in a corner room. There were boat rides on the lake, funiculars up the small mountains, long walks along the lakeshore promenade. I actually forgot the rubble of the past which, to a considerable extent, formed the scene of German cities. I noticed, however, that Lugano was a city kept neat by Swiss Germans while preserving the chaotic hodgepodge of Italian charm.

Next came a bus ride to and along Lake Como, past the spot where Mussolini was spotted, and then back into the mountains, via Malojapass to Davos and St. Moritz. There are always wealthy people in the world, and they started to gather there, but it wasn't particularly prevalent. From there, the Rhäticon train, an unbelievable engineering feat composed of curved tunnels and bridges with a continuously varying scenery to gawk at. Then on to Chur, where I visited, believe it or not, the roomer we had had in 1937. And then back home. In order to "defray" some of the travel expenses, I tagged on a business trip. As you can see, I remember the trip of 1953, which happened 46 years ago, in great detail, every ride, sequence of scenes and views, walks, even the people sitting next to me in the hotel earlier. It sure helped me to compensate for the miserable years.

-35-

FROM A JOB TO A PROFESSION

Life was, of course, not just a sequence of vacations. Let's say that my initial apprenticeship had matured by the time of my 1952 vacation. I'd become proficient in pursuing the protection of inventions through appropriately formulating, in various ways, the underlying concepts and describing the principles and uses involved. I'd also learned to oppose the patent grants of competitors by showing that what they claimed wasn't in fact an invention. Others tried to do the same with the stuff I'd prepared. This wasn't done out of nastiness, but you didn't want others to interfere with what you were doing, while you wanted very much to interfere with what competitors were doing; that's just the name of the game. Since industrial electronics was a very active field in the sense of extensive and intensive, inventive activities, the whole area was very active, not just by AEG but many other domestic and foreign companies. There are some technical fields where very little happens; things remain basically the same, but such was not the case in industrial electronics.

Because of such lively activity, it soon developed that I had to travel to Munich with increasing frequency, sometimes once a month, to attend hearings with patent office personnel, but mostly to argue cases before an appeal tribunal. Due to his handicap, my mentor Dr. Barz wasn't keen on travelling and after initial successes on my part, he let me be.

Of course I flew. I was the first to do this; the others followed quickly. I was 24 years old and loved these trips. There was always a little time for sightseeing, particularly when the hearing was in the early morning, and you flew in the day before. The patent office was housed in the so-called German Museum, a very fascinating place. They'd reconstructed the lab set-up where Hahn and Strassmann had discovered nuclear fission. I came to enjoy Munich. Many parts of the city were still in ruins but the rebuilding progressed at a ferocious pace.

Industrial electronics wasn't limited to steel rolling control, and it wasn't just practiced in Berlin facilities, but in some other places as well, in the Ruhr-district and in a little village called Belecke, halfway between the Ruhr district and Hanover. After an initial introduction by Dr. Barz, I occasionally went there alone. As an aside, it was a mistake for the company to have this Belecke facility; there was a bunch of very brilliant engineers, a good management staff, but it was in the middle of nowhere. There was nothing to do and gradually, they drank themselves into a stupor.

Back to industrial electronics: there were other fields, such as spot-welding (we had a great edge there), and another field that commanded lots of activities was multi-color printing, not by way of nice individual plates, but on a mass production basis. Colored magazines were new then. For this, you have different rollers, each printing a different color for the same picture, one after the other; the pictures have to be exactly aligned. For example, you must print the red picture component exactly on top of, say, the earlier-printed, blue picture component or you will get funny-looking edges. To accomplish this, you need precisely-working electronic gadgetry.

AEG had a rather basic patent on this from earlier times. There were other inventions I was working on. I don't want to bore you with technical details, but there is purpose to my accounting. But before I go on here, I want to turn to some companion matter.

I've mentioned the so-called German economic miracle and how my work related to it; but there was another, more visible aspect. The wonderment of Zurich, seeing it twice in a row as an example of an intact city, was gradually balanced by seeing the ruins of Berlin rapidly vanish and being replaced by, well what? There was developing a sometimes interesting mixture of restoration, i.e. repairing the damage if possible and leaving the architecture as it was. And then, there was the new stuff. Often pragmatic, cost effectiveness dictated the looks, and style had to yield – not always though, but often. Of course, anything is better than burnt-out ruins and empty façades. But the cities became a hodgepodge of often clashing styles; So, the memory of Zurich persisted in a way to this day, supplanted however by the restored Vienna. My occasional travels to Munich, with increasing frequency – but also Frankfurt and the Ruhr district – gave me ample opportunity to witness the rebuilding not just of Berlin.

On a more personal level, my daily routine of going to work led me fortunately through parts of the city with damage that could be repaired. So, from 1949 onward, you could begin to forget the years of deprivation. As I have said, following the lifting of the Berlin blockade, the stores were soon filled with goods and remained so. Department stores opened up, and the abundance of available goods was remarkable. But of course, there was the matter of money. That had a very controlling effect. People needed many things, but bought with care; quality was king. Consider the contrast to today's world, where impatience dictates that everybody wants everything now and in unlimited abundance. There was probably much greater enjoyment in buying a suit, replacing china (I still have it). You don't need two or three dozen of pairs of shoes; a few will do, and so will (and did) two or three suits, preferably tailor-made, one or two sports jackets, a few slacks, half a dozen shirts will do nicely, particularly when top quality. So, from my own experience and observation, the economic miracle, with its broadly-based increase in production, was balanced by strong demand. The miracle was limited by people's means to acquire anything, so the years of deprivation didn't result in an orgy explosion for amassing large quantities of everything at low quality. Quite to the contrary, people's fussiness in that regard increased; quality was tops. Some puritanical souls complained that nothing was good enough; indeed, and why not?

Now, a British company violated the color printer patent by having such a multicolor print control installed with a big publishing house in Hamburg. Since this was a rapidly growing, expensive business, we had to stop it. Dr. Barz and I flew to Hamburg to consult with an attorney because the matter would be litigated before the regular courts. For some reason, I began to feel that he felt uneasy with complicated control devices and he wanted me to handle this.

It's somewhat difficult to explain: he was more at home with electronic structure and devices, up to that time used in relative simple systems; I, on the other hand, felt more at home in complex systems, never mind the components.

The matter became rather important for several reasons. First of all, it was the first litigation of that kind in the entire company after the war. As I've said, the patent department was organized not only in Berlin but in many other parts of Germany, with a senior patent engineer having one or more junior or apprentice engineers as an assistant. The relationships between mentors and apprentices (i.e. seniors and juniors) were mixed; by and large, the seniors held the juniors at leashes of differing tightness; not so Dr. Barz nor Dr. Steinbach, the mentor of my friend Keller; and there were a few other exceptions. So, Dr. Barz let me handle this matter more or less on my own, just as I'd handled, on my own, more appeal matters in

Munich than other junior patent engineers had been allowed to. All this was of great interest to all these junior patent engineers; added to that was that I was youngest of them all, so they paid attention.

In Hamburg, we conferred with a regular attorney who would formally represent the matter before the regular court. Actually, I don't know why Dr. Barz came along; apparently he felt that, in such a matter, there should be somebody else with the attorney other than that kid – meaning me. The attorney, a very charming lady, filed the suit relying completely on what I had told her. As is customary in such cases, the other side filed a counter-suit in the Patent Office in Munich, asserting invalidity of our patent. If the Patent Office agrees with the invalidity claim, that ends the infringement matter. For such a suit before a tribunal in the Patent Office you don't need a lawyer. Our boss, the head of the patent department, could have claimed to handle the matter, just to add weight to our position but I think he didn't like it because it was too complicated.

Dr. Barz had enough confidence in me to let me handle the matter before the Patent Office. There was some paperwork, and my first impression was that the patent attorney representing the British company wasn't too sharp. Then came the crucial point, the hearing in Munich. Dr. Barz came along to lend me moral support; it's always good in important matters to have at least two people on the scene. The German patent attorney for the other side was accompanied by a British attorney who spoke no German; a rather ridiculous set up because the German attorney was often busy translating and couldn't concentrate on what was going on. We all met in the waiting room and the German attorney, who was about twice my age – I was 26 – said with a smirk on his face; "Ah, you are actually my opponent."

He presented the opening argument asserting invalidity of the patent, and, too sure of himself, he was rather sloppy and perfunctory. I had rehearsed my argument with alternative, contingency versions, walking for hours, back and forth and around in our garden. In his argument, there were no surprises, and I had no problem countering his position point by point. Sort of half-way through my argument, while carefully observing the judge's reaction, I began to sense that I'd won already. One of the judges (the one most familiar with the case before the hearing) began to ask me questions, much more to the point than what the attorney had presented. But I was even better prepared for that. Of course, all cases have their weak spots, and I sensed that this judge was approaching one of them. But, right then and there, the attorney for the other side felt "left out" and asked to be heard; he said something quite irrelevant, which indicated that he hadn't been aware there was a point approaching something that could be turned to his favor. The judge, realizing the attorney's incompetence, decided not to pursue the matter and it was all over. After a conference of less than half an hour, the Court unanimously turned them down and upheld the patent.

A few months later, we were in Hamburg on the infringement matter since the patent had been held valid. Our Hamburg attorney gave a brief formal introduction, then let me have my say. Of course, I'd prepared very well, again with lots of walking in the garden. Actually, it was the easier part of the matter; the infringement was pretty clear-cut. The other side, too, had a regular attorney; they'd fired their patent attorney, and there was new one, much more competent. I, in my arrogance, thought this to be more fun. I didn't get cocky, though, and at least we had a good debate, which the judge obviously enjoyed. In a few days, he decided, yes, the patent was infringed by the other side.

As I pointed out, all of the junior patent people in the company, particularly those held in tight rein by their senior mentors, had eagerly awaited the outcome. Since, as I've said, I was the youngest of the bunch, my winning all the way had the effect in breaking down the "generation gap" in the firm. And don't forget, the litigation took place in what was still a British occupation zone; we'd won against the occupier!

Matters became easier for many of our junior group. Dr. Barz was very generous and kind. He didn't claim at all that it "really" had been his victory, and from then on, treated me as an equal. All that helped morale, but for me even more; I'd shown to myself that I wasn't only capable of dabbling in esoteric matters of pure science but could also make it in the real world. I was by then 27, with five years of patent experience behind me: now what? By nature, I was obviously too young to stop looking for more to learn, to just continue doing what I was doing.

-36-

GETTING OUT

Through a fluke I came across an ad in which an American company (Dresser Industries) was looking for engineers and scientists on a broad scale, not for a position in Europe but in the United States. Later, I found out that quite a number of U.S. corporations embarked at this time on regular "fishing expeditions" all across Western Europe, in a rather indiscriminate fashion, to scoop up technically-versed people. I found it astonishing, because at that time the parents (i.e. people in the U.S. of my age or at least of the same generation) were then producing the so-called Baby Boom and were, in the early '50s, in the same situation we were in Europe. They had finished college and, on what you may call a wholesale basis, were invading the job market. You might expect this to be the set-up of a large-scale scenario of unemployment, but the American economy was booming because of the continued armament, as well as the post-war boom. The preceding depression had been stifling housing construction. Even though there'd been hardly any destruction on account of the war, the economic scene was cluttered with lots of outdated stuff. Civilian goods like apartments, houses, and cars hadn't been produced. Most of that demand was beginning to be satisfied but the boom held on while, apparently, the colleges and universities produced fewer graduates than the economy needed; and so, they canvassed Europe for people.

It was a part of my job, as I've described, not just to seek patent protection for company inventions in Germany but also in important cases in other countries. Many European countries had patent systems similar to the German one, or actually systems that had been directly copied, so they didn't offer any particular challenge to me. However, I also handled several U.S. patent applications through an American patent attorney, and I had to confess that the American system was very different from the German one and from other European systems, and rather mysterious at that. So, I figured I should go to the U.S. for a while and study on location what their patent system was all about. I was also mindful that, in Germany at that time, any advancement of any substantial nature in general was predicated on having had "foreign experience." For example, an individual had hardly any chance ever becoming a plant manager or a manager of a division or even a department, unless he had successfully worked in or managed a sales or engineering support office in a foreign country. Today, with the European integration, the situation may be different, because foreign exposure is rampant and inevitable.

So, just for the fun of it, I answered this Dresser Industries ad, not really expecting an answer, until I received a letter. A Mr. McLemore would be on such and such date and time in the Kempinski Hotel in Berlin. In the past, the only contact I had had with any Americans were with visiting professors, and on vacation, I had encountered some rather boisterous soldiers, not making the best of impressions. I went to the interview primarily to meet the man. He was charming and friendly, and we had a good talk. Still not taking this matter very seriously, I made no effort to impress him, to present a favorable image or façade. I told him what I did professionally, what I knew, and what I didn't know. Obviously he was very experienced in judging people and he undoubtedly realized very quickly that I wasn't playing any games or tried to put something over. When I left, I believe after about an hour, I thought to myself, what an interesting experience; but I also believed that, most likely, that was it. Later, I realized that, if he hadn't been interested, the interview may have lasted not more than 10 minutes.

Much to my surprise, I got another letter within a few weeks for another interview. Obviously, matters became now serious and without saying so, even to myself, I believe that I made up my mind right then and there: if they made me an offer and it was at all reasonable, I would accept it.

I saw Mr. McLemore again. He didn't have a written offer yet but gave me a description of a very interesting job position, and he wanted to know whether I would be interested. The job was, in effect, to build up a foreign (as to the U.S.) patent department for the company. Their patent affairs had been handled on a local level (i. e. individual divisions had their own patent departments), and the foreign matters were apparently in a kind of disarray. Their Dallas patent counsel wanted to clean things up and to put some international position into his (own) operation– there was also a power play involved. Whatever his motivation (and we all have motives behind our actions), this proposition fit me perfectly. I would handle their patent applications for the purposes of seeking patent protection abroad, meaning mostly Europe, and that was my field of expertise; but the underlying substance was American patent applications, and that was exactly the subject matter I wanted to learn. I really doubted that I could be that lucky, but I didn't question Fortune.

Mr. McLemore advised me of the soon-to-be forthcoming written offer, and that would include an offer to pay for my trip across the ocean. Arrogant as I was, I told him that I would pay my own way. Intuitively, right from the beginning, I wanted to avoid the impression that they were dealing with a poor immigrant with low potential, one of the huddled masses etc. as per the New York harbor Statue of Liberty, begging to come ashore. Well, he insisted that this was simply a part of the offer, and that trip payment didn't entail any obligation on my part. I think that he had a pretty good idea about my independent way of thinking and liked it. I had also told him that I had a three-month termination clause in my contract with AEG, but that because of my wide range of duties, I believed that my employer needed more time to replace me. I didn't want to leave them in a quandary, and I would like to give them half a year notice. On my part, this was done in a very non-committal fashion, but in retrospect I believe that Mr. McLemore was impressed by my sense of responsibility. Only later, I learned that in the US, just two weeks' notice was customary, and that people usually didn't extend their duty beyond that of what was called for in a written contract.

Shortly after the second interview, I received a written contract offer which offered me a salary about three times my current one in terms of a currency conversion ratio. That, of course, was misleading, because at that time the Dollar was still over-valued. Since I didn't know details, I'd started my own investigation on purchasing power, using U.S. magazines and friends' advice as a basis. Accordingly, my salary would be about double what I made then, not counting the trip payment. So in the late winter/spring of 1956, I accepted the offer to become the foreign patent counsel of Dresser Industries at some point in time in 1956.

On October 1, 1956, I boarded a Pan American DC-7 in Düsseldorf for New York. When I said goodbye to my mother at the Düsseldorf airport, I undoubtedly didn't comprehend her anguish as I was too engulfed by the forthcoming adventure. We took off for Amsterdam and London to take on more passengers; flying across the ocean was not yet a matter of common occurrence. Next to me sat a truly kind gentleman, an American (I don't know whether there were many non-Americans on board). I didn't understand too much what he was saying, but he showed me all kinds of literature and overwhelmed me in what I soon came to learn was American friendliness. Looking back after all these years, I think that with this man as my seating companion, I became immediately enthralled in a very important aspect of the American culture, namely, the compassionate interest in another person.

We landed in Gander, Newfoundland for refueling; it was dark and raining. But soon after take-off, the day broke and we were winging into New York. I was glued to the window as we descended along the East Coast, beginning the descent shortly after passing Boston and then Long Island. Then we landed.

Idlewild Airport – as it was called then – was being rebuilt to accommodate New York's soon-to-be expected influx of masses of passengers. The arrival hall was a barrack-like structure, and my first contact there was with a big, black, broad-shouldered immigration official who inspected my X-rays very carefully. At that time, apparently, the main concern of the U.S. authorities was to not to import life-threatening diseases through the influx of emaciated outsiders. Not spotting any cancerous or tuberculosis shadows on my X-rays, he broke into a broad smile, almost as good as Louis Armstrong could produce, and welcomed me to the U.S.

The bus ride from the airport to downtown New York offered me the first glimpse of the city. It was clear that I was surrounded by people to whom this kind of trip was something perfectly ordinary, and why shouldn't it have been? WWII had been over for 11 years – ah yes, there had been another war in the meantime, in Korea, but that too was over. The American economy was booming (after all, that was the reason I was there). When rolling into Manhattan, I got my first inkling what this city was really like, in terms of demonstrations of power and wealth. It was only four years before that I had walked through Zurich in wonderment of what an intact, undamaged city was. And now, I felt th e same feeling in New York.

I got to my hotel, not too far from the bus terminal on 7ᵗʰ Avenue near 52nd Street. The hotel was modest but comfortable, I think about $6 a night. I hadn't slept for who knows how many hours but was wide awake. I knew I was just a few blocks away from Times Square, so after dumping my stuff, I set out to look around.

To me, I was approaching the center of the universe. The details didn't matter; there's something about Times Square which is so glamorous, in spite of the unbelievable degree of decrepitude. It has always attracted people from all parts of the world. When I stood there, then walked and walked along the streets of New York, to Rockefeller Plaza, to the Empire State Building, to the UN and down to Wall Street, I somehow felt I had arrived. I cannot identify specifically what and where it was I had arrived; what is exactly the point of identification? I was in Times Square: a German who, 11 years ago, had been hiding from artillery bombardment a few blocks away from Hitler's bunker. I had arrived, not because of- any grant or gift, and not because I was considered by somebody to be worthy of the honor, but I had arrived on my own, because people wanted what I had to offer. Actually, I had come here to increase my expertise and to return to Germany at some time in the future. But I believe that, subconsciously, I decided – right then and there – that I had been on the wrong side without any fault of my own, and that I never would turn my back on a power that will never lose.

Made in the USA
Las Vegas, NV
10 February 2022